Uniform Behavior

Uniform Behavior

Police Localism and National Politics

Edited by

Stacy K. McGoldrick
and
Andrea McArdle

Stacy K. McGoldrick: To my grand father James McCloskey, a dedicated Philadelphia police officer.

Andrea McArdle: To my parents, the late James and Gloria McArdle.

UNIFORM BEHAVIOR

© Stacy K. McGoldrick and Andrea McArdle, 2006.

First published in 2006 by
PALGRAVE MACMILLAN™
175 Fifth Avenue, New York, N.Y. 10010 and
Houndmills, Basingstoke, Hampshire, England RG21 6XS
Companies and representatives throughout the world.

PALGRAVE MACMILLAN is the global academic imprint of the Palgrave Macmillan division of St. Martin's Press, LLC and of Palgrave Macmillan Ltd. Macmillan® is a registered trademark in the United States, United Kingdom and other countries. Palgrave is a registered trademark in the European Union and other countries.

ISBN-13: 978–1–4039–7170–8
ISBN-10: 1–4039–7170–6

Library of Congress Cataloging-in-Publication Data is available from the Library of Congress.

A catalogue record for this book is available from the British Library.

Design by Newgen Imaging Systems (P) Ltd., Chennai, India.

First edition: May 2006

10 9 8 7 6 5 4 3 2 1

Printed in the United States of America.

Contents

List of Tables

Introduction

Stacy K. McGoldrick and Andrea McArdle

In August 1997, Abner Louima was tortured and sexually assaulted in Brooklyn's 70th Precinct station house. As this incident began to create national shock waves, a personal advisor to Louima suggested he say that during the attack one officer had asserted that it was "Giuliani time," meaning that the police could act with relative impunity (Kocieniewski 1997, Toobin 2002). Although Louima later recanted this statement, the retraction came only after the quote had saturated media coverage of the event. Despite the fact that it turned out to be untrue, local communities were galvanized by the comment because they thought it embodied police culture under Mayor Giuliani. The brutality that Louima experienced and the discourse that swirled around his assault will likely be long discussed by urban sociologists and historians as evidence of New York City's political culture in the 1990s.

Beneath the sensational and polemically charged facts of this case is a mundane reality that may become far more noteworthy in the years ahead: in 1997 the public conceived of responsibility for police behavior as residing with the mayor of the city. Thus "Giuliani time" was different from "Dinkins time" or the time of any other mayor. In protests over the brutality and the controversial trials of the officers involved, demonstrators focused on the police chief and mayor. In other words, public discourse about city policing had a local context; the communities who were subject to those police forces drove debates and discussions, and new policing policies were rooted in local politics.

As we write this introduction, the catastrophe of hurricane Katrina is unfolding in the Gulf Coast. If Abner Louima personifies a sad legacy of police-community relations in the 1990s, Katrina may well come to characterize Homeland Security and policing during the war on terror. While most of us are haunted by the images of evacuees stranded in the New Orleans Convention Center without food and water, the scope of the suffering needs to be considered in terms of the failure of local police forces to maintain order and public safety; the failure of the national guard and other U.S. security forces to move quickly, efficiently, and humanely; and the failure of the Department of Homeland Security and its federal emergency management agency to safely evacuate a dangerous city. The inability of various branches of law enforcement to coordinate, resulting in part from confused jurisdictional lines and overlapping geographic territories, speaks to the challenges ahead for any Homeland Security force to be able to deal with human disasters, either man-made or natural. The organization and management of police forces, along with the cultural understandings that develop around their practices and deployment, are not just about politics and power. As we have seen in the early fall of 2005, there are enormous consequences and many lives at stake when police work is carried out without proper care for human life and suffering.

Historically, American police forces have always been intimately connected to local political parties and the concerns of the local populations, usually the elites of that local population. In the case of the United States, the first police forces were institutionalized slave patrols that operated in southern cities. In the northeast, cities like New York and Boston developed police forces in response to calls for social order and those forces developed under the heavy influence of local political machines. As William Allison demonstrates in his piece for this volume, until calls by reformers during the Progressive era changed some departments, municipal police forces commonly replaced most of their patrolmen and officers when a new party came to power in the city council. Thus the connection between localism, municipal politics, and social order of policing was true from the inception of American police forces.

This tradition has been complicated by various interventions from the federal and state governments. The Progressive Era marked the beginnings of more complex interactions between local forces and federal authorities, especially in eastern cities. Chapters in this volume by William Allison, Val Marie Johnson, and Joseph Varga examine the nuances of these federal-local engagements during that period. More recently these interventions have included grant money to buy equipment and lawsuits over racial profiling, as chapters by Marilynn S. Johnson and Andrea McArdle demonstrate. Nevertheless, police departments varied largely from city to city, and they were shaped both institutionally and culturally by the cities, suburbs, and rural areas they policed. As this history of police localism has played a part in the vast political differences we have seen across the American landscape, one of the goals of this book is to reflect on the complicated relationships between police forces and the communities they police. Several chapters in this book, including Marilynn S. Johnson's and Andrea McArdle's accounts of New York City's police department, Kris

Erickson, John Carr, and Steve Herbert's analysis of local dynamics in Portland, Oregon, that ultimately led Portland to withdraw from formal cooperation with the FBI, and Anthony Pereira's study of policing in New Orleans, explicitly demonstrate this inherently American phenomenon by drawing on local experiences with police forces and the regional particulars of community struggles for police reform.

Perhaps the best way to understand the role of local politics in police operations is to investigate that ambiguous distinction with which citizens most often concern themselves—the line between formal and informal police duties. By informal policing we mean the casual (not explicitly managed or mandated) activities police officers engage in, which can include profiling, patrolling, or stop-and-frisks. The conflation of formal and informal elements in police work can be described through the metaphor of distance; if the informal activities of police reflect a conception of the proper distance between police and the community to be rather intimate, then police reform can be seen as the result of new debates and new powers seeking to reconfigure that distance.[1] At moments reformers have sought to widen the distance between police force and communities through professionalization (such as formal education and recruitment processes), militarization (formal tactics favored over the informal inquiries of the beat officer), and removal of the influence of municipal government over hiring and promotion. More recently, community policing and team policing have sought to reintegrate police officers into the communities they police. Finally, the policies of the Department of Homeland Security have had the effect of distancing police forces from communities by mandating certain activities over others (guarding the power plant because of the yellow alert instead of patrolling the neighborhood, for example). The salience of informal policing and community perceptions of police activities resurfaces in many periods when crises of urban identity appear.

William Thomas Allison provides us with one example of how struggles over informal policing represented a call for greater distance between police and communities with his discussion of the prevalence of the military metaphor and its link to professionalization among police forces in the first decades of the twentieth century. Reformers thought that separating police from local political machines, among other efforts to professionalize police officers, would help create a force less susceptible to corruption. In contrast, the first police forces in southern and northern American cities in the first half of the nineteenth century were intimate with local political structures and any attempt to separate the police from their patronage position within municipal governments was met with fierce and often violent resistance. The intimacy of local police departments with both the elites in the local community and political parties helped create an informal legitimacy necessary within the American republican context. For example, Joseph Varga's chapter detailing the enforcement of a police commissioner's English-only mandate at a tenants' rally in Brooklyn, New York, during the post–World War I Red Scare examines how the police, in maintaining order, reflected the prevailing interests and insecurities of the most powerful members of the community.

In the post–September 11 world, U.S. police forces are experiencing an ever-increasing pressure to respond to the enforcement initiatives of the national government and its new Department of Homeland Security—from enforcement of civil immigration law to responding to the national color alert systems that register apparent shifts in levels of vulnerability to terrorist acts. Exploring the greater implications of Homeland Security and the "War on Terror," scholars in this collection address the extent to which the changes and enforcement priorities introduced with the creation of the Department of Homeland Security will lead to a change in both the culture of policing and the locus of responsibility for the actions of police forces. While authors in this volume analyze the lineage of the localist orientation toward policing and moments of police reform, we also take into account the growing challenges of "Homeland Security" and its possible implications for the tradition of local control and accountability in policing. For example, if police are accused of abuse while enforcing their new national responsibilities related to antiterrorism, the question of political accountability becomes more complicated. While it is now politically untenable at best and absurd at worst to blame the president for municipal police abuses, there is increasing reason to believe that the expectation of purely local accountability for police forces is now being ruptured. With the onset of Homeland Security initiatives, the USA PATRIOT Act, and other legislation that seeks to coordinate the antiterrorist tactics of police forces, a new dynamic in local police work has come to the forefront. In the post–September 11 era the police force is national, even international, rather than local, in its vision.

In the first years of the twenty-first century we appear to be undergoing a sea change in the scope of police operations and this anthology will explore the implications of new national priorities for community-police relationships. Bringing together the work of a diverse group of authors, this collection offers a new perspective on police studies, focusing on the impact of national policy imperatives on the tradition of localism and on the meanings attached to the dynamic, mutable relationships between local police forces and communities. We consider the impact of these significant if underappreciated changes in policing against other moments of shift in the culture, organization, and mission of U.S. police forces.

This book does not seek to analyze approaches to policing (i.e., community policing vs. zero-tolerance initiatives) or simply to offer case studies that document the experience within particular localities. Rather, the discussion of local policing will be more conceptual as we seek to draw insights into how various frameworks for police deployment illuminate social and cultural struggles. Thus, the anthology addresses how the conceptualization of policing and police culture as local has changed over time, how national and geopolitical imperatives of the moment are affecting communal and informal systems of governance, and what the history of state-or nationally imposed police reforms can tell us about the likely consequences of national antiterrorist initiatives such as those under the rubric of Homeland Security.

Foundational to any theory of policing is the idea that policing is not simply a matter of the formal laws that police enforce, or the kind of state that has jurisdiction over them, but is made up of informal, on-the-spot decision making that reaffirms, or can damage, police legitimacy. In such engagements, the police force acts outside its bureaucratic role as enforcer of the formal written law. A close examination of officers' actions in these gray areas can provide us with significant information about how police forces interact with local communities, and whose community interests are being advanced or attended to. Hegemonic community pressures on the police departments often get articulated both in the culture of policing and in the day-to-day ways in which police interact with nonhegemonic members of the community. For example, when a police officer decides to "stop and frisk" individuals in poor or racially segregated neighborhoods, the decision may reflect cultural conceptions of race, class, criminality, and hegemonic desires about enforcement priorities and the populations that the police should target. Joseph Varga's chapter on public-order policing targeting local tenant activism in New York City during the Red Scare, Val Marie Johnson's study of private and state policing of immigrant women's morality during the Progressive Era in New York City, and Anthony Pereira's examination of how policing in New Orleans has operated in a context of grave inequalities and social deprivation, illuminate this theme.

Another important aim of this anthology is to recover evidence indicating that great struggles over the scope and function of policing have occurred before, to account for how these battles have led to transformations in the distribution of authority between local and national levels of government, and to identify the altering dynamics of class, race, and gender in police-community relations. For instance, historically, police forces have developed locally in the framework of the political, cultural, and racial realities of the place being policed. In those contexts, there has been tension between communities' political desire to maintain local control over their police forces and the occasional push for statewide or national control. We can see this struggle in the state takeover of the New Orleans police force in the wake of Reconstruction, for example, and in the White League assaults on police officers that resulted. Although it springs from a different set of concerns, this dialectic is once again in evidence in the war on terrorism. The tensions between local and state or federal institutions are documented in differently nuanced ways here in Marilynn S. Johnson's chapter on how federal intervention has followed a pendulum-like pattern, periodically advancing the struggle against police misconduct but at other times encouraging local police to engage in political surveillance and repression, and Erikson, Carr, and Herbert's analysis of tensions between the federal and local scales of governance of policing.

The political struggle over police roles now under way is being waged increasingly on the national and international as well as local fronts. Police forces are now expected to carry out national government initiatives in unprecedented ways. For example, Andrea McArdle addresses how local police forces are being recruited to enforce federal civil immigration laws and generally to protect the nation state in their role as "first responders" in the event of terrorist attack. Stacy K. McGoldrick's chapter traces how these changes in expectation and practice have been accompanied by a more nationalized discourse concerning crime and policing.

In addition to dealing with local crime, police now operate in the context of international events. Peter Manning's chapter on the emergent growth of cooperation among police agencies points out that a broader transnational security perspective, one that extends beyond the new priorities that police forces face as a result of the terrorist attack on September 11, has been transforming policing in the United States, particularly at the local level. Anthony Pereira's examination of local context in policing in New Orleans occurs within a larger framework of the state and its repressive mechanisms and relates policing to the salience of the right to human security and the rule of law in democracies. Joanne Klein's chapter examining the failed British policy of criminalizing terrorism in Northern Ireland during the "Troubles," the mid-1970s-to-1998 period of civil war between Northern Irish Catholics and Protestants, offers a comparative perspective on antiterrorist policing. It resonates strikingly with recent experience in the United States.

This book places in historical context the continuing push-pull dynamics between national politics and the entrenched tradition of local control over law enforcement in the United States. Drawing on the present sense of urgency around the war on terror and earlier national political initiatives that have sought to influence law enforcement at the local level, this book addresses key questions about how national and geopolitical developments come to shape local policing and inform who decides how, and to what end, local police forces will maintain public order, interact with local communities, and address issues of accountability, oversight, and reform.

Note

1. Stacy K. McGoldrick was inspired to use this metaphor from a similar usage in Davis, Diane E. "The Power of Distance: Rethinking Social Movements in Latin America." *Theory and Society*, 24(4) (1999), pp. 589–643.

References

Kocieniewski, David, 1997, "Officers Investigated in a Suspect's Injuries," *New York Times*, August 13, pp. A1, B1, B3.
Toobin, Jeffrey, 2002, "The Driver: Did the Prosecutors in the Louima Case have the Right Man All Along?" *The New Yorker*, June 10, pp. 35–39.

1

The Militarization of American Policing: Enduring Metaphor for a Shifting Context

William Thomas Allison

During the last decades of the nineteenth century, many Progressive police reformers developed what came to be known as the military analogy to promote the professional model of police reform. The Progressives, social and political reformers active between the 1890s and early 1900s, wanted to clean up corrupt cities, and police forces seemed a logical place to focus their efforts; the military analogy's model and its accompanying rhetoric provided an apparently quick-fix, depoliticized framework to rid police forces of graft and corruption, and remold police into model agencies to maintain law and order in American cities. The concept applied military-style organization, structure, practice, and purpose to the professional model of policing. Furthermore, professional policing emphasized decentralized local organization rather than national centralized authority, which had been popular in Europe but did not articulate well with the American tradition of localism.

The military analogy also applied war-like terminology to crime policy and police theory, creating rhetoric and a vernacular that remain even though the analogy's use as a reform tool has waned. Indeed, the rhetoric may well be the lasting legacy of the militarization of American policing. Despite much criticism, the idea of a "war on crime" remains a consistent theme in American police and crime policy. This is the case even more so today as police agencies are expanding their mission to include the domestic "war on terror" and still grappling with the implications of decentralization versus centralization for police organization.

The Military Model and the Spirit of Reform

As part of the Progressive Era effort to clean up city politics and attack vice and other social evils, reformers demanded effective and efficient police departments.[1] Progressive reform set police on the path of professionalization and community-oriented policing methods that would achieve prominence in the last quarter of the twentieth century. During the Progressive Era, police departments experimented with civil service, training and education, and sharing experiences through nascent professional organization. Police work, like many other fields, such as law, medicine, education, even the military, evolved into a profession, in which practitioners of a career field established educational, ethical, and organizational standards. Indeed, the U.S. military had been one of the earliest career fields to become a profession in the nineteenth century. Progressives applied scientific management and corporate organization models to administering city governments and providing efficient city services. Ward politics and city boss machines complicated such concepts, especially in regard to police reform.

The military model and its rhetoric of police reform seemed to offer an alternative paradigm more fitting to what Progressives thought police ought to be doing—fighting a "war" against crime and vice. For example, Progressive politicians, such as then New Jersey Governor Woodrow Wilson (a great proponent of public administration) and New York City Police Commissioner William McAdoo, compared police in the United States to an army in both method and purpose.[2] The military model provided the organizational, strategic, and tactical reforms and methods to "fight" a "war on crime." The military analogy's rhetoric provided the rousing martial language that accompanied the military model to inspire police and assure the public.

During the Progressive Era the military analogy resonated with reformers, especially in overcrowded industrial cities, where crime had become a critical political and social problem. Police now warred on crime and the principal battleground was the American city. This characterization continued well into the twentieth century, and in 1929, New York City Police Commissioner Grover Whalen, who once commented "There is plenty of law at the end of a nightstick," filled in the players in the vernacular of the analogy: criminals were the enemy, lawyers served criminals as diplomats, police manned the trenches as the last line of defense, and civilians played the role of unwilling combatants. However exaggerated, "good" and "evil" fought for control of American cities. Unlike World War I, where "peace without victory" was the objective, nothing short of unconditional surrender would suffice in the war against crime. A small minority of Progressive police reformers, such as Raymond Fosdick and August Vollmer, feared the potential threat of militarism and its tactics to a free civil society and preferred a less-militarized model of reform that focused on education and scientific methods to promote police professionalism. But the ringing military rhetoric that dominated public debate often overshadowed their dissent.[3]

Police historian Robert Fogelson correctly asserts that the military analogy legitimized Progressive reformers' attempts to separate police from partisan local politics. Furthermore, moving from political organization to "professionalization" was a common Progressive theme. For example, the U.S. Army and Navy had spent much of the nineteenth century depoliticizing their respective officer corps and striving toward becoming a professional fighting force. Generally, the military had avoided the corruptive grasp of party politics. Nor had it succumbed to unionization. Since police and the military shared somewhat common purposes, Progressive Era reformers saw military organization as a good model for policing. According to reformers, to successfully conduct a war on crime in American cities, police had to be truly independent of party machines and avoid the temptation of organized labor. By presenting police as a top-down military rather than a political organization, reformers boldly hoped to eliminate corrupt relationships between police and boss politics.[4]

These attitudes toward policing loosely resembled those in Europe, where police forces had long operated along military lines, much more so than American police ever dreamed of doing. Britain's "bobbies," the Italian Carabinieri, and French *Gendarmes*, along with Spanish, Russian, and Swiss police all followed a military organizational model under centralized state management rather than local control. The strong European tradition of centralized authority allowed for the success of the military model of policing in Europe. The significant absence of the military analogy's rhetoric in European policing, however, made such a system palatable for European citizens and their sense of rights and civic responsibility. In the United States, tradition and history dictated the opposite—the traditional disdain for and fear of centralized authority had been so deeply rooted in American society that a sense of rights and civic responsibility forcibly forbade an armed centralized national police force. In the United States, then, police would come to be militarized but not on a national level, and not without some trepidation. Authority and control would have to remain primarily local.[5]

The military analogy of police reform had its initial impact on police reorganization and reform during the Progressive Era. By 1900, Los Angeles and

Milwaukee, among several other cities, had reorganized police departments along military lines and had even enthusiastically courted former as well as active military officers to command police departments. In accordance with military organization, departments became more locally centralized by consolidating precincts and streamlining chains of command and more specialized by adding detective bureaus, traffic departments, and vice squads. Departments added more administrative and operational support for patrolmen on the streets, much like industrialized armies had increased logistical and other support for troops in the field. Local centralization, consolidation, specialization—these became the watchwords of Progressive professionalized police reform according to the military analogy.[6]

Teddy Roosevelt's Experiment: Police Professionalization and the Military Ideal

Theodore Roosevelt practiced the military analogy perhaps with greater zeal than any other reformer and certainly became its most popular advocate. With impressive energy, Roosevelt applied the military analogy model to the New York City Police Department (NYPD) as a member of the New York City Board of Police Commissioners from 1895 to 1897. The epitome of the nonprofessional military enthusiast, Roosevelt resigned his position on the Federal Civil Service Commission to serve as a police commissioner for New York City. He recognized this was a risky move, especially for a politician with national ambitions. In few places in the United States were corruption and police so intertwined as in New York City. Tammany Hall had controlled police graft since before the Civil War, and its grip on the NYPD was solidly entrenched despite efforts by reformers to loosen its hold. Up to that time, the commission had made little effort and less progress toward reform, even though establishing the commission itself was supposed to have been a move toward that very end.[7]

As a police commissioner, Roosevelt is more popularly known for his exploits, such as going on patrols and personally involving himself in several investigations. Often accompanied by Progressive journalists Lincoln Steffens, Stephen Crane, and Jacob Riis, he reveled in his "midnight rambles," calling them "great fun." All three journalists filled their newspaper pages with stories of Roosevelt, the hands-on reform police commissioner.[8] Roosevelt's proactive approach seemed more intent on catching police who were not working than watching police at work. He enjoyed finding startled cops who were supposed to be on patrol sitting instead in a saloon with brew in hand or, worse, yet, caught in the act of accepting a bribe from a saloonkeeper or madam of a house of prostitution.[9]

Roosevelt promoted the military analogy through bellicose pronounce-ments that set an early standard for military analogy oratory. He claimed that no other city in the United States had "such desperate enemies to fight as ours," and that the commission was "attacking corruption as it never before has been attacked."[10] In *Cosmopolitan*, he described the police as a "half-military" organization that required the same structure, discipline, and values as "obtain to the Army and Navy." Like soldiers, Roosevelt, wrote, police had to exhibit "vigilance, good judgment, . . . great energy, courage, and determination in the performance of their regular duties."[11] In an essay in *American Ideals*, he beat the drums of war, calling for a "war against corruption," "resolute warfare against every type of criminal," and "war upon all criminals alike." He promised to turn the NYPD into a force of "fighting efficiency."[12] In *The Forum*, Roosevelt expressed his politically astute resolve to uphold the rule of law through clean police work:

> In the end, we shall win, in spite of the open opposition of the forces of evil, in spite of the timid surrender of the weakly good, if only we stand squarely and fairly on the platform of honest enforcement of the law of the land. But if we are to face defeat instead of victory, that would not alter our convic-tions and would not cause us to flinch one hand's breadth from the course we have been pursuing. There are prices too dear to be paid even for victory. We would rather face defeat as a consequence of honestly enforcing the law than win suicidal triumph by a corrupt conviction at its violation.[13]

His use of such military rhetoric was not lost upon his fellow commissioners. Avery Andrews, a Democrat, had graduated from West Point and Republican commissioner Frederick Grant, son of General Grant, had been a successful soldier in his own right, serving in the Indian Wars. Both championed the military analogy.

Roosevelt even allowed his military fervor to influence his opinions on the ethnicity of police officers. He despised Irish immigrants, who made up a large portion of the force and who had, he thought, a propensity toward corruption. Because of his idealized view of Prussian military tradition, he believed German immigrants should have made excellent policemen, but they, too, disappointed him.[14] Overall, he preferred native-born Americans who had recently served in the Army or Navy, which should come as no surprise considering the militaristic attitudes, such as duty to country, honor, and courage, Roosevelt championed.[15]

Roosevelt's martial verse was not without substance. He instilled military discipline in the police force in order to weed out corrupt and incompetent officers. Whereas previously recruits had bought their way into the police force, rigid mental and physical examinations awaited recruits hoping to join the force under the Roosevelt Board. Over a third of the applicants failed either or both examinations. Writing that like soldiers the best police should be those "who win promotion by some feat of gallantry on the field of battle," Roosevelt put in place awards and promotion for meritorious conduct and bravery. He ordered precincts to conduct drill twice a week, marching in tight formation and practicing baton use. He instituted pistol practice and shooting competitions. His famous bicycle squad developed into what Roosevelt called a "remarkable . . . *corps d'elite*" that exhibited "devotion to duty" and "daring and skill." Roosevelt wrote with great pride that "the police service is military in character, and we wished to encourage the military virtues."[16]

Roosevelt met his end in New York City by insisting on enforcing Sunday liquor laws. Saloons and other establishments that served liquor had either ignored the law or paid off cops to look the other way on Sundays. Tammany Hall had openly flaunted its success in breaking the law. Roosevelt, a politician at heart, realized that sacrificing himself for the Sunday liquor law was not worth his political future. He resigned from the commission in April 1897 to take up duties as Assistant Secretary of the Navy for the McKinley administration. Neither Tammany Hall nor the state Republican machine in Albany mourned his departure and both had a hand in moving Roosevelt along to Washington. His impact on the NYPD in the short term suffered, as Tammany Hall experienced a brief resurgence at the beginning of the new century and reversed several of the Roosevelt Board's reforms. Like many Progressive Era reformers, Roosevelt had attempted too much too fast, but he had brought national attention to the military analogy.[17]

The military analogy did not die with Roosevelt's departure from police work. Just after World War I, New York City Police Commissioner Arthur Woods encountered problems similar to those that had confronted Roosevelt. A veteran of the war, Woods strongly supported the military analogy as the path to a solution. Writing in his *Policeman and Public*, published by Yale University Press in 1919, Woods promoted *esprit d'corps* among police, training and education, and professionalism in police departments to better wage war on crime. Woods maintained that the "departmental instinct of courage" made policemen "brave," ready to face "danger in ways that are not commonly realized." This danger in American cities was of a "different kind," according to Woods, from "that which the soldier faces." Whereas a soldier knew his enemy, a policeman did "not know who may be his enemy, and he must not be too quick to conclude that anyone is hostile." For that reason, Woods warned that the military analogy must not be overzealous. Police, according to Woods, functioned as peace officers first and foremost: it would be "absurd if [policemen] appeared warlike." He believed the crime problem in American cities required a war to fight it, but he also recognized the delicate position of domestic police forces in a free society. If police became de facto military soldiers, the values and institutions of free society could be threatened. Still, Woods maintained that in some ways police were fighting a tougher war than soldiers in the military fought. Police faced "unceasing warfare" that required constant vigilance, lest they lose the "fight."[18]

Woods believed that training and professionalism based upon military ideals would enable police to prevail in the war on crime. Police officers had to undertake continuous and effective training just as military officers underwent throughout their careers. Ongoing training and promotion based upon merit, according to Woods, would allow knowledge, skill, discipline, and efficient organization to improve police work at all levels. He recommended that police training schools and academies be established across the United States and be made mandatory for police service. It is important to remember that in 1919 police training was still an embryonic and somewhat unpopular concept in many American cities, especially those with strong political machines involved in police politics.[19]

Woods's thinking represented a faddish crossover between the military and police work that had currency from the early 1900s through the 1920s. The linking of police reform with the use of the military analogy received great attention across the nation. Police departments of all sizes endeavored to apply the military-like methods that Roosevelt, Woods, and others championed. Several departments turned to military officers, hoping that the experience of military life and wartime campaigns could help lead cities to victory in the war on crime.

The Military Model and Reform in Philadelphia:
The Machine Fights Back

By far the most famous and extreme of these experiments of putting the military analogy to work under the command of a military officer was the experience of Philadelphia in the 1920s. Mayor W. Freeland Kendrick, a machine politician but nominal reformist elected in 1923, applied a radical form of the military analogy to superficially clean up the Philadelphia Police Department and curb crime. Using an active-duty senior general officer of the U.S. military to run a city police department represented a dangerous involvement of the military in domestic affairs. His choice for the job was renowned Marine Corps General Smedley Butler. A veteran of the Spanish American War, the Boxer Rebellion, and the occupations of Haiti and Nicaragua, Butler had earned a reputation as both a fighter and an administrator. He had twice been awarded the Congressional Medal of Honor and had declined to accept a third citation. In the eyes of reformers, his colorful combat record and harshly efficient colonial administrations in Haiti and Nicaragua had prepared him well for ridding one of the largest American cities of crime. Mayor Kendrick wanted Butler because he was well known, full of bravado, and, as an officer, could be expected to follow orders, in this case from the Philadelphia political machine. The press praised the choice. John Stuart, writing for *Collier's*, called Butler the right "fighting cuss" for the job: "A hot time was promised."[20]

Speak-easies, prostitution, gambling, and a multitude of other vices that shocked the strict moral mindset of the city's upper-middle-class reformers ran rampant in Prohibition Era Philadelphia.[21] Deeply rooted in the fertile dirt of machine politics, ward bosses had managed to prevent long-term meaningful police reform. Butler was the man, the machine thought, who could lead a superficial reform of the police and wage a spurious war on crime, and thus satisfy public concerns while allowing the machine to maintain control of its lucrative illegal schemes. The bosses never intended that Butler win the war; only fight it so that it looked like he was winning. He had been hired as a "smokescreen."[22]

Butler took office in 1924 and immediately went on the offensive, dashing Mayor Kendrick's hope that he would follow orders. This was indeed "a new type of war for a Marine." Butler pledged to "wage ruthless war on crime, vice, and to enforce prohibition."[23] He gathered the Philadelphia police force in the opera house and delivered speeches urging the cops on to the fight as if they were about to go into battle in the Philippines or France. He boldly offered a promotion to the first cop who killed a gangster. To the press and city leaders, he promised to rid Philadelphia of vice in a mere forty-eight hours. Within those forty-eight hours, 75 percent of the 1,300 salons in Philadelphia had been closed down. The infamous "Tenderloin" district of the city had been wrecked, but only temporarily, as many of these establishments reopened in a matter of weeks. The *New York Times* ran the headline: "Butler Begins War: Undesirables Flee from Philadelphia." Police in east coast cities set up roadblocks and posted extra patrolmen at train stations in the hope of preventing these "undesirables" from adding to their already infested streets.[24]

Butler took the concept of "war on crime" literally. He militarized the Philadelphia police force. Patrolmen sported new grayish-blue uniforms complete with Sam Brown belts, holsters, and bandoliers. Butler himself wore a custom uniform loosely modeled after his Marine dress uniform, adding a blue cape with two gold stars on its stiff collar symbolizing the rank of major general (Butler was only a brigadier general at the time). He set up military-style outposts on street corners and organized a special "bandit squad" armed with armored cars and sawed-off shotguns to raid prostitution houses, bootleggers, and crime dens. His attitude toward criminals was not in the mold of the Progressives and reflected his own attitudes toward the occupied peoples over which he had reigned during his military career. He publicly claimed, "The only way to reform a crook is to kill him," and gave several similarly belligerent performances in speeches, radio addresses, and newspaper interviews.[25] That his administration epitomized the dangers of military rule was of little doubt, as *Literary Digest* concluded: "The inauguration of a military dictatorship in the city where the Declaration of Independence was signed is a sign of tendencies which distinguish American political currents in the twentieth century. In the very cradle of liberty, the civil government has been made subordinate to military government."[26]

Butler attacked the police department itself with equal vigor. Bucking the police reform trend of education and training, Butler abolished the department's School of Instruction and revamped promotion guidelines. All training would be on-the-job and under Butler's command. He notoriously barged into a station house, located the nearest sergeant who appeared to have "leadership qualities," and promoted him on the spot. It was about as close to a battlefield promotion as one could get in the "war on crime" under Smedley Butler. He took personnel and other resources from the traffic department and detective bureau and added to his patrol squads and special raid teams. Police themselves came up with creative names for various squads, such as the "Alcohol Expeditionary Force." He created a handpicked "shoe-fly" squad to rat out corruption within the police department. Butler centralized police organization along strict lines. He needed a "disciplined army in the war against crime," and thus had little choice but to try to remove the control of the bosses. Much to the chagrin of the bosses, but with Mayor Kendrick's grudging approval, Butler completely reorganized the city's police districts, consolidating them by half to twenty-two. To command each district, he personally appointed a new captain and two lieutenants, chosen from other neighborhoods in an effort to avoid the controlling arms of local ward bosses. Like his *gendarmes* in Haiti, Butler's Philadelphia police would not be manipulated by local political factions.[27]

Philadelphia, however, was not Haiti, and in the end the political machine of the City of Brotherly Love found Butler's tactics incompatible with its own strategic objectives. Even Mayor Kendrick had reached his limit with the flamboyant Marine general. Butler's tenure ended after less than two contentious years. Like Roosevelt in New York, Butler was too much, too fast, and showed that reformers using the military analogy had perhaps pushed their case too well. With one of the most famous military officers brought in to run the police, Philadelphia's experience with Butler received widespread publicity, which in the end was not flattering to either side. Butler and Kendrick publicly argued over who had the final say over police appointments and dismissals. This small feud festered into a much larger crisis as the Philadelphia political machine pressured Kendrick to force Butler to relax enforcement of prohibition laws so that the machine could recoup some of its losses from Butler's antivice activities in 1924.[28] In late December 1925, Kendrick ordered Butler to step down as Director of Public Safety, declaring that "I had the guts to bring General Butler to Philadelphia, and I have the guts to fire him." As word spread of Butler's imminent departure, Philadelphia hotels planned New Year's Eve celebrations replete with flowing fountains of liquor. On December 26, Butler left Philadelphia for his home in San Diego.[29]

Butler's tenure in Philadelphia received mixed reviews. The *Christian Science Monitor* praised him for an effective war on robbery and violent crime, but took him to task for losing the battle to enforce prohibition. The *New York Times*, however, claimed that getting a drink in Philadelphia was nowhere near as easy as it was before General Butler took command. Few, not the least of whom was President Calvin Coolidge, enjoyed the idea of an officer of the American military being involved in the messy slander of big-city machine politics. The *New York Times* praised Coolidge's conclusion that Butler was no longer effective in Philadelphia and was not doing the Marine Corps good service by wishing to continue to work there. In a short time, Philadelphia returned to its pre-Butler ways and corruption again infected the police force. Butler never claimed to be a reformer, a notion he detested, but rather naively thought himself an officer doing his duty as ordered by his commander, the mayor.[30]

He would not leave police work for good after Philadelphia. For the rest of his life he campaigned for reorganization of local and state law enforcement along military structures that he outlined, including enlistment periods, housing of patrolmen, military organization of police bureaucracy, and combat-like methods to capture criminals.[31] Butler told the Philadelphia *Evening Public Ledger* that "Sherman was right about war, but he was never head of police in Philadelphia."[32]

Despite the varied results of using military officers to run police departments, the use of the military analogy as a model for police reform had proven resilient among city officials and the general public. It helped establish more separation between police and local politics, and weakened the grip of police machines on municipal graft. It helped make local centralized police organization more efficient and professional. Moreover, citizens seemed to relate to the rhetoric and vernacular of the military analogy. The mission of American policing had been narrowed and clarified. Crime fighting (police work) and crime prevention (social work) now defined the role of police in American cities. Still, problems remained.

Heads of public safety and police chiefs in many cities had no tenure-like protection and thus only lasted two or three years before being run off by local political forces. Police reformers, both those supporting and opposed to the military analogy, agreed that for any reform of American police to be successful, the police executive needed more autonomy from the political whims of city boss machines.[33]

The Military Model and National Government

Additionally, critics of the military analogy and the "war on crime" began to complain of police abuses of civil rights and other police "lawlessness." By the 1930s, several large cities had established crime commissions not only to study crime but also to expose the entrenched military power of police. The "this is war" argument seemed to be wearing thin. Instead, the commissions suggested that economic, social, and educational "rearrangements" be put in place to address society's ills and thus remove the impetus for crime. Although various crime commissions criticized police corruption and incompetence, they almost universally returned to the rhetoric left over from the military analogy. Even at the federal level, the rhetoric sometimes overshadowed substance. President Calvin Coolidge's National Crime Commission, meeting off and on from 1925 to 1929, supported a renewed "war on crime," but did little to back up its call to arms.[34] President Herbert Hoover replaced Coolidge's commission with his more effective advocate of a "war on crime," the National Commission on Law Observance and Enforcement, which gave much-needed strength to the "war on crime" rhetoric, but, like its national and local predecessors, Hoover's commission wanted it both ways. Police should fight crime like armies fight a war, but with limitations that did not infringe upon civil rights. One volume of its massive fourteen-volume report on crime in America heavily criticized police abuses, notably the "third degree." While Americans seemed to support a war on crime, the methods that police used in this war made them a bit squeamish. Even more troubling for local law enforcement authorities was the threat of growing federal involvement in what had been largely a local issue.[35]

Diehard crime fighters found their most able and vocal campaigner in the young, brash director of the Federal Bureau of Investigation (FBI), J. Edgar Hoover. Leading the charge for federal intervention in the crime problem, Hoover championed President Franklin Roosevelt's law-and-order emphasis, which became popular among local police agencies, and was a staunch advocate of a federal role in local law enforcement. Hoover promoted a professionalized war on crime throughout the 1930s and

1940s. According to Hoover, the increase in crime represented a clear danger and threatened all Americans: "This army of crime is larger than any unified force in history. If this tremendous body of evil doers could be welded into a unit of conquest, America would fall before it not in a month, not in a day, but in a few hours."[36]

In fighting crime, Hoover strongly supported using the new investigative science called criminalistics. He established national fingerprint catalogs and crime labs, and placed highly trained agents in the field to assist local law enforcement. Hoover brought the power and resources of the federal government to bear locally on the crime war. While Hoover led the charge in the war on crime, he also came to symbolize the pinnacle of police professionalism. More than any single individual during the pre–World War II period, Hoover encouraged professionalized police by promoting the image of law enforcement officers as highly trained, skilled, and ethical defenders of the public good. Despite criticism Hoover received during his later years as the director of the FBI, he did at least publicly advocate a strict policy against use of the "third degree" and condemned police abuse of any sort. Hoover successfully infused professionalism with the rhetoric of the military analogy.

Hoover's prize accomplishment during the 1930s was probably the establishment of the National Police Academy in 1935. This national training school gave select local law enforcement officers extended training in the latest crime-fighting techniques from the best instructors in the nation, while Hoover used the academy to increase federal influence on local law enforcement. The FBI helped train local officers and improve crime-fighting techniques while crime commissions focused on improving local administrative and organizational capabilities. Both approaches aimed toward the common goal of efficient locally centralized policing through professionalization. Hoover, however, wanted a more national approach. Initiatives like the National Police Academy were directed at bringing together what Attorney General Homer Cummings called the "disorganized army" of law enforcement officers that had to this point "sought to contest the underworld in disjointed groups."[37]

A better-organized army to fight the war on crime was indeed a popular prescriptive suggestion. Justin Miller, Dean of the School of Law at Duke University, stated to a national radio audience in 1934 that "Consideration of a better army for the war against crime necessarily requires comparison with the existing army, and frank and honest recognition of present weaknesses." Instead of recommending reform from the federal level down, as Hoover wished, Miller wanted the stronger army to originate at the local level. Community leaders needed to take charge to recruit better personnel and cut away waste from local police agencies. Local police needed to improve coordination with state and federal law enforcement authorities. He went so far as to suggest that county law enforcement agencies were outdated, even "utterly inexcusable," considering that "modern developments" had "wiped away county lines." He advocated federal standards but with local implementation and enforcement. Miller concluded his address with a call to arms: "Let us go forward on all fronts in our battle against crime."[38]

The Durability of the Military Analogy

World War II and the early years of the cold war interrupted the war on crime as war of the traditional sort had to be fought elsewhere. Since the 1950s, the military analogy has overshadowed the military model of policing. When the report of the national commission on law enforcement and administration of justice in 1968 highlighted the need for police departments to become more adept at recognizing and responding to social change in the communities they served, and proposed that police take the initiative in community outreach as opposed to the traditional practice of citizens approaching police,[39] the commission identified a change in strategy, not a doctrinal shift, in policing. And while it has been possible to assimilate this community-based policing model to the rhetoric of the "war on crime" in which police forces could enlist citizens as crime fighters,[40] community policing has served more as a model for preventing crime rather than "fighting" it.[41]

Today, the program of Homeland Security has shown how serviceable the military analogy continues to be both in the tradition of police localism and federal programs. Emphasizing the need for cooperation among law enforcement agencies at all levels, the rhetoric of federal-level initiatives identifies state and local police forces as the key first responders in efforts to combat terrorism in American cities.[42] If Roosevelt's work in New York City and Butler's effort in Philadelphia represented the high points of the military model as a basis for militarized police professionalization, the military analogy has remained remarkably resilient and versatile, even as its context and raison d'etre have continued to shift.

Policing an open society based upon democratic ideals is a difficult task with no easy or even obvious solutions. The military analogy, its model for police professionalization, and its stirring rhetoric have endured for over a century at the forefront of American policing. Its tactics and strategies have changed, but its rhetoric has remained constant. Debate, however, continues as to just how effective police are in the "war on crime." Is the "war on crime" preventing crime? Is there substance behind the rhetoric? Is it time for a new analogy to reflect a paradigm that has already shifted?

Notes

1. From the Latin *vitium*, meaning default or defect, and first used in English in the thirteenth century in reference to immoral or depraved behavior.
2. Michael McGerr, *A Fierce Discontent: The Rise and Fall of the Progressive Movement in America, 1870–1920* (New York: The Free Press, 2003), p. 79; Paul Boyer, *Urban Masses and Moral Order in America, 1820–1920* (Cambridge: Harvard University Press, 1978), pp. 175–204.
3. Samuel Walker, *A Critical History of Police Reform: The Emergence of Police Professionalization* (Lexington, Massachusetts: D.C. Heath, 1977), pp. 128–129.
4. Robert Fogelson, *Big-City Police* (Cambridge: Harvard University Press, 1977), pp. 54–57.
5. Raymond Fosdick, *American Police Systems* (New York: The Century Company, 1920), pp. 3–57; Clive Emsley, "The Origins of the Modern Police," in Terence J. Fitzgerald, ed., *The Reference Shelf: Police in Society* 72:2 (New York: H. W. Wilson Company, 2000), pp. 9–17.
6. Fogelson, *Big-City Police*, pp. 54–57.
7. Jay Stuart Berman, *Police Administration and Progressive Reform: Theodore Roosevelt as Police Commissioner of New York* (New York: Greenwood Press, 1987), pp. 33–123; Samuel Walker, *A Critical History of Police Reform: The Emergence of Professionalization* (Lexington, Massachusetts: D. C. Heath, 1977), pp. 25–25; James F. Richardson, *The New York Police: Colonial Times to 1901* (New York: Oxford University Press, 1970), pp. 248–257; Theodore Roosevelt to Henry Cabot Lodge, April 3, 1895, Elting E. Morrison, ed., *The Letters of Theodore Roosevelt, Volume 1, The Years of Preparation, 1868–1898* (Cambridge: Harvard University Press, 1951), p. 439 (hereafter referred to as *The Letters of Theodore Roosevelt*); Theodore Roosevelt to Anna Roosevelt, April 14, 1895, *The Letters of Theodore Roosevelt*, p. 442; Theodore Roosevelt to Avery Andrews, April 25, 1895, *The Letters of Theodore Roosevelt*, p. 45.
8. Jacob Riis, *Theodore Roosevelt the Citizen* (New York: The Macmillan Company, 1918), p. 134.
9. Lincoln Steffens, *Autobiography of Lincoln Steffens* (New York: Harcourt Brace and World, 1931), pp. 257–258; Riis, *Theodore Roosevelt*, pp. 129–154; Richardson, *The New York Police*, pp. 260–261.
10. Theodore Roosevelt to Lucius Burrie Swift, July 12, 1895, *The Letters of Theodore Roosevelt*, p. 465.
11. Theodore Roosevelt, "Taking the Police Out of Politics," *Cosmopolitan* 20 (November 1895), p. 45.
12. Theodore Roosevelt, "Administering the New York Police Force," *American Ideals and Other Essays, Social and Political*, 3rd ed. (New York: G. P. Putnam's Sons, 1899), pp. 184–187.
13. Theodore Roosevelt, "The Enforcement of the Law," *The Forum* 20 (September 1895–February 1896), p. 10.
14. Theodore Roosevelt to Cecil Spring Rice, August 5, 1896, *The Letters of Theodore Roosevelt*, p. 555.
15. Theodore Roosevelt, *American Ideals*, p. 185.

16. Roosevelt, "Taking the Police Out of Politics," p. 45; Roosevelt, *American Ideals*, pp. 160–188.
17. Berman, *Police Administration and Progressive Reform*, pp. 119–121.
18. Arthur Woods, *Policeman and Public* (New Haven: Yale University Press, 1919), pp. 86–89, 136–137, 148–165.
19. Ibid.
20. John Stuart, "A Leatherneck Wallops the Small Gods," *Collier's* (January 17, 1925), pp. 18–19.
21. "How Wet is Philadelphia?" *Literary Digest* (November 10, 1923), pp. 28–44.
22. Hans Schmidt, *Maverick Marine: General Smedley D. Butler and the Contradictions of American Military History* (Lexington: University Press of Kentucky, 1987), pp. 144–145; Lowell Thomas, *Old Gimlet Eye: The Adventures of Smedley D. Butler* (New York: Farrar and Reinhart, 1933), p. 263.
23. Thomas, *Old Gimlet Eye*, p. 262.
24. *New York Times* (January 9–13, 1924); Schmidt, *Maverick Marine*, pp. 146–149.
25. *New York Times* (December 24–29, 1925); Schmidt, *Maverick Marine*, pp. 156–157; Thomas, *Old Gimlet Eye*, p. 270.
26. "Butler: A 'Devil Dog' in Philadelphia," The *Literary Digest* (January 26, 1924), p. 44.
27. Fogelson, *Big-City Police*, p. 78; Schmidt, *Maverick Marine*, pp. 151–152; Thomas, *Old Gimlet Eye*, p. 267.
28. C. K. Taylor, "Baiting a Marine," *The Outlook* (October 8, 1924), pp. 199–200.
29. *New York Times* (December 24–29, 1925); Schmidt, *Maverick Marine*, pp. 156–157; Thomas, *Old Gimlet Eye*, p. 270.
30. *Christian Science Monitor* (December 24, 1925); New *York Times* (December 27 and 29, 1925); Fred D. Baldwin, "Smedley D. Butler and Prohibition Enforcement in Philadelphia, 1924–1925", *Pennsylvania Magazine of History and Biography* 84:3 (July 1960), p. 356; Walker, *A Critical History of Police Reform*, pp. 66–67; Schmidt, *Maverick Marine*, pp. 158–159.
31. Smedley D. Butler, "Making War on the Gangs: A Plan to Take the Police Out of Politics," *The Forum* (March 1931), pp. 134–141.
32. Quoted in Baldwin, "Prohibition Enforcement," p. 356.
33. Fosdick, *American Police Systems*, 379–383; Fogelson, *Big-City Police*, p. 61.
34. Nathan Douthit, "Police Professionalism and the War Against Crime in the United States, 1920s–1930s," in George L. Mosse, ed., *Police Forces in History*, vol. 2 (London: Sage Publications, 1975), pp. 323–335.
35. National Commission on Law Observance and Enforcement, *Report on Lawlessness in Law Enforcement* (Washington, D.C.: Government Printing Office, 1931).
36. Quoted in Douthit, "Police Professionalism," pp. 330–332.
37. J. Edgar Hoover, "The Confession and Third Degree Methods," *Law Enforcement Bulletin* 5 (January 1936), pp. 11–13; J. Edgar Hoover, "Law Enforcement as a Profession," *Law Enforcement Bulletin* 6 (November 1937), pp. 3–4; Walker, *A Critical History of Police Reform*, pp. 159–160; Douthit, "Police Professionalism," pp. 330–333; Herbert Corey, *Farewell Mr. Gangster: America's War on Crime* (New York: Century Company, 1936), p. 266. See also

the International Association of Chiefs of Police *Proceedings* and *Yearbook* from 1935 to 1940.

38. Justin Miller, "A Better Army for the War Against Crime," one of a series of four broadcasts on "Coping with Crime" sponsored by the American Bar Association, delivered on NBC Radio under the auspices of the National Advisory Council on Radio in Education, May 19, 1934, transcript from Duke University Library.

39. The President's Commission on Law Enforcement and Administration of Justice, *The Challenge of Crime in a Free Society, Task Force Report: The Police* (Washington, D.C.: Government Printing Office, 1967), pp. 1–221; Robert W. Winslow, ed., *Crime in a Free Society: Selections from the President's Commission on Law Enforcement and Administration of Justice, the National Advisory Commission on Civil Disorder, the National Commission on the Causes and Prevention of Violence, and the Commission on Obscenity and Pornography*, 3rd ed. (Belmont, CA: Dickenson Publishing Company, 1977), pp. 322–359.

40. Ramsay Clark, *Crime in America: Observations on its Nature, Causes, Prevention, and Control* (New York: Simon and Schuster, 1970), pp. 132–149.

41. Orin F. Nolting, ed. *Municipal Police Administration* (Chicago: International City Managers Association, 1961), p. 55; O. W. Wilson and Roy C. McLaren, *Police Administration*, 3rd ed. (New York: McGraw Hill, 1972), pp. 56, 117.

42. See, e.g., http://www.dhs.gov//dhspublic/display?content=119, Department of Homeland Security, Press Release, January 24, 2002 (describing "America's first line of defense in any terrorist attack as the 'first responder' community— local police, firefighters, and emergency medical professionals").

2

"Arriving for Immoral Purposes": Women, Immigration, and the Historical Intersection of Federal and Municipal Policing

Val Marie Johnson

In the Progressive Era the efforts of reformers, especially women reformers, to mobilize, protect, and discipline women influenced the development of an apparatus bridging national and local jurisdictions that was used to police immigrant women and women's moral delinquency more broadly, and to deport immigrant women from the United States. In continuity with the workings of the earliest U.S. police forces, these developments around policing and immigration were grounded in local politics. In the context of New York City and Ellis Island, struggles around nation, ethnicity and race, class, and their links with electoral politics, also helped to produce a reform of policing. Private groups' attempts to regulate the morality of women were crucial to mobilizing these multifaceted politics and the policing reforms they spurred. Acting on behalf of or as a supplement to state regulation, representatives of private reform organizations extended policing at both the international and local levels into immigrants' private practices and spaces, thereby facilitating legislative reform and a higher number of public prosecutions.[1] This chapter examines how fear and social biases combined with unequal power relations to shape policing and law, both discursively and materially, and how invoking concerns about "white slavery," immigrant prostitution, and immigration itself, contributed to sensationalized and flexible vocabularies that helped fuel the building of a new state and private forms of policing.

The Municipal and Moral Roots of Immigrant and Immigration Policing

Local political battles and their connections with moral reform crucially shaped the policing intersection that federal authorities and municipal state and private groups forged in the early twentieth century. One of the main ways in which native-born whites responded to immigrant working-class men's entry into formal political citizenship in cities like New York and Chicago was to implicate them in "white slavery" (or forced prostitution) conspiracies and in tales of political corruption. As I have analyzed elsewhere, Eastern European Jews were a particular target of these conspiracies, as they settled *en masse* in this era and became engaged in municipal party and radical politics. In the New York City municipal electoral campaigns of 1893–1894 and 1900–1901 native-born, elite, Gentile and Jewish reformers, with the help of commercial newspapers such as the *New York World*, *Sun*, and *Journal*, mobilized cross-class and cross-ethnic alliances against a Democratic machine dominated by working-class immigrant men and alleged to have links to prostitution in immigrant neighborhoods. Local campaigners produced noticeable anti-immigrant and anti-Semitic strains in the major official documents on municipal political and police corruption, such as the Lexow and Mazet Commissions of 1894 and 1899.[2]

Eastern Europeans and other immigrants did participate in prostitution and local politics, just as local officials extorted money from commercial vice. However, beginning in 1893 and as late as 1909, campaigns against corruption targeted immigrant neighborhoods because they were home to influential political constituencies. Immigrant Jews on New York's Lower East Side, for example, were renowned for their links with the machine, for their independence from the Democratic and Republican Parties, and for their leadership in political movements that were even more unsavory to established interests: industrial and trade unionism, socialism, and anarchism. "White slavery" facilitated scintillating stories about the corruption of the body politic through Jewish immigrants, political bosses, and radicals. In the 1909 municipal election campaign, muck-raking journalist G.K. Turner and publisher S.S. McClure broadcast these tales nationally through *McClure's Magazine*, asserting that "certain political associations on the [Lower] East Side" were "composed almost entirely" of men who combined "the proceeds of the shame of women with that of procuring white slave victims," and provided "the backbone of the fraudulent voting." Turner provided a long list of alleged Eastern European and Italian "traders." His hyperbolic claims were presented as "a recital of the *facts* brought out in official investigations" by local antivice organizations, but also the "investigations of the Ellis Island authorities," and the federal and state immigration commissions.[3]

It was through these localized and yet translocally resonating politics that the policing of corruption through *urban immigrant vice* was transformed into a more urgently perceived need to police *immigration and the importation of crime.* If "immigrants" were responsible for degrading the nation's cities then immigrant passage and integration into the nation were obvious channels for greater scrutiny. The ideas, techniques, and personnel deployed in these local urban contests fed directly into the making of federal law and policy targeting immigrant prostitution and "white slavery." These electoral campaigns and linked reform activity began the formation of a loose web of reformers who worked on the regulation of immigrants through their influence on and enactment of immigration and postsettlement policy. They did so through private and state entities ranging from the informal surveillance networks of social settlements and antivice organizations like the Committee of Fourteen, to the New York Police Department (NYPD) and Night Court, the New York State and U.S. Immigration Commissions, programs for "immigrant inspection" at Ellis Island and the Port of New York, to the White House of New York reformer Theodore Roosevelt and international organizations mobilized against "white slavery."

Immigrant Policing Becomes Immigration Inspection

Private reform entities, and women reformers, played a crucial part in extending the role of the state through the regulation of immigrants and through forging links between national government and local policing. The first federal restrictions on immigrant entry were actually centered on moral and racial regulation: the Immigration Act of 1875 banned prostitutes and persons convicted of crimes of moral turpitude, and was aimed at excluding Chinese immigrants in particular. However, it was not until 1903 that reformers extended the moral regulation of immigrants to the borders of the nation in a serious way. In that year the New York Council of Jewish Women (CJW), under the direction of the aptly named Sadie American, initiated the inspection of Jewish steerage passengers through a partnership with the U.S. Immigration and Naturalization Service. Building upon moral reform activism in local campaigns, and work against "white slavery" by international women's organizations such as the Jewish Association for the Protection of Girls and Women, American and the CJW established an Ellis Island Department of Immigrant Aid. After affiliation with the state the CJW's work at the Island continued to be partially funded by Jewish philanthropists.[4]

Also in 1903, prominent Anglo-Protestant reformers—including Margaret Dye Ellis, Josephine Shaw Lowell, Grace Dodge, and Florence Kelley—and Jewish reformers such as American, lobbied for Immigration Service posts for women to inspect first- and second-class cabin passengers when they docked at the Port of New York. Because of a complex combination of male immigration officers' gendered professional gatekeeping, their differing views of the state, and the class and ethnic hierarchies among immigrants, the moral inspection of cabin passengers met with resistance from the outset, and the documentation of its continuance is concentrated between 1903 and 1905. In keeping with the generally more rigorous screening that steerage—that is, working class and primarily Eastern and Southern European—passengers received at Ellis Island, women reformers' moral inspection of immigrant Jewish women without means appears to have continued unabated at least into the mid-1910s.[5]

At Ellis Island, CJW representatives worked through interpreters to interview Jewish immigrants perceived to be in danger. This encompassed all single women between twelve and thirty years old. Like their male counterparts with the Hebrew Immigrant Aid Society (HIAS), CJW representatives helped immigrants through processing at Ellis Island, and in making connections to transportation elsewhere or with family members in New York. The HIAS and the CJW could prevent immigrants from being held or deported by officials. CJW aid workers also had the "power to detain" women, and often did so until it was verified that their destinations and escorts were suitable with regard to the regulation of immigrants' postsettlement behavior.[6]

Many women were shepherded on their way, but others emigrating as cabin and steerage passengers who were perceived to be immoral or "adrift" experienced a range of discipline. Women inspectors ferreted out flirtatious women and cases of extramarital sex or pregnancy. They sent immigrants with confused stories or unsuitable escorts and destinations to local reform institutions. They forced unmarried emigrating couples to marry at Ellis Island before they entered the country. Moreover, women immigrant aid leaders and frontline workers envisioned immigrant inspection to include the discernment of women "brought in for immoral purposes," to use Sadie American's words. When the cabin inspection project was under threat women reformers and their male allies launched a public relations campaign to save the initiative. In significant part this was directed toward President Theodore Roosevelt, who was the central executive-level liaison for Anglo-Protestant women reformers in the establishment of women cabin inspectors. In this context, a letter from Cabin Inspectress Mathilde Wichmann urged Roosevelt that the official state "badge of the inspectress" was essential to the authority required to facilitate "the prevention of disaster to individuals" and "the exclusion of unqualified aliens."[7]

Reformers and officials involved in regulating immigration thus created a loop of intensified criminalization and policing between the national and local levels. Although small numbers of immigrant men were impacted by the morals policing described here, a gendered double standard in morals policing and the workings of a liberal state reluctant to police property owners ensured that women defined as public (and propertyless) were the primary practical targets of state discipline at the national and local levels.[8] From the late–nineteenth century through the years of the first Red Scare, vastly more women were barred or deported from the United States in connection with alleged *immorality* than were men and women who were so policed for their political allegiances (as anarchists, Wobblies, and so on). The dynamics that led to the targeting of women intensified after 1904. Even though antiprostitution language in the 1903 Immigration Act was theoretically directed at agents and procurers (and thus also at men), the slippage endemic to all private and state efforts at moral regulation meant that rhetoric about protecting women translated through policing and prosecution into their punishment.[9]

Immigration Inspection and Immigrant Policing: Fortifying the Loop

More rigorous moral screening at the nation's border fed back into municipal policing. There, immigration reformers and their allies were involved in the establishment of a more tightly configured private-state network for the local policing and discipline of immigrant (and nonimmigrant) women's moral delinquency. These local mechanisms in turn informed a more intensive federal-level moral cleansing of tenuously settled immigrant women. By way of illustration, the records of the CJW's Ellis Island project, and those of the private reform organizations with which the CJW was connected, document how the policing of immigrants at Ellis Island and the Port was linked with an informal but influential network of regulatory endeavors that reached out into the city. CJW members—such as Sadie American, Lillian Wald, Belle Israels, Maude Miner, and Stella Miner—and their Anglo-Protestant reform allies worked to morally assimilate immigrants.

This meant placing women into the poorly paid forms of industrial work where they already predominated. Reformers offered assistance finding housing, but also trained immigrants in the skills of domesticity, and monitored their private lives and spaces through a system of home visiting. Between 1906 and 1908, for example, CJW representatives made 4,314 "friendly" visits to young immigrant women or their families. CJW members undertook a range of educational and supervisory projects to prevent or manage women's fall from virtue: public sex education advocating the sanctity of marriage, a maternity home, leisure venues supervised by reformers, dance hall regulation through licensing, probation work, and a home for women first offenders. CJW members cooperated with other women reformers—from local social settlements, and reform organizations such as the Society for the Prevention of Cruelty to Children and the Association for Improving the Condition of the Poor—in the moral surveillance of families in immigrant neighborhoods. Wald, Israels, and the Miner sisters also cooperated with local police, courts, and private antivice organizations like the Committees of Fifteen and Fourteen, in the morals policing of working-class immigrants.[10]

"Keep These People Out": Frances Kellor and the Reform of Immigration Law

By 1906 or 1907 the private-state apparatus for the moral inspection and surveillance of immigrants entering the country and settling in the city began to include local policing tactics that were more formally intertwined with federal immigration law and policing procedures. In part this reflected the fact that by 1907 federal authorities were undertaking a more intensive campaign against immigrant prostitution and "white slavery" with the cooperation of local state and private actors.[11]

Again, women reformers played important roles in this process. A key figure in this regard was Frances Kellor. Trained in law, sociology, and social work, Kellor had a life-long professional focus on immigrants. In 1906, she was Director of the Inter-Municipal Research Committee. In 1907, she became a member of the antivice Committee of Fourteen. After serving on the New York State Immigration Commission (1908–1909), she became director of the state Bureau of Industries and Immigration. She went on to work as a key committeewoman for Theodore Roosevelt's Progressive Party. Kellor's primary focus was on immigrant labor conditions and Americanization, but she was keenly interested in the *moral* vulnerability of immigrants. The fact that her first degree was in law helps to explain her significant influence on legal matters: protective legislation, immigration law, and the reform of how morals offenses were prosecuted domestically.[12]

From 1906 on, Kellor corresponded and met with powerful men about the illicit importation of women: President Roosevelt, high-level local and federal immigration officials, and locally based reformers such as Republican Congressman William Bennet. After graduating from Albany Law School, Bennet served as a State assemblyman in 1901–1902, a municipal court justice in 1903, and was then elected to three Congresses from 1905 to 1911. He was a prominent member of the Committee of Fourteen and the U.S. Immigration Commission (1907–1910). In 1906 Congressman Bennet asserted to top immigration officials and the press that women were being imported through the Port in a "wholesale fashion . . . for immoral purposes." Frances Kellor was Bennet's source.[13]

New York City Immigration Commissioner Robert Watchorn met with Kellor on the matter in late 1906 and recalled her proclaiming: "I know how difficult it is for the Government to keep these people out, because you have no means of determining whether they are virtuous or not at the time of arrival. Nevertheless shortly after they are admitted they do pursue this unlawful and deplorable course." Importantly with regard to both immigrant women's complicity in "white slavery," and the surveillance and policing of settled immigrants, Kellor implied to Watchorn that immoral women were entering the country clandestinely. He reminded her that immigrants were "paroled at the time of arrival" and could be deported if they were admitted under false pretenses. She then claimed that she would provide a list of immigrants who were currently "living unlawful lives" and thus should be deported. Kellor was given "full access to the ships' manifests," but after "several interviews" with her, the Immigration Commissioner was unable "to get any definite information" confirming her allegations. This was *not* broadcast in the press, and did not appear to mitigate the increasing criminalization of immigrant women.[14]

Kellor's references to the inscrutability of immigrant virtue on landing, her attempts to document their postsettlement "unlawful lives," and Watchorn's reminder of immigrant parole all alluded to the legal ambiguity around entry restriction and deportation that was enshrined in the Immigration Acts of 1891 and 1903. The former in effect elongated the tenure of entry restrictions by authorizing the deportation of aliens who, within one year of arrival, became public charges from causes allegedly existing prior to landing. As Daniel Kanstroom has noted, this 1891 provision "began to bridge the conceptual gap between extended border control and post-entry conduct." This prolonging of entry restrictions was further extended with the two-year statute of limitation for deportation in the 1903 Act.[15]

In January 1907 Kellor contacted President Roosevelt about the new Immigration Act that would be passed the following month. The president's secretary communicated to the federal secretary in charge of immigration—German Jewish New Yorker Oscar Straus—that Kellor urged the inclusion of a provision in the new Act that would enable federal officials to prosecute proprietors of "houses of prostitution to which immigrant girls are enticed" in U.S. cities. At this point Kellor explicitly emphasized policing proprietors (who would mostly be men by this date in New York City), but her general rhetoric and practices around immigrant women implicated *them* in the policing dynamic. Her use of the term "enticed" highlights the nebulous way in which women's agency was framed through the policing of "white slavery," which theoretically involved forced prostitution but in practice encompassed women who *chose* prostitution. Kellor's references to women's dubious virtue at landing and after settlement in her meeting with Commissioner Watchorn indicates that she wanted the state to exclude and deport *women*, and not just men who profited from vice.[16]

Kellor's goals with regard to the policing of immigrant morality implied both the necessity of stronger federal-local links in enforcement, and shifting conceptions of the proper lines of authority for federal and municipal government and the state more generally. Regardless of whether or not Kellor intended the 1907 Immigration Act to police proprietors, within two days of the receipt of her January correspondence on the Act an official Memorandum for Secretary Straus indicated that proprietors were no longer central to the policy discussion. The memo noted that reports that Kellor had provided to officials documented New York City disorderly houses inhabited by a range of "women with immoral tendencies." While "most of the brothels" were reportedly "peopled by women of foreign nativity," the records suggested that "in only a small number of instances" were girls "enticed or decoyed to such places." Kellor's interest in policing the *importation* of women for nefarious purposes, and her highlighting of postsettlement immigrant misconduct, translated into a practical focus on *urban, largely voluntary*, prostitution involving immigrant women. The author of the memo recommended that these were "matters for the municipal authorities."[17]

In less than a week, the Department of Commerce and Labor's Acting Solicitor was discussing Kellor's reports in a second memo headed thus: "In re power of Secretary *to deport prostitutes* under the Act of March 3, 1903, *who have become such since admission to the United States*." This memo foreshadowed the 1907 Immigration Act and how the U.S. Supreme Court in 1909 would interpret it in its opinion in *Keller v.* United States. It emphasized that the "regulation and control of *houses* of prostitution is a matter which is unquestionably left to the State or municipal control." The memo noted, however, that Kellor's reports had led authorities "to a considera-tion of the powers vested in the Department with reference to *exclusion and deportation of prostitutes.*" Both early 1907 memos shifted attention from proprietors to prostitutes, but in the second Acting Solicitor Nesbit argued forcefully against the assumption that a woman practicing prosti-tution after entering the country had necessarily done so before entry:

> it would be highly unreasonable to hold that an alien who before admission had never committed a crime involving moral turpitude but after admission . . . committed such a crime would be liable to deportation. In such a case the remedy would not be deportation, but . . . punishment by enforcement of the criminal laws of the jurisdiction in which the offense was committed. The right of deportation is the exercise of a high sovereign power and great care should be taken that the authority conferred is not exceeded.

He concluded the memo with a clear assertion that "immigrants who were not prostitutes at the time they entered" were "not deportable" under cur-rent statutes.[18]

The Acting Solicitor's opinion on this point was ignored, and his memo was the ironic harbinger of a shift in Immigration Law. The Immigration Act of 1907 deemed that "any alien woman or girl [found to be a prostitute] . . . within three years after she shall have entered . . . shall be deemed to be unlawfully within the United States." Deportation applied to women entrapped or coerced into prostitution or engaged in any "immoral purpose."[19] By September 1907 the Bureau of Immigration defined the enforcement of the Immigration Act as follows: "The fact that an alien, when apprehended, is found practicing prostitution . . . is so strong an indication that the alien was a prostitute . . . at the time of entry . . . as to raise a presumption of fact that such alien belonged to one of the excluded classes in question at the time of arrival." Immigrant immorality *after* landing was sufficient evidence of immorality *upon* landing. This interpre-tation was further legitimized in 1909 by the legal arguments of the U.S. Attorney General and U.S. Supreme Court Justice Holmes's dissenting opinion in *Keller v. United States.*[20] These changes in immigration law and policy, compounded with the impact of already gender-biased policing, meant that after 1907 the number of women barred and deported in this manner rose dramatically. By 1915, approximately 2,500 women had been barred from the United States in connection with prostitution, and hundreds had been deported.[21]

It is unclear from Immigration Bureau correspondence whether Frances Kellor's interest in policing disorderly houses linked with immigrants was informed by her perception of the demographics of proprietors as a group. In October 1907, Kellor produced a report that claimed to document "the social evil as it relates to the importation of women." In it she asserted the existence of a "syndicate" which imported women from Europe, but the detailed description that she provided was once again of the "disorderly house business in New York," which Kellor claimed to be controlled by the French and Jewish "nationalities." Kellor argued that while "the French houses" were reputed "to be worse," they were actually not "to be so much feared as the Jewish." She drew upon an acknowledgment of both the moral propriety of respectable Jews and the money-grubbing stereotype: because "The Jew" had been raised to know "the value of morality and decency," if they were linked with prostitution they were "thoroughly vicious and bad." The French were "not so grasping in their desire for business." Kellor warned that New York was a haven for the worst of the worst: Jewish men running houses in the Tenderloin district had "been chased out of Pittsburgh, Newark and Philadelphia." She concluded: "They are Jews and I have yet to find a city . . . in which they have not succeeded in corrupting and demoralizing both the police and the politician."²²

Like other reports documenting antiprostitution campaigns involving Jewish immigrants, this one is held in the papers of settlement and moral reform leader Lillian Wald. The connections that Kellor and Wald enjoyed make it probable that this report circulated among officials at multiple levels of the state. Wald is credited with convincing Governor Charles Hughes to establish the New York State Immigration Commission (NYSIC). Wald, Kellor, and fellow immigrant, vice, and municipal reformer James Bronson Reynolds, all served on this body. I detail below how elements of Kellor's 1907 report were reiterated in later documents produced through the "white slavery" panic, including those of the U.S. Immigration Commission.²³

"Special Inspectress" Helen Bullis: Immigration Policing in the City Streets

The 1907 Immigration Act led to an increase in barred and deported women in part because of intensified federal involvement in the policing of domestic prostitution. Greater involvement by the federal government and reformers such as Frances Kellor in turn heightened the municipal policing and prosecution of immigrant women's prostitution. The operation of this local-national policing loop is directly confirmed by Helen Bullis, a "Special Inspectress" for the Immigration Service at Ellis Island who also cooperated with the Committee of Fourteen in its vice investigations. Bullis reported to New York City Immigration Commissioner

Watchorn that by August 1907 "the recent efforts of the [federal] Government toward the suppression of the traffic in immigrant women" had led to "accompanying unusual activity of the Police Department in raiding and closing disorderly houses." By 1907 or 1908 immigration officials were directly aiding the local police in Tenderloin vice raids. By October 1907 at the latest Special Inspectress Bullis was in regular communication with Immigration Commissioner Watchorn and the Fourth Deputy Police Commissioner of New York City with regard to her surveillance of landing and settled immigrant women. She worked in tandem with the Police Department, instigating investigations and raids, and the prosecution and deportation of immigrants allegedly involved in prostitution.[24]

Through their communications with other reformers, officials, politicians, and the press, reformers such as Kellor and Bullis helped to produce social paranoia about the clandestine importation of alien immorality. Kellor asserted that immigrants appeared "virtuous," but pursued an "unlawful and deplorable course" after landing. Bullis warned that women were "arriving for immoral purposes," but were "taking precautions" which made it "very hard to discover them upon landing." Bullis' suspicions—at times based on anonymous tips—were not always groundless and her investigations did unearth the practice of prostitution by recent immigrants. However, like Kellor's nebulous assertions to Commissioner Watchorn, Bullis' surveillance reports reveal the tenuous evidence upon which many of her assertions were founded. A recently immigrated woman was presumed immoral who was "alone and not met by anyone," who was followed to resorts that were "under suspicion," who was "in the company of a known prostitute," or who sent her baggage to an address on "a block where there [was] scarcely one decent place."[25]

Bullis' construction of guilt by association was formally codified in Immigration Service policy and Immigration Law. A 1909 "Confidential Circular" from Commissioner-General of Immigration Daniel Keefe ordered all Commissioners and Inspectors of Immigration to fully investigate any "woman or girl applying for admission" who was suspected of "being destined to a life of prostitution" because her destination was "within the confines" of officially defined "restricted districts" in U.S. cities. The Immigration Service mapped whole sections of urban space as indicative of moral turpitude for all immigrants (and particularly immigrant women) landing there. The 1910 Immigration Act further embedded a reliance on postsettlement conduct and guilt by association as indicative of immigrant conduct and character before migration: it deemed any immigrant "employed by, in, or in connection with any house of prostitution or music or dance hall or other place of amusement . . . frequented by prostitutes" as "unlawfully in the United States" and *subject to deportation until such time as they became U.S. citizens.*[26] Today, this slippery legal logic around entry restriction and deportation operates through the Immigration Act of 1990. Immigrants "engaged in prostitution within 10 years" of entry are deemed "inadmissible at time of entry" and thus deportable.[27]

In the early twentieth century, Kellor and Bullis ensured an active link between morals policing at the nation's gates and within the city, through the reform and rigorous enforcement of both Federal immigration law, and local policing and court procedure. Bullis produced the same sort of slippage from targeting men to women in morals policing that characterized Kellor's work. Judging by Bullis' correspondence with Watchorn, she may have come to focus on the misconduct of recently immigrated women because they were easier to police than procurers and importers. In October 1907, Bullis was concerned with immoral women immigrating to the city clandestinely, but like Kellor she also targeted brothelkeepers and "houses of ill-fame" to which immoral women were "manifested." In November, Commissioner Watchorn responded to Bullis' reports with the sort of caution that he had expressed to Kellor: "What you state tends to confirm but does not conclusively prove the existence of what is commonly called 'the White Slave Traffic' . . . Proof—nothing but proof—sufficiently strong to convince a jury will accomplish the purpose we have in view. Is there no way in which you can take one concrete case and pursue it to a conclusive issue?" By the spring of 1908, Bullis was fully concentrated on unmasking and deporting immoral immigrant women. In December 1908, Bullis wrote to Commissioner Watchorn that "the pimps" were "a class unquestionably more criminal than their women," but there is no evidence that Bullis pursued these men. Rather, Bullis again communicated to the commissioner that she had "the honor" to report that seven more women arrested for morals offenses were deported with her assistance.[28]

The Politics of Disciplining Immigration and the City Courts

The national-local policing intersection targeting immigrant morality also played a key role in the reform of the local court system. By 1908, some local Night Court officials, including President of the New York City Board of Magistrates Charles Whitman, and members of the Police Department, were cooperating with the Immigration Service in order to enforce the 1907 Immigration Act clause that allowed women to be deported for immorality within three years of landing. This team of federal and local officials sought to ensure that immigrant women arrested on morals charges uniformly answered under oath the question "How long have you been in the U.S.?" and had their affidavits stamped with an immigration date. The key question thus was temporal: A finding that an accused woman was guilty of engaging in prostitution during the legally defined postsettlement probationary period for the scrutiny of immigrant morality,[29] would become the basis for concluding that the woman had been immoral *before* landing (and thus should have been excluded).

The 1907 Immigration Act question for accused women was almost certainly inserted into Night Court procedure at the urging of reformers such as Frances Kellor, William Bennet, and court insider Charles Whitman. The web of reformers and officials linking immigration policy, local courts, private reform organizations, and electoral politics that makes this explanation plausible also illustrates the complexities of the national-local policing intersection. Congressman and Committee of Fourteen member Bennet was a municipal judge only a few years earlier. As Bennet's 1906 dissemination of Kellor's assertions about the importation of women foreshadowed, by 1907 her work was linked with the Immigration Service and the Fourteen. Through the Fourteen's legal research committee Kellor was active in reforming the municipal prosecution of vice. Reformers from the Fourteen and court officials such as Whitman *created* the specialized Night Court for morals offenses in August 1907, the same month that Bullis highlighted the impact of federal efforts on local policing in her correspondence with the New York City Immigration Commissioner. The Fourteen's research committee was staffed and funded by women reformers, and committee members Kellor, Mary Kingsbury Simkhovitch, and Ruth Standish Baldwin linked this research body with the immigrant surveillance network provided through institutions such as Simkhovitch's Greenwich House settlement and the New York Probation Association (NYPA). Both Baldwin and Simkhovitch were active directors of the NYPA. The Council of Jewish Women's Maude Miner cofounded the NYPA with Charles Whitman, who had appointed her a probation officer in the new Night Court, where immigrant women were her primary concern.[30]

"Special Inspectress" Bullis acted as the New York City Immigration Commissioner's eyes in the Night Court, where in April 1908 she discovered that some police officers were advising women to answer the 1907 Immigration Act question in such a way as to avoid "being turned over at once to Ellis Island." Some court clerks were not demanding that women appear "in person to answer" the question, and were taking answers from arresting officers instead. Many affidavits for "alien prostitutes bore no immigration stamp" as a result. Bullis pushed for the removal of the offending officials and for enforcement of the requirement that women swear to their immigration date before the court. One culprit for the missing stamp was "an assistant clerk," who "when directed to put it on in future, refused, saying that this kind of procedure was 'damned nonsense.' " The clerk was "under charges," but his bold refusal to cooperate suggests the likelihood that more low-level functionaries may have resisted policing immigrants.[31]

Some officials did more than refuse to police. In the spring of 1909 federal-local cooperation unearthed an alleged "racket" in false documentation of landing dates operated by vice practitioners in the Tenderloin and federal and local officials. One accused official investigated by the Immigration Service was a Night Court interpreter, Solomon Lubliner, who had previously been employed at Ellis Island. He and his "confederates" were allegedly assisting immigrant women accused of prostitution "to frustrate deportation proceedings" by providing them "with names and other data regarding arrival beyond the statutory period." It was precisely this sort of resistance by low-level officials and the accused that led to the 1910 Immigration Act's elimination of the three-year statute of limitation on immigrant moral parole.[32]

In assessing the motives of resistant officials we must weigh the fact that officials like these were sometimes engaged in exploiting the survival strategies of working-class immigrants, including prostitution. Reformers such as Frances Kellor critiqued employment and travel agencies that took advantage of immigrants in this manner. In the case of immigrant women in the Night Court, police officers resisting the 1907 Act argued that if pimps were alarmed by women being deported efforts to "secure" the pimps would be made more difficult. The low policing and prosecution rates for men connected with vice in this era undermine any simple assertion of police strategy or chivalry. Given that policemen and low-level officials were working class and recently immigrated or the children of immigrants, empathy may also have informed their actions.[33]

Charles Whitman, however, acted as a key liaison on court reform for private organization reformers and immigration officials in ways that advanced his own judicial and political career. In 1909, Congressman William Bennet conducted the *failed* reform mayoral campaign of Otto Bannard. In the same year Charles Whitman finessed an alliance with reformers and a campaign highlighting Tammany's links with "white slavery" into his election as District Attorney (D.A.) (by 1915 he was governor of New York State). As D.A., Whitman promptly appointed as his assistants two lawyers who had been engaged in reform efforts around immigrants, crime, and political corruption since the 1890s: Frank Moss and James Reynolds. These men and their allies in private organizations and higher levels of government continued to construct vice in immigrant neighborhoods and at the nation's gates as an urgent menace, and the reform of the city's courts as a crucial solution. Through the continued influence of Whitman, the final report by the

Committee of Fourteen's research committee, produced under the supervision of Frances Kellor, was an influential document in the further reform of the Night Court into an even more specialized and punitive Women's Court for morals offenses in 1910.[34]

The insistence that strong links between immigration and crime required the reform and operational intersection of policing and prosecution at all levels of the state was further legitimized by the U.S. Immigration Commission's 1910 report on the *Importation and Harboring of Women for Immoral Purposes.* As a prominent member of the USIC, Congressman Bennet submitted this "white slavery" report to Congress in December 1909. The USIC, and the *New York Times'* coverage of it, presented international "white slavery," immigration, and urban vice controlled by "foreigners," as overlapping phenomena. According to the *Times,* the USIC report recommended more stringent policing and placing "the burden of proof . . . on the immigrants." The perspective and recommendations of the USIC clearly reflected the influence of New York City reformers. The *Times,* paraphrasing the USIC, specified that the alien threat was centered in "two organizations of importance, one French, the other Jewish." The echo of Frances Kellor's claims here is unsurprising if we recall her links with Bennett, other reformers and officials, and the New York State Immigration Commission. She was also now the director of the New York State Bureau of Industries and Immigration.[35]

The USIC and the *Times* also presented the corruption of New York's courts as an aspect of international "white slavery." To illustrate how "the agents of the traffic keep their eye on . . . law officers" the *Times* quoted the USIC's commentary on the workings of the Night Court: "The women arrested . . . soon learned to know the temper of each Magistrate . . . The severest Judges had few cases . . . and the lenient one had his courtroom filled . . . It is a common occurrence for women to be placed on probation even though they had previously served several times in the Workhouse." Here women's resistance to the legal system and judicial discretion are used to demonstrate the conspiratorial evils of "white slavery."[36]

This USIC assessment and the evidence that Helen Bullis uncovered suggest that while reformers set up an apparatus to police immigrants, local groups—the accused and some officials—worked to subvert these efforts. Federal investigators such as Bullis found that this directly impacted the national-local policing intersection. Varied police conduct at different ranks and in varied situations—like the resistance of court officials and the cautionary notes of Immigration Commissioners—illustrate the fragmented and contradictory workings of the local and federal state, and the policing intersection between them. Local police raided or tolerated vice venues, fought members of the judiciary in an effort to convict women, and (with other officials) helped women subvert judicial process and avoid deportation.[37]

Morals policing also demonstrates how the workings of the local state in the management of immigrants was linked with municipal institutions such as the courts and extended to the federal jurisdiction of Ellis Island. The actions of Ellis Island officials outlined above suggest parallels to the sort of urban machine resistance to the efficient discipline of working-class conduct that maddened municipal reformers in this era. In some ways the Ellis Island administration did operate like the municipal machine, but through New York State Republican, and federal Democratic and Republican networks. Top New York immigration officials, staff, and Ellis Island contracts followed federal-level political party shifts, with top officials having more rapid turnaround. Thus the Republicans held federal power from 1897 to 1913 but federal Democratic staff appointees from the Cleveland administration were still in their posts well into the twentieth century. Serious enforcement of the civil service requirements instituted in 1896 was slow in coming. Moreover, as they remain today, arriving immigrants were inherently vulnerable to bribery, extortion, theft, and fraud. Charges and investigations of corruption among Ellis Island officials, and concession owners and employees, began surfacing by the late 1890s. All of these sociopolitical factors motivated the three investigations into corruption on the Island undertaken between 1898 and 1906, the last by municipal reformer James Reynolds.[38]

It is important to appreciate the imperfect operations of the local and federal state, and the policing intersection constructed between them by private and state actors in the Progressive Era. This must not, however, diminish our recognition of the ways in which this intersection seriously impacted immigrant and nonimmigrant, working-class women. After 1907 and especially 1910, the linked reform of local courts and federal immigration law, and more intensive screening, surveillance, and policing of immigrant women, combined with other local reforms in the policing and prosecution of vice to create a noteworthy web of moral discipline. By 1911–1915 New York City's Women's Court conviction rates ranged between 84 and 93 percent. In 1912–1913 this was accompanied by an incarceration rate of 87 percent, almost half of whom were first offenders. After 1915 the Court's conviction rates dropped into the seventieth percentile, but astonishingly first offenders made up almost 60 percent of this lower percentage. In these same years, hundreds of women were barred and deported from the country as allegedly immoral criminals. Many of the deported would have been convicted in the city's reformed Women's Court. Moreover, the policing of landed immigrants through a local-national intersection that was pioneered via

Ellis Island and New York City spread to other cities such as Chicago and San Francisco.[39]

Finally, the municipal campaigns against immigrant prostitution and the local-national loop that shaped a punitive local apparatus for the policing of morals offenses ultimately had the harshest local impact on those New York women who were denied the possibility of assimilation: African Americans. The possibility of whiteness shaped social, political, and economic integration and resources after settlement, and thus kept even the most racialized European immigrant groups and their children from being represented in Progressive Era vice prosecutions beyond their level in the general population.[40]

African Americans of multiple generations were denied this level of integration and resources, which created cruel ironies in local morals policing. The construction of an elaborate and intensive apparatus for policing and prosecuting prostitution in New York City was initiated primarily to regulate the conduct and spaces of working-class European immigrants, especially Eastern European Jews on the Lower East Side. It was pursued and elaborated by reformers intent on regulating immigrants as they entered the nation and settled in the city. Yet by the mid-1910s the local apparatus most singularly targeted African American women in Harlem. In 1914, African Americans made up about 2 percent of the city's population, but provided approximately 35 percent of Women's Court cases. African American women were also most likely to be sentenced to the workhouse for their first offense, and by 1916–1917 were estimated to make up 36 percent of the female population incarcerated there. This meant that they were overrepresented in this institution at over fifteen times their city population. The fact that this level of what Loïc Wacquant has termed "racialized hyper-incarceration" was produced through the citizenship battles of whites served as the ultimate concrete and symbolic denial of citizenship to African American women.[41]

Some Concluding Questions

I end with a few questions that this history of morals policing raises for present concerns. Historically distinct conditions apply to the Progressive Era and our own. Yet the analysis here of the development of federal-local intersections in policing and immigration at the turn of the last century suggests that these earlier intersections were constructed through historical specificity in ways that may illuminate contemporary manifestations.

Important shifts in the role of the state and private entities in social regulation, reforms in policing, and intensified federal and local cooperation in policing, marked both eras. In the Progressive Era, these shifts were informed by profound changes in political economy attending the growth of industrial capitalism and transnational shifts in populations and power. Although the attacks of September 11, 2001, have facilitated drastic changes in the way police personnel are deployed, current United States policing tactics (and their links with the regulation of immigrants) are grounded in, and consequential for, the broader political economy.

Just as it is unhelpful to conceive of recent shifts in policing as unprecedented, it will expand our understanding of crisis-inspired changes to consider how they are made possible and unfold in relation to long-term developments associated with the rise of advanced capitalism: the intense globalization of economic production, the rise of a corporate model of governance that in the name of global competitiveness prioritizes the dismantling of the welfare state in the economic north and the austerity of "structural adjustment" in the economic south, the radical domestic and international concentration of wealth, and the linked policy ascendance of internationally circulating strategies for "governing through crime" and risk management.[42]

In the Progressive Era, key questions around policing were channeled through struggles concerning gender and the sexual morality of women because the regulation and mobilization of women were at the crux of fundamental sociopolitical and economic shifts: in the division of labor, in the growth of cities, in the construction of citizenship and entitlement, and of the public and private spheres. If racialized men—men perceived to be Arabic or South Asian—are the overwhelming target of the current intersection between policing and immigration, a crucial question is whether this targeting is exclusively linked to the demographics of Al Qaeda or with broader factors of global political economy.

The history of morals policing recounted here highlights the importance of paying attention to how immigration, national and local security, and the links among them, are grounded and deployed in the political strategies of the Republican and Democratic Parties, and state and private actors linked with various levels of the state. The current linking, for policy and/or rhetorical purposes, of national security and immigration issues raises similar questions and implications for contemporary U.S. elections, appointments, policy victories, and socioeconomic resources. By way of just one example, massive funds are being tacked onto the coattails of the war on terror.[43]

The earlier history of women's participation in the relations among immigration, law, and policing also highlights the need to pay close attention to the nonelectoral politics shaping current "reforms" and their impact. How are private organizations, such as anti-immigration groups

9/11 Families for a Secure America and The Federation for American Immigration Reform, or "inbetween" groups, such as The Council on American-Islamic Relations, involved in influencing and/or resisting the development of a contemporary national-local apparatus to police and deport immigrants?[44]

The complexity of the history around policing and immigration in the late-nineteenth- and early-twentieth century also encourages us to look for contemporary contradictions and forms of fragmentation in the state and linked forms of policing. How, for example, do conflicts of interest or differing views of the state's role and scope within and between relevant state and private groups impact policing in the post–September 11, 2001, climate? What are the consequences as shifts in priorities in policing work through existing political, legal, policing, and criminal justice systems at various levels of the state? Are longstanding or new checks and balances operating to temper the impact of social panic on policing practice? Is anyone, like Immigration Commissioners Watchorn in 1907, asking for "Proof—nothing but proof"?

Perhaps the most important questions to emerge from this history of a federal-local policing initiative center around how fear and bias combine with unequal power relations to shape policing and law both discursively and materially, on the ground. In the Progressive Era, people used concerns about "white slavery," immigrant prostitution, and immigration itself, as sensationalized and flexible vocabularies through which to debate a range of topics. The inflammatory and shape-shifting character of the languages that helped to fuel the building of new state and private forms of policing in this earlier era is evident in present-day vocabularies deployed in the war on terror. How are contemporary conceptions of threat and protection framed through nebulous narratives of conspiracy to construct citizenship, community, and professional expertise for particular groups and discipline, suspension, or refusal of citizenship and human rights for others? How are features that characterized this earlier policing history— the construction of status crimes (from being a "prostitute" to being an "undocumented person"), guilt by association, and the legal elision of entry restrictions and deportation for post-entry conduct evident in today's context?

I have touched on the fact that African Americans were unintended victims of this federal-local policing initiative in the Progressive Era. How do the dynamics of slippage and unintended consequences in the war on terror impact groups who are generally vulnerable to policing? At a recent Canadian Colloquium on the Criminalization of Poverty, for example, an advocate for the homeless described how state and private policing of the urban spaces where many of the poor live has markedly intensified in the post–September 11, 2001, climate,[45] suggesting that the criminalization of particular groups spills over into broader ideas and policies. Has the United States come to define policing internationally, at the nation's borders, and in its cities, as fundamental to the character of citizenship and democracy? These questions are as relevant today as they were in 1907.

Notes

1. The author offers her sincere thanks to editors Stacy McGoldrick and Andrea McArdle for their contributions to this chapter. For her intrepid research assistance, I also offer thanks to Cynthia Pierce, City University of New York School of Law, J.D. Candidate (May 2006).

2. For analysis of political campaigns against prostitution, and press and Jewish involvement see Johnson, "Protection, Virtue, and the 'Power to Detain' " and chapter three of Johnson, "Defining 'Social Evil': Moral Citizenship & Governance in New York City, 1890–1920," Ph.D. dissertation., New School for Social Research, 2002. See also Edward Bristow, *Prostitution and Prejudice: The Jewish Fight Against White Slavery, 1870–1939* (New York: Schocken Books, 1983). The chief counsel for the Lexow and Mazet Commissions, Frank Moss, undertook an additional study in 1897 that devoted almost a hundred pages to organized Jewish crime in the city. See Marc Connelly, *The Response to Prostitution in the Progressive Era* (Chapel Hill: University of North Carolina Press, 1980), pp. 60–61, 118–119. For Moss's 1897 report and the Mazet Commission see Arthur Goren, *New York Jews and the Quest for Community: The Kehillah Experiment, 1908–1922* (New York: Columbia University Press, 1970), p. 134; Bristow, *Prostitution and Prejudice*, pp. 46–47, 175. For the alleged moral and political corruption of immigrants in New York City and Chicago see the following: George Kibbe Turner, "Tammany's Control of New York City by Professional Criminals," *McClure's Magazine* (June 1909); S.S. McClure, "The Tammanyizing of Civilization," *McClure's Magazine* (November 1909); George Kibbe Turner, "The City of Chicago: A Study of the Great Immoralities," *McClure's* Magazine (April 1907), pp. 581–582; T. Bingham, "Foreign Criminals in New York," *North American Review* (September 1908), pp. 383–394; "Congress Receives White Slave Report," *New York Times* (December 11, 1909).

3. On New York City politics at the turn of the last century, and the place of Jewish New Yorkers in it, see David Hammack, *Power and Society*: Greater New York at the Turn of the Century (New York: Columbia University Press, 1987), pp. 137, 151, 175–176; Angel and Gurock in Jackson (ed.), *Encyclopedia*, p. 621; Rudolf Glanz, *The Jewish Woman in America: Two Female Immigrant Generations 1820–1929*. Volume I the Eastern European Jewish Woman (New York: Ktav Publishing House, 1976), 110, p. 189, note 27; Connelly, *Response to Prostitution*, pp. 60–61. The Turner quotation is from "The Daughters of the Poor," *McClure's Magazine* (November 1909), pp. 45–61 (emphasis in original).

4. On the 1875 Immigration Act see the following: Mae M. Ngai, "The Strange Career of the Illegal Alien: Immigration Restriction and Deportation Policy in the United States, 1921–1965," *Law & History Review*, 21 (2003), pp. 73–74; Daniel Kanstroom, "Deportation, Social Control, and Punishment: Some Thoughts About Why Hard Laws Make Bad Cases," *Harvard Law Review*, 113 (2000), p. 1889; Lucy Salyer, *Laws Harsh as Tigers: Chinese Immigrants and the Shaping of Modern Immigration Law* (Chapel Hill: University of North Carolina Press, 1995); Lucie Cheng Hirata, "Free, Indentured, Enslaved: Chinese Prostitutes in Nineteenth-Century America," *Signs* 5 (1) (1979), pp. 3–29. Sadie American's father changed the family name from Abraham. The National CJW joined England's Jewish Association for the Protection of Girls and Women in 1902 (through the persuasion of Sadie American). Faith Rogow, *Gone to Another Meeting: The National Council of Jewish Women, 1893–1993* (Tuscaloosa: University of Alabama Press, 1993), pp. 136–138, Linda Kuzmack, *Woman's Cause: The Jewish Women's Movement in England and the United States, 1881–1933* (Columbus, OH: Ohio State University Press, 1990), p. 69.

5. Documentation of the morals policing of immigrants can be found in *Records of the Immigration and Naturalization Service*, microform, Series A: Subject Correspondence Files, Part 3: Ellis Island 1900–1933, Reel 5 (hereafter cited as RINS 3:5), and Part 5: Prostitution and "White Slavery," 1902–1933, Reels 1, 4, and 7 (hereafter cited as RINS 5:1 or 4 or 7). Other immigrants were inspected for virtue by Ellis Island "matrons," but Immigration Service records suggest that this effort was not as systematic (or well-documented) as the CJW and cabin passenger ventures. For more detailed analysis of women reformers' moral inspection of steerage and cabin immigrants (including the complex dynamics limiting cabin inspection) see Johnson, "Protection, Virtue, and the 'Power to Detain,' " and Johnson, "Defining 'The Social Evil,' " pp. 257–280. Thomas Monroe Pitkin, *Keepers of the Gate: A History of Ellis Island*, notes the fact that Ellis Island matrons were generally on the lookout for immigrant "prostitutes" (New York: New York University Press, 1975), p. 101.

6. Statement by Sadie American to Secretary of Commerce and Labor George B. Cortelyou, describing a May 22, 1903 meeting on the retention of inspectors for cabin passengers (hereafter cited as Statement by American), in RINS 3:5: 0082–85. In this period the Immigration Commissioner was within the Department of Labor and Commerce, after which the unit migrated bureaucratically. See *Records of the Immigration and Naturalization Service*. The CJW claimed to have prevented the deportation of 1,327 Jewish women from 1908 to 1911. The CJW's work paralleled that of the Hebrew Immigrant Aid Society (HIAS), which processed men and families at Ellis Island. Although it involves the HIAS, the oral history of woman who emigrated from the Ukraine in 1914 illustrates how immigrant aid worked, including help finding housing and employment. EIOHP #123, 7–9, 11–13. For immigrant aid work see the following: *Proceedings of the Triennial Conventions of the National Council of Jewish Women* (Chicago: Toby Rubovits, 1908), pp. 147–148, 154–155, 208–209; Rogow, *Gone to Another Meeting*, 136–142, 146–147, 148, 151; Kuzmack, *Woman's Cause*, p. 72; Kathie Friedman-Kasaba, *Memories of Migration: Gender,*

Ethnicity, and Work in the Lives of Jewish and Italian Women in New York, 1870–1924 (Albany, New York: State University of New York Press, 1996), pp. 102–103, 119; Susan A. Glenn, *Daughters of the Shtetl: Life and Labor in the Immigrant Generation* (Ithaca, New York: Cornell University Press, 1990), pp. 51–53, 256, note 6.

7. For the range of discipline enacted by immigration aid leaders and frontline workers see the following: Margaret Batchelder to Hon. Theodore Roosevelt, June 18, 1903, in RINS 3:5: 0026–0027, 0032, 0033; Mathilde Wichmann to President Roosevelt, May 26, 1903, in RINS 3:5: 0048–0057; Wichmann to Cortelyou, May 26, 1903, in RINS 3:5: 0126–0136; "Examples of Women Aliens" (March 22, April 1 and 14, May 2, 1903), in RINS 3:5: 0051–0052; Williams to Commissioner-General of Immigration, April 16, 1903, in RINS 3:5: 0185, 0186, 0187; Josepha Lassoe to Roosevelt, June 18, 1903, in RINS 3:5: 0035–0040; Williams to Commissioner-General, December 1, 1904, in RINS 3:5: 0242; Williams to Commissioner-General, March 9, 1903, in RINS 3:5: 0192–0194. Cortelyou to Roosevelt, July 29, 1903, in RINS 3:5: 024–027; Margaret Dye Ellis to V.H. Metcalf, February 2, 1905, in RINS 3:5: 0228; Ellis to Roosevelt, March 27, 1903, in RINS 3:5: 0012; Williams to Commissioner-General, June 3, 1904, in RINS 3:5: 0252; Statement by American in RINS 3:5: 0082–0085; Ellis, "Statement Concerning Women Immigration Inspectors" (1903) in RINS 3:5: 0077, 0078, 0072. The cabin inspection campaign was initiated in January 1903 by a meeting between President Roosevelt and Margaret Dye Ellis, who urged that cabin passengers deserved as much "care and protection" from "evil disposed persons" as steerage passengers. Within a month, five women were appointed. Ellis to Metcalf, February 2, 1905, in RINS 3:5: 0225. For analysis of Roosevelt's involvement see Johnson, "Protection, Virtue, and the 'power to detain'." Correspondence to the Commissioner-General of Immigration (who was also the Secretary of Commerce and Labor) was addressed to one of these titles or the name of the person holding them. I have tried to remain true to the originals in my citations.

8. From 1904 through 1907, 81 women versus 10 men were barred in connection with prostitution. From 1907 to 1909, 326 women and 32 men were deported under moral justification. See "Arrest and Deportation of Prostitutes and Procurers of Prostitutes," Department Circular no. 156, Bureau of Immigration and Naturalization, Department of Commerce and Labor, Office of the Secretary, September 26, 1907, in RINS 5:1. Connelly, *Response to Prostitution*, pp. 56–58, 175, note 7. With regard to the general operation of a gendered double standard in morals policing the numbers tell the tale. In 1912 and 1913 there were 8,299 arraignments in Manhattan's Women's Court, with conviction rates of 84% and 93% respectively. In twelve months from 1912 to 1913 there were *thirty-seven* cases brought against men in connection with commercial vice. Seventy-six percent were convicted. See Committee of Fourteen, *Annual Report* (New York: Committee of Fourteen, 1913 [hereafter cited as C14AR (1913)]), pp. 24–25, 31, 43; C14AR (1929), p. 33; C14AR (1914), pp. 9, 31–32 and "Summary of Progress." The federal White Slave Traffic Act (or Mann Act) is considered to be the most serious tool for the moral discipline of immigrant

men. From 1910 through 1915 there were only 1,057 Mann Act convictions *nationally* (Maude Miner, *Slavery of Prostitution: A Plea for Emancipation* [New York: MacMillan, 1916], p. 118). This is less than half the 3,411 women convicted in Women's Court in 1915 alone. C14AR (1929), p. 33. For a detailed analysis of the gendered double standard in morals policing in New York City in this era see Johnson, "Defining 'The Social Evil,' " chapter 5. On the morals policing of men see especially pp. 538–548. For discussion of the Supreme Court ruling that vice proprietors were not under federal jurisdiction, see Johnson, "Defining 'The Social Evil,' " chapter 3, and Connelly, *Response to Prostitution*, pp. 50–54, 175, note 7.

9. From 1904 to 1908, 205 women were barred in connection with prostitution. From 1908 to 1915 2,317 women were so barred. In addition to deportation figures in the previous note, 392 women were deported in 1914, and 204 in 1915. "Arrest and Deportation of Prostitutes and Procurers of Prostitutes," and Connelly, *Response to Prostitution*, pp. 56–58, 175, note 7. The deportation of radicals peaked with the uncharacteristically high number (446) expelled in 1921. Before 1921 a tiny number of "anarchists" were excluded. A small number of IWW members were deported during and after World War I, and a small number of anarchists were deported in 1918–1919. William Preston Jr., *Aliens and Dissenters: Federal Suppression of Radicals, 1903–1933*, 2nd ed. (Urbana: University of Illinois Press, 1994), pp. 33, 99–100, 206.

10. For information on early NYCJW moral reform efforts see *Proceedings of the Triennial Conventions*, pp. 147–148, 154–155, 208–209; Elizabeth I. Perry, *Belle Moskowitz: Feminine Politics and the Exercise of Power in the Age of Alfred E. Smith* (New York: Oxford University Press, 1987), pp. 30 ff. For Miner, the New York Probation Association (NYPA), and Waverly House, see her *Slavery of Prostitution*. For analysis of her work with immigrant women see Johnson, "Defining 'The Social Evil,' " pp. 306–312. For the NYPA's surveillance of immigrants see the NYPA FOLDER and the Correspondence 1912–1913 folder, box 18, Series II: Director's and Executives' Records, *Greenwich House Records, 1896–1956* (New York: Tamiment Institute Library Microfilm, 1995) Reel 2198. For attempts at leisure supervision see Perry, *Belle Moskowitz*, pp. 43–57, Moses Rischin, *The Promised City: New York's Jews, 1870–1914* (Cambridge, MA: Harvard University Press, 1962), p. 207. The text of 1910s laws regulating dance halls is in Arthur Spingarn, *Laws Relating to Sex Morality in New York City* (New York: Century Co., 1917), pp. 51–52. See also Peiss, *Cheap Amusements*, chapters 4 and 7. On women's cooperation with the Committees of Fifteen and Fourteen see Johnson, "Defining 'The Social Evil,' " chapters 2–5, and Belle Israel, "The Way of the Girl," *The Survey*, 22 (July 3, 1909), pp. 486–497.

11. Pitkin, *Keepers of the Gate*, p. 102.

12. For a summary of Kellor's work, especially with regard to immigrants and her influence with top officials, see John Higham, *Strangers in the Land: Patterns of American Nativism 1860–1925* (New York: Atheneum, 1971), pp. 44, 239. John Higham's assessment of Kellor's leadership in the Americanization movement is an apt one for her work with immigrants: "In one breath she preached social

welfare and national discipline" (239). Kellor manifested her interest in the orderly integration of immigrants into the nation's social fabric through a concern with assimilation, disciplining delinquency, and mitigating the exploitation of immigrants. What was most evident in her work around immigrant prostitution was her concern with social discipline. For Kellor's ideas on delinquency and discipline see her *Experimental Sociology* (New York: MacMillan, 1901) and her analysis of "Reform and Industrial Schools" in Charles Henderson, *Outline of Study, for Officers of Correctional Institutions* (Jeffersonville, IN: Indiana Reformatory Printing Trade School, 1900), pp. 7–21. For Kellor and the Committee of Fourteen see their *Annual Report* (New York: Committee of Fourteen, 1907), pp. 6–8, 12–13. Kellor was born in Ohio and raised by her mother. Her father abandoned them. She began her career as a reporter, and went on to earn a Cornell law degree and a doctorate in sociology at the University of Chicago. She was a resident of Hull House. Once in New York she worked through the College Settlement and the New York Summer School of Philanthropy. By 1905, Kellor lived with Women's Trade Union League leader Mary Dreier. *Notable American Women. The Modern Period. A Biographical Dictionary* (Cambridge: Belknap Press, 1980), p. 395. In this same era Kellor was extensively involved in "protective" work with African Americans migrating from the South to Northern cities. See Johnson, "Defining 'The Social Evil,' " pp. 384–392.

13. For Kellor's meetings and correspondence see William Loeb (secretary to the president) to Hon. Oscar Straus (secretary of Commerce and Labor), January 13, 1907, in RINS 5:1: 0494; (authorship unclear) Memorandum for the Secretary (Department of Commerce and Labor), January 15, 1907, in RINS 5:1: 0496; Acting Solicitor Nesbit, Office of the Solicitor (Department of Commerce and Labor Memorandum), January 19, 1907, in RINS 5:1: 0499–0500; "Memorandum" (by Commissioner Robert Watchorn), January 25, 1907, in RINS 5:1. On W.S. Bennet (1870–1962) see Biographical Dictionary of the U.S. Congress, online at <http://bioguide.congress.gov/scripts/biodisplay.pl?index = B000370>. On Kellor's exchange with Bennet see the next note.

14. The exchange between Kellor, Bennet, the press, and the commissioner is recounted in "Memorandum" (by Commissioner Robert Watchorn), January 25, 1907, in RINS 5:1.

15. Kanstroom, "Deportation, Social Control, and Punishment," p. 1889.

16. William Loeb to Hon. Oscar S. Straus, January 13, 1907, in RINS 5:1: 0494; "Memorandum" (by Commissioner Robert Watchorn), January 25, 1907, in RINS 5:1. On male proprietorship of vice by 1907 see Timothy Gilfoyle, *City of Eros: New York City, and the Commercialization of Sex, 1790–1920* (New York: W.W. Norton, 1992), p. 417.

17. [Authorship unclear] Memorandum for the Secretary (Department of Commerce and Labor), January 15, 1907, in RINS 5:1: 0496.

18. Acting Solicitor Harrison Nesbit, Office of the Solicitor (Department of Commerce and Labor Memorandum), January 19, 1907, in RINS 5:1: 0497–0498 [emphasis added], 0499–0500. *Keller v. United States*, 213 U.S. 138 (1909). For details on how the U.S. Supreme Court interpreted immigration

law with regard to individual prostitutes versus disorderly house owners see Connelly, *Response to Prostitution*, pp. 51–54 and Johnson, "Defining 'The Social Evil,' " pp. 288–1289.

19. The prostitution provision in the 1907 Act is quoted fully in Connelly, *Response to Prostitution*, p. 50. As Kanstroom indicates, this change in emphasis "from entry control to post-entry social control" was rooted in the long-term "attempt to prevent the entry of prostitutes into the United States. The proof of post-entry conduct was temporally linked to entry. The use of the words 'deemed to be unlawfully' also shows this link" ("Deportation, Social Control, and Punishment," p. 1910).

20. "Arrest and Deportation of Prostitutes and Procurers of Prostitutes," Department Circular no. 156, Bureau of Immigration and Naturalization, Department of Commerce and Labor, Office of the Secretary, September 26, 1907, in RINS 5:1. Connelly, *Response to Prostitution*, pp. 53–54. Supreme Court Justice Oliver Wendell Holmes clearly articulated this idea in his dissent in *Keller v. United States*, 213 U.S. 138, 149–50 (1909): "If a woman were found living in a house of prostitution within a week of her arrival, no one, I suppose, would doubt that it tended to show that she was in the business when she arrived. But how far back such an inference shall reach is a question of degree, like most of the questions of life. And, while a period of three years seems to be long, I am not prepared to say, against the judgment of Congress, that it is too long." The main opinion in the *Keller* case held unconstitutional the provisions of the 1907 Act that authorized criminal prosecution of persons who supplied housing to immigrant women engaged in prostitution.The court held that these provisions entailed the exercise of a police power that Congress had not been granted and that was reserved for the states. *Keller v. United States*, 213 U.S. at 144–45, 148.

21. From 1904 through 1907, 81 women were barred in connection with prostitution. By 1908 this figure had reached 205. From 1907 to 1909, 326 women were deported. From 1908 to 1915, 2,317 women were so barred under moral justification. An additional 392 were deported in 1914 and 204 in 1915. Connelly, *Response to Prostitution*, p. 175, note 7, and Miner, *Slavery of Prostitution*, p. 116.

22. Kellor Manuscript (October 17, 1907), folder 6.3, LWP1. The Tenderloin district stretched on the West Side of Manhattan between approximately 20th and 59th Streets. By this date campaigns against prostitution had pushed many houses of prostitution out of the Lower East Side. For documentation on the northward movement of prostitution from 1890 to 1920 see Gilfoyle, *City of Eros*, p. 384, note 3.

23. For other prostitution reports that addressed Jewish immigrants see the following from box 91, LWP1: 1905 Prostitution Cases; Prostitution Reports: Resorts, folder 6.8; Boarding House Reports, folder 6.4. For Wald and Kellor's roles in the state Immigration Commission (NYSIC) see Higham, *Strangers in the Land*, p. 240. For the overlap between Kellor's report and that of the USIC see below and "Congress Receives White Slave Report," *Times* (December 11, 1909).

24. Helen Bullis to Robert Watchorn, October 28, 1907, in RINS 5:1: 0056–0059. Arthur Woods (4th Deputy Police Commissioner) to Helen Bullis, October 12, 1907, in RINS 5:1: 0069, 0083; Bullis to Watchorn, October 11, 1907, and attached documents in RINS 5:1: 0073–0078, and also RINS 5:1: 0084. The fact that Helen Bullis was stationed at Ellis Island indicates that she investigated women who emigrated in steerage. For Bullis' cooperation with the Committee of Fourteen see her 1913–1914 correspondence with Frederick Whitin in box 13, C14. On federal participation in Tenderloin raids see Pitkin, *Keepers of the Gate*, p. 103. Pitkin notes that by 1908 the Immigration Service at Ellis Island was also cooperating with the "Italian Squad" of the New York Police Department in their battles against the organized crime alleged to be connected with Italian immigration (100).

25. Bullis to Watchorn, October 28, 1907, in RINS 5:1: 0056–0059. Kellor's quote is from "MEMORANDUM" (by Commissioner Watchorn), January 25, 1907, in RINS 5:1. For similar sentiments about the clandestine importation of immoral women communicated to officials see Josephine Shaw Lowell to Hon. George B. Cortelyou, June 12, 1903, in RINS 3:5: 0061, 0097; Statement by Sadie American, in RINS 3:5: 0082, 0083, 0084, 0086. For Bullis' surveillance reports see the following: Woods to Bullis, October 12, 1907, in RINS 5:1: 0069, 0083; Bullis to Watchorn, October 28, 1907, in RINS 5:1: 0056–0059; Bullis to Watchorn, October 11, 1907, and attached anonymous letter and followup report, in RINS 5:1: 0073–0078, and RINS 5:1: 0084.

26. March 19,1909 "Confidential Circular/To All Commissioners of Immigration and Inspectors in Charge" from Commissioner-General of Immigration Daniel Keefe, in RINS 5:4: 0159. Act March 26, 1910, Sec. 3, 36 Stat. 264, and ch. 128, 36 Stat. 263 (1910). For case law see Bugajewitz v. Adams, 228 U.S. 585 (1913); *Ex Parte Cardonnel*, 197 F. 774 (N.D. Cal. 1912). *See also* Kanstroom, "Deportation, Social Control, and Punishment," p. 1889, and Louis Anthes, "The Island of Duty: The Practice of Immigration Law on Ellis Island," *New York University Review of Law & Social Change*, 24 (1998), p. 563.

27. 8 U.S.C. § 1182, and 8 U.S.C. § 1227(a)(1) (2003).

28. Robert Watchorn to Helen Bullis, November 19, 1907, in RINS 5:1: 0042. Bullis to Watchorn, October 28, 1907, in RINS 5:1: 0056–0059; 4th Deputy Police Commissioner Arthur Woods to Helen Bullis, October 12, 1907, in RINS 5:1: 0069; Bullis to Watchorn, April 7, 1908, in RINS 5:1: 0659–0761; Bullis to Watchorn, December 29, 1908, in RINS 3:3: 0576–0577. Interestingly with regard to Kellor's focus on Jewish immigrants and her downplaying of French involvement in prostitution in the city, in this correspondence Bullis primarily focused on French immigrants.

29. Pitkin, *Keepers of the Gate*, p. 103; Inspectress Bullis to Commissioner Watchorn, April 7, 1908 in RINS 5:1: 0659–0761; Bullis to Watchorn, December 29, 1908, in RINS 3:3: 0576–0577.

30. The Committee of Fourteen's legal research committee consisted of Columbia law professor Francis Burdick, Kellor, Simkhovitch, and Ruth Standish Baldwin, who chaired the committee and also largely financed its work. See C14AR 1907, pp. 6–8, 12–13. Women's central role (especially Kellor's) in this

research committee's work is partially obscured in the Committee of Fourteen's records, and has to be carefully pieced together from their Annual Reports and *The Survey* (November 5, 1910), p. 172. For Baldwin's provision of $3,900 of $5,000 budgeted for research see the undated Baldwin letter to Mr. Slade, box 14, C14. For Miner's work with immigrant women in the Night Court see her *Slavery of Prostitution*, pp. 30, 31, 32–33, 53, 55. On the NYPA see the following: "Whitman Tells of White Slave Trade," *Times* (December 1, 1909); "White Slave Proof," *Daily Tribune* (January 8, 1910); and the NYPA folder and the Correspondence 1912–1913 folder, box 18, Series IIA: Director's Records in *Greenwich House Records, 1896–1956* (New York: Tamiment Institute Library Microfilm, 1995), Reel 2198 (hereafter cited as GHR 2198).

31. Bullis to Watchorn, April 7, 1908 in RINS 5:1: 0659–0761. Bullis to Watchorn, December 29, 1908, in RINS 3:3: 0576–0577. Daniel J. Keefe (Commissioner-General of Immigration) to Robert Watchorn, March 19, 1909, in RINS 3:3: 0585–0586.

32. Pitkin, *Keepers of the Gate*, p. 103; Commissioner-General of Immigration (Keefe) to Robert Watchorn, March 19, 1909, in RINS 3:3: 0585–0586. It is unclear from the documentation whether Bullis was involved in the investigation of the Night Court interpreter and his colleagues at Ellis Island who were helping accused women to avoid deportation. On "the apparent conspiracy of the underworld to avoid expulsion by lying about the critical date" see note 128 in Kanstroom, "Deportation, Social Control, and Punishment."

33. On agencies exploiting immigrants and migrants (including their alleged links with vice) see Frances Kellor, *Out of Work: A Study of Unemployment* (1904; reprint, New York: G. P. Putnam's Sons, 1915). The material on the police explanation is from Bullis to Watchorn, April 7, 1908, in RINS 5:1: 0659–0761. For statistics and analysis on the extremely limited policing of men connected with vice in this era see Johnson, "Defining 'The Social Evil'," pp. 538–548.

34. Bennet's campaign management is noted in "Moral-Rakers and Bond-Rakers Make Muck of Excise Question," *Morning Telegraph* (December 2, 1909) covered scrapbook, box 96, C14. For Whitman's career and the place of antiprostitution agitation in it see the following in the same covered scrapbook: "General Sessions is Blamed," *Times* (December 22, 1906); "Night Court Stops Police Bail Graft," unidentified (August 18, 1907); "Whitman Tells of White Slave Trade," *Times* (December 1, 1909); "Rockefeller in Earnest," *New York Daily Tribune* (January 5, 1910); "Mr. Rockefeller Causes Raines Law Hotel Raids," *Evening Telegraph* (May 19, 1910). Frank Moss was a Methodist, counsel for the Society for the Prevention of Crime, and the Lexow and Mazet investigating committees, Police Board president, and president of the City Vigilance League during the 1901 electoral campaign. "Frank Moss Favors a Single-Headed Police Control," *Democracy* (November 27, 1909), covered scrapbook, box 96, C14. James B. Reynolds was University Settlement headworker and the executive director of Seth Low's 1901 reform mayoral campaign. After Low became mayor, Reynolds became his private secretary. Reynolds was also a member of the New York State Tenement House and Immigration Commissions. See Hammack, *Power and Society*, pp. 143–144,

150–152, 249, 311, 353, note 49. For analysis of the long and complicated process that culminated in the Women's Court and its continued reform into the 1910s see Johnson, "Defining 'The Social Evil', " Chapter 5.

35. "Congress Receives White Slave Report," *Times* (December 11, 1909). Connelly notes the likelihood that G.K. Turner's writings influenced the Commission, but Kellor's work communicated similar ideas to Bennett and immigration officials from 1906 on (*Response to Prostitution*, p. 178, note 33). I have seen no evidence of Turner's inclusion of the French in his exposés. For the alleged link between Jews and "white slavery" in the USIC report see U.S. Senate, *Reports of the Immigration Commission*, vol. 19, *Importation and Harboring of Women for Immoral Purposes* (1910), pp. 62–65, 77–78. For evidence of further overlap between the USIC's recommendations and the advocacy of New York reformers see Brief by A.N. Parker (Chief, Law Division) to Commissioner-General of Immigration F. P. Sargent, May 28, 1908, re: Frances Kellor Report On The Problem Of Immigrants in RINS 5:1: 0484; Wald Speech given at National Conference on Charities and Correction in Buffalo, New York, June 16, 1909, LWP2.

36. "Congress Receives White Slave Report," *Times* (December 11, 1909).

37. For Williams' caution see the following: Williams to Commissioner-General of Immigration, March 9, 1903, in RINS 3:5: 0192–0194; Williams to Commissioner-General, April 16, 1903, in RINS 3:5: 0185, 0186; Williams to Commissioner-General, May 6, 1903, in RINS 3:5: 0168–0169; Williams to Wm. Loeb Jr. (Secretary to the President), June 10, 1903, in RINS 3:5: 0010; Williams to Commissioner-General, December 1, 1904, in RINS 3:5: 0243. For analysis of Williams' motives see Johnson, "Protection, Virtue, and the 'Power to Detain'." For Watchorn's concerns see the following: "Memorandum" (by Commissioner Robert Watchorn), January 25, 1907, and Watchorn to Bullis, November 19, 1907, both in RINS 5:1: 0042. For documentation and analysis of the fragmented and contradictory character of the policing and prosecution of morals policing in New York City, especially before 1910 see Johnson, "Defining 'The Social Evil', " pp. 475–485. The chapter also examines the relatively successful efforts of reformers to remedy these fissures and contradictions, with extremely punitive results.

38. Pitkin, *Keepers of the Gate*, pp. 27–41, 48–49, 81. For Reynolds' 1906 investigation see *Records of the Immigration and Naturalization Service*, microform, Series A: Subject Correspondence Files, Part 3: Ellis Island 1900–1933, Reels 1 and 9.

39. For the intertwined workings of Women's Court and deportation proceedings see the following in the THD—Prior to 1915—ii folder, box 21, C14: "Confidential Bulletin"; "Tenement House Cases, May 1913"; "Tenement Houses Cases, April, 1914"; "Disorderly House Cases Tried in Special Sessions." See also George J. Kneeland, *Commercialized Prostitution in New York City* (1913; reprint, Montclair, New Jersey: Patterson Smith, 1969), pp. 274–275. For the extension of the national-local policing of immigrants to other cities see Pitkin, *Keepers of the Gate*, p. 104.

40. The only European immigrant group that was overrepresented in incarceration dynamics was the Irish, and this was only until the very early 1890s.

Despite the prominent place of Eastern European Jewish immigrants in campaigns against prostitution and "white slavery" they were never overrepresented in policing and incarceration. See Johnson, "Defining 'The Social Evil', " pp. 217–220 and especially note 8 on 218. For background on how European immigrants negotiated whiteness see Matthew Frye Jacobson's *Whiteness of a Different Color: European Immigration and The Alchemy of Race* (Cambridge, MA: Harvard University Press, 1998).

41. For the New York City population of African Americans see N. Kantrowitz in Jackson (ed.), *Encyclopedia*, pp. 920–921.For the Women's Court and incarceration figures see C14AR (1914), pp. 30–33 and Fernald et al., *A Study of Women Delinquents* (201). For further analysis of the racialized consequences of morals policing in New York City see Johnson, "Defining 'The Social Evil'," Chapter 4 and pp. 558–570. Loïc Wacquant uses the term "racialized hyperincarceration" to explain the overincarceration of African American men in the contemporary era, but the historical and cross-gender parallel is apt. See his "Deadly Symbiosis: When Ghetto and Prison Meet and Mesh," *Punishment & Society* 3 (1) (2001), pp. 95–134.

42. On neoliberalism, the global economy, and political rationalities see Joseph E. Stiglitz, *Globalization and its Discontents* (New York, W.W. Norton, 2002), L. Duggan *The Twilight of Equality? Neoliberalism, Cultural Politics, and the Attack on Democracy* (Boston, MA: Beacon Press, 2003), J. Comaroff and J.L. Comaroff, "Millennial Capitalism: First Thoughts on a Second Coming," *Public Culture*, 12(2) (2000), pp. 291–343, W. Larner, "Neo-liberalism: Policy, Ideology, Governmentality" *Studies in Political Economy*, 63 (2000), pp. 5–25, Ronaldo Munck, *Globalization and Labour: The New "Great Transformation"* (London: Zed Books, 2002). On neoliberalism, "risk society," and crime, see the following: Richard V. Ericson and Kevin D. Haggerty, *Policing the Risk Society* (Toronto: University of Toronto Press, 1997); Pat O'Malley, ed., *Crime and the Risk Society* (Brookfield: Ashgate, 1998); Pat O'Malley, "Uncertain Subjects: Risk, Liberalism and Contract," *Economy and Society*, 29(4) (2000), pp. 460–484; Barbara Adam, Ulrich Beck, and Joost Van Loon, *The Risk Society and Beyond: Critical Issues for Social Theory* (London: Sage, 2000); Jonathan Simon, "Governing Through Crime," in G. Fisher and L. Friedman, eds., *The Crime Conundrum: Essays on Criminal Justice* (Boulder, Colorado: Westview Press, 1997), pp. 171–190.

43. An unprecedented $12.2 billion, for 2, 671 "pork barrel" budget earmarks, was attached to the 2004 U.S. Defense Appropriations Bill. Republican Senator Arlen Specter described one such $1.25 million earmark on the defense bill, for Night Vision Equipment Co., in the following terms: "These projects, key to our nation's defense, will be invaluable in our continuing war against terror." Silverstein, "The Great American Pork Barrel," *Harper's* (July 2005), pp. 31–38, and especially (including the quotes) pp. 37–38. In 1980, there were sixty-two earmarks attached to the Defense Appropriations Bill. The unprecedented current level of pork barrel politics linked with the Defense budget is part of a general streamlining of fiscal corruption in Washington in the past few years. Earmarks on appropriation bills have doubled since 2001, and tripled since 1998.

44. For information on FAIR's Board of Directors, their media profile, political and law enforcement connections, and their activities see http://www.fairus. org/About/About.cfm?ID = 2337&c = 22 For media clips produced by FAIR, including the September 11 anniversary TV ad produced with 9/11 Families For a Secure America and calling for "an immigration time-out" because the immigration system "couldn't tell a terrorist from a tourist" see http://www. fairus.org/Media/MediaList.cfm?c = 36. For information on 9/11 Families For a Secure America see http://www.911fsa.org/. For this organization's lobbying for "enhanced cooperation with and training of state and local law enforcement officers on immigration law" see "Testimony presented to the House of Representatives by Rep. John Hostettler (R-IN), September 28, 2004" on this site. For information on The Council on American-Islamic Relations and their civil rights and advocacy work see http://www.cair-net.org.

45. Wayne MacNaugton, "Being Homeless Post-9/11." Presented at "The Criminalization of Poverty": A Colloquium and Public Meeting, Halifax, Nova Scotia, November 2004.

3

"For Speaking Jewish in a Jewish Neighborhood": Civil Rights and Community–Police Relations during the Postwar Red Scare, 1919–1922

Joseph Varga

On October 4, 1919, Louis Goldberg was arrested by officers of the New York City Police Department (NYPD) and charged with disorderly conduct for violating a police directive that public gatherings be addressed in the English language. Goldberg's arrest came at a time of actual crisis in the local housing market, and of a perceived crisis, the Red Scare, at the national level, when foreign language speakers were considered to be sympathizers with radical causes. Goldberg was later released from custody and the charges against him were dismissed, but his preemptive arrest by the NYPD denied him the opportunity to address the gathered crowd for his intended purpose. Although a person could be arrested under the disorderly conduct statute for threatening a breach of the peace, the police arrested Goldberg without any basis for concluding that the impact of his speech was a threat to public order. Goldberg's case thus illustrates the problems of the use of discretionary authority by police officers in their attempt to control public space. The incident also reveals the tensions that existed in the practice of police work between the maintenance of public order and the protection (or suppression) of basic individual rights, a tension mediated by the rule of law and the ability to utilize discretionary authority.

This chapter uses the Goldberg case as a lens through which to examine how the application of laws conferring discretionary police authority to regulate public order play a crucial role in the policing of public space, often at the expense of individual rights. The Goldberg case occurred during a time when courts' delineation of the scope of free speech protections was still evolving[1] and before the Supreme Court had clarified that the protections of the First Amendment applied to states as well as the Federal Government.[2] However, this case shows how the exercise of police power to maintain order serves, as a practical matter, to define the actual scope of individual liberties. And the chapter considers more broadly how the interplay of a variety of factors, both structural and historically contingent, encompassing national policies and local conditions, informs the analysis of when and how police use their authority to maintain order and control public space.

Moving Day

For landlords and tenants in New York City in the early decades of the twentieth century, October 1 was the traditional, unofficial "moving day." By unwritten agreement most city landlords, many of whom were sublessees, renting buildings from the owners and turning what profit they could from their tenants, ran their one-year leases from October to October. Many leases were not in written form, but based on verbal agreements between landlord and lessee.[3] Each October 1, thousands of tenants changed locations, some voluntarily, others as a result of eviction.[4] Moving Day not only crowded the city's streets with carts, trucks, and vehicles of every description, but also clogged the city's lower courts with landlord-tenant disputes over rent, repairs, and the legal rights of the respective parties. While the courts certainly favored landlords in most disputes, the rights of renters, who made up a majority of the city's population, could not be ignored. Even when the landlords had the law on their side, the renter countered with two powerful weapons: the tenant organization and the rent strike.[5]

The year 1919 was particularly troublesome for all parties as moving day approached. The postwar housing shortage, brought on by decreases in the rate of new construction, increased demand, and rampant speculation, had caused rents in New York City to rise significantly.[6] Wartime inflation of construction costs had resulted in a 94 percent decrease in tenement construction from 1915 to 1919.[7] Coupled with the steady rise in population from both immigration and the migration of workers from rural areas in the southern United States to wartime industrial jobs in New York City, the limited availability of housing units had led to a yearly state of crisis in city rental housing during the war years, a crisis that peaked in 1919. Building owners sought to maximize their profit margins while the market was tight, using their legal standing as property owners and the unregulated housing market to their advantage. Renters countered the legal power of landlords by organizing rent strikes and forming tenant associations to defend their rights and negotiate disputes. Although spontaneous rent strikes had been a well-established practice in the prewar years,[8] the acute housing shortage of 1915–1919, in conjunction with an increase in the organizing efforts of Socialist groups in both industry and housing, had markedly changed the power dynamic of landlord-tenant relations.

The formation of tenant organizations during the war years was largely the work of trade unions and Socialists, who sought to encourage worker solidarity by linking shopfloor struggles to the struggles for decent, secure living conditions.[9] Just as the increased demand for wartime production workers accelerated the process of union organizing, the shortage of housing encouraged the establishment of tenant associations.[10] Rent strikes in 1916 and 1917, which resulted in mass evictions of tenants in Lower Manhattan, the Bronx, and parts of Brooklyn, convinced many renters that their strength lay in solidarity. Tenant association membership rose rapidly in 1918 and 1919, as organized renters made demands for repairs, rent control, and written leases, while also demanding to be recognized by the courts as having rights equal to that of the property-owning landlords.[11]

Several other factors in addition to the yearly tenant/landlord disputes combined to make Moving Day 1919 a confrontational scene. The city had been the site of major strikes and labor actions in various industries. Dockworkers, compositors, millinery workers, tugboat operators, and a host of other city workers had either walked off their jobs or threatened to in the summer and fall of 1919. Strikes and job actions occurred throughout the country: steel industry strikes in Gary, Indiana, Pittsburgh, and Chicago, dock strikes in major ports, and even a strike by fertilizer workers in the Deep South. These labor actions, as well as unrest and rioting in Chicago and St. Louis, led many Americans to fear that a "red" revolution was at hand.[12] In New York, rallies by labor radicals and Socialist groups fueled this feeling, prompting a backlash against public demonstrations, including meetings of women discussing birth control. The city was also faced with a transportation crisis brought on by the continuing battle between the Public Service Commission and private rail owners over control of the subway and mass transit lines. Fall of 1919 saw the suspension of service of several surface rail lines, mainly serving passengers traveling between Brooklyn and Manhattan, drastically curtailing the ability of workers to get to and from their places of employment.[13]

October 1, 1919, saw over 50,000 families change addresses, and many of these faced the possibility of homelessness, in both the short and long term.[14] While many families moved voluntarily because of expired lease agreements, thousands of families refused to vacate apartments, insisting on their right to lease extensions at existing rates. As a result, the Bronx and Brooklyn Municipal Courts attempted to handle some four thousand proceedings calling for the forced eviction of over twenty thousand renters.[15] In Manhattan, Mayor "Honest" John Hylan's newly established Office of Rent Profiteering was besieged by both renters and landlords, and the chaos resulted in the near lynching of one landlord for questioning the "respectable status" of a female tenant.[16] As the week wore on, tenants and landlords battled in both the courts and in the buildings and streets for control over scarce housing.

In Brooklyn, tenant activism was organized, as in the Bronx and Lower Manhattan, by trade union leaders and members of Socialist organizations. By 1919, organizing efforts, often financed by union locals and Socialist organizations,[17] but carried out by women activists,[18] had reached its apex in Brooklyn, spearheaded by an umbrella organization, the Brooklyn Tenants Union. The BTU was an amalgam of local tenant organizations formed in mainly Jewish, Italian, and Eastern European neighborhoods throughout the borough, with strongholds in Williamsburg, Flatbush, and Brownsville.[19] In early fall, the BTU leadership announced a series of public meetings to be led by tenant advocacy lawyers in October to inform members of their legal rights and encourage membership and steadfast resistance to landlord evictions and rent increases. In an attempt to maintain "public order" during the crisis period, New York City Police Department Commissioner Richard Enright had issued a directive stating that all public meetings were to be conducted "in the English language" to prevent the dissemination of "dangerous propaganda."[20] Any meeting not conducted in English, according to Enright's order, would be a violation of New York State Penal Law Section 43, disturbing or endangering the public order.

By Moving Day, many tenant activists were aware of the commissioner's English-only directive, including Louis P. Goldberg, a leading legal counselor for the BTU. Scheduled to address a group of predominantly Jewish tenants in the Brownsville section of Brooklyn on October 4, Goldberg decided to test the commissioner's directive. As the crowd gathered on the corner of Dumont and Sheffield Avenues in mid-morning of October 4, the preliminary speakers were introduced and addressed the crowd, by prearrangement, in English, an unusual circumstance in a neighborhood where the predominant public language was Yiddish.[21] When Goldberg was introduced, he addressed the crowd in Yiddish and was promptly arrested, and the public gathering was forcibly dispersed. Goldberg was charged with violating Penal Code 43, "disturbing and endangering the public order," forced to pay a $500.00 bond, and to appear in court for trial.[22] However, he was discharged the following day and all charges against him were dropped. Goldberg then brought a false imprisonment suit against Police Commissioner Enright and arresting officers Adam Kletz and Michael Singer. The suit was dismissed by the trial court, but the dismissal was overturned and the complaint in the suit reinstated by the Appellate Division, Second Department, of the New York State Supreme Court.

In the course of that decision, the Appellate Division indicated that Goldberg was not guilty of any wrongdoing and that Enright's English-only order was illegal.[23] The language of the Appellate Division reversing the dismissal of Goldberg's civil lawsuit for false imprisonment is unambiguous about the lack of justification for Goldberg's arrest: "[O]n these pleadings, no justification appears for this interference with the right to speak in a citizen's native tongue." The appellate decision is particularly harsh on Commissioner Enright's English-only order, stating that "said police order was illegal and affords no justification for arrest."[24] The court indicated that had there been some showing that the meeting was set for an unlawful purpose or that Goldberg's speech "tend(ed) to defy authorities"[25] it might have approached the case differently. But the court was clear that the fact that the police did not understand Goldberg's speech or its potential to cause disruption could not justify the order, stating that "it would be beyond the power even of the legislature."[26]

Yet in spite of the court ruling the police had achieved their immediate goal of breaking up a public meeting that Enright and others saw as a dangerous challenge not only to public order, but to the property rights of landlords. Using a preemptive arrest, the police clearly curtailed the ability of both Goldberg and those attending the public meeting[27] to communicate ideas and share information. Though the use of preemptive arrest on public order charges was a common police tactic, police officers just as often did not attend to the content or effect of public speech at mass meetings, concentrating instead on maintaining the flow of pedestrian and vehicular traffic, while physically containing crowds. In other words, although the maintenance of public order was a primary reason for the existence of urban police forces, public order policing did not necessarily imply a diminution of demonstrators' rights to speak and assemble in public space.

A critical element in public-order police responses is thus the discretionary authority that the police exercise whenever they enforce, or decline to apply, a law. Broadly worded order-maintenance codes, such as a statute prohibiting disorderly conduct, embed this discretionary authority and serve as the requisite "cover" for police actions such as the preemptive arrest in the Goldberg case that suppressed the content of speech. Using the Goldberg arrest and the suppression of "Jewish" speech at the height of the Red Scare as a case study, the following section examines how local application of disorderly conduct statutes and other low-level order-maintenance codes play a crucial role in policing public order and maintaining control of public space during periods of heightened fear. And it considers how use of this embedded discretionary power is affected by a variety of factors.

A Framework for Analyzing Public-Order Police Actions

Multiple factors inform the local application of disorderly conduct statutes as a tactic for maintaining order and controlling public space. These include the occurrence of a period of overall tension or crisis, the ideology of municipal leadership, the dynamics of community–police relations, the perceived goals of the local police force, and interpretation of local statutes. These factors when listed stand as structural elements that frame police activity in any period, but their importance depends on historically specific conditions that affect the decision-making process of police officers at the point of interaction with the public.[28] Whether officers act as disinterested, objective guardians of public order, neutral guarantors of individual rights, or overt violators of those rights, depends largely on how these structurally conditioning factors operate in a given historical time frame. The structural and historically contingent are thus mutually implicated in any analysis of the dynamics of public-order policing.

The postwar years, 1919–1921, were a period in which many Americans felt a heightened sense of crisis, and many were concerned with the public manifestations of conflict and tension that existed among competing factions in American society. As real income fell amidst the doubling of prices for many consumer goods, the conflict between capital and labor reached a crescendo. Every major U.S. industry experienced strikes in 1919–1920, including steel, coal, textiles, telephones, metalwork, meat-packing, and freight handling. In spite of the efforts of both national and local law enforcement to weaken and repress the radical elements of the labor movement (Eugene Debs was in jail, the International Workers of the World had been virtually destroyed) the extent of labor unrest was unprecedented.[29] Of central concern to Federal, state, and local authorities was not merely the outbreak of a strike wave, but efforts by labor leaders and Socialists to organize across industries and in nonwork, nonindustrial areas like tenant associations. The election in New York of Communist

Party representatives to the New York State Assembly, the strong showing of Socialist Party members in local elections,[30] and the ability of radicals to organize into effective political groups outside of the workplace, coupled with revolutions in Russia, Eastern Europe, and colonial struggles, all contributed to a rising sense of fear among the general population and business and political leaders, in the nation in general and in New York City. This overall climate of fear made it relatively easy for landlord groups to redbait newly formed tenant associations. Landlords attempted to label all tenant groups as "Bolsheviks" and claim that all threats of rent strikes were the actions of tenant "Soviets."[31]

While police were often sympathetic to individual families in the eviction process, and could be sympathetic to mass gatherings, they often had little regard for radicals, who, more often than not, returned their contempt. In the past, New York City police had admitted to a desire to "punish crowds who were hostile to authority" and the added pressures of the Red Scare only intensified this desire.[32] The general feeling of fear of Bolshevik revolution was manifested in both the issuance of the English-only order and its subsequent enforcement. Enright and his officers defended the directive on two grounds: first, they cited the arrest of an actual anarchist in 1917, who did, in fact, exhort a crowd in Union Square Park to openly defy the military draft, with the express purpose of weakening the U.S. government and preparing for a revolutionary overthrow.[33] Second, they pointed to the fear that non-English speakers would be able to convey a similar seditious message to a crowd without the knowledge of the authorities, if the address was in a language other than English.

These concerns about speaking in languages other than English reflected pervasive cultural anxieties in the United States during the early decades of the twentieth century when language learning and other Americanization initiatives emphasized the connection between language and thinking: to think American required that one speak "American."[34] Thus, the overall feeling of crisis, brought on by the heightened tension between capital and labor, and labor's ability to organize beyond the shopfloor, and anxiety about foreign-language-speaking subversive elements within the labor movement, created conditions that were conducive to the use of discretionary authority under the public-order statutes to curtail speech and assembly.

The actions and attitudes of municipal leaders further contributed to an atmosphere in which expressive conduct could be openly suppressed. Given the limitations of space, I will focus here on two key figures in New York City law enforcement, Mayor "Honest" John Hylan and Police Commissioner Richard Enright. Both seemed determined to keep radical forces in check among city residents and within the police force itself.

Hylan's administration is viewed by historians as largely inept and inconsequential.[35] While this evaluation may not be completely fair, Hylan was the candidate of the remnant of Tammany Hall, who defeated a reform/fusion mayor, John Purroy Mitchell, and did attempt to reinstall some of the worst abuses of the party patronage system. On the issue of tenant/landlord relations, Hylan's cost-conscious administration slashed the budget of the Tenement House Department, which meant cutbacks in inspections on conditions in city buildings. Thus, while wartime conditions drastically lowered rates of new construction, existing rental stock continued to deteriorate.[36]

Forced by 1919 to respond to the crisis, Hylan created the Mayor's Committee on Rent Profiteering, staffed largely by Democratic loyalists and chaired by property lawyer Nathan Hirsch. While the Committee proved very successful in finding temporary dwellings for evicted renters, and in hearing thousands of arbitration cases in all boroughs, it failed to enforce many of the arbitration decisions, and served mainly to give jobs to Hylan supporters while steering tenants away from the Socialist-led associations.[37] The Committee also testified before the state legislature, convincing a special session that there was no need to mandate temporary rent freezes, mandatory one-year leases, and restrictions on landlords' right to evict, measures that had been recommended by many municipal court justices.[38] Instead, the committee convinced the lawmakers to pass a relatively toothless and unenforceable bill that did little to help the renters. Hylan's main goal seems to have been to lessen the appeal of the Socialist-led tenant associations. He recognized and actively worked with only those associations that had some official connection to his party.

Police Commissioner Richard Enright, a Hylan appointee from the ranks (he had been president of the Lieutenants Association, a rank-and-file benevolent organization), had been elevated to the Commissioner's Office to soothe the rank-and-file during a period of police actions over wages and work conditions in Boston, Cincinnati, and other cities.[39] While Enright's tenure was without the major scandals that plagued other commissioners, he was not without critics, both in his internal handling of the department and in relations with the public. Enright won wage increases and improved working conditions for patrol officers, but was accused of playing favorites with Democratic Party loyalists who had been either removed from the force or suspended due to behavioral infractions. Enright reinstated a number of expelled or suspended officers, which led to the claim that his administration operated on the basis of patronage and spoils.[40] Based on his record of obtaining better conditions for his troops and his consistent attention to the needs of patrol officers, it would appear that Enright's main function, within the city's administration, was to head off any hint of the labor radicalism that was gaining ground in police forces in other cities, particularly Boston, where police had walked off the job.

Like most police commissioners of the era, Enright viewed his job as establishing and maintaining public order. And like many of his contemporaries, particularly during the Red Scare, Enright tended to view ethnic neighborhoods of the working classes as dangerous and as threats to public order. His order prohibited not only non-English public speech, but also banned the sale of any literature or the collection of money, lest the radical organizations grow stronger. His consistent defense of the English-only order as necessary to "preserving the order of a large community of cosmopolitan character"[41] was at once self-contradictory and blatantly xenophobic, with its explicit assumption that non-English speech would be radical in nature and thus a threat to the community. His further insistence, both in court and in official documentation, on referring to Goldberg's language as "Jewish" demonstrates a profound lack of understanding of ethnic communities that was all too commonplace among police officials and patrolmen. In short, the mayor and police commissioner were responsive to anxieties about labor unrest and radical activism, and Enright in particular linked concerns about radical influences with foreign elements and language.

The attitudes and actions of the city's leadership bear on a third factor, community/police relations, including both the attitudes of police officers toward citizens and citizen perceptions of the police. Police attitudes can be discerned from two directions: their actions in handling the daily routine and the more visible realm of public crowd control. From the perspective of city residents, alternating waves of scandal and reform, highlighted in the sensationalist press, worked in combination with ethnic, class, gender, and racial identities, to form a perception of whether the police acted "fair" in their interactions with the city's various publics.

The main duty of daily policing in New York and other large cities during this period (and before, and still) is the use of order-maintaining authority and discretionary judgment by applying state and local ordinances to regulate and control the use of public space.[42] In carrying out these duties, officers develop attitudes toward citizens that are often based in preconceived notions regarding class, ethnic, and racial links to criminal behavior. Most historians have recognized that public-order arrests are linked to ethnicity and class. Eric Monkonnen terms nineteenth-century police policies in U.S. cities "class control."[43] When New York City police officers patrolled crowded areas with high concentrations of apartment renters, the majority of whom were considered noncitizen "immigrants," the relationship between authority and immigrants posed special problems. Police often used their authority in preserving public order to thwart what many residents considered legitimate economic activity, such as selling from pushcarts and displaying wares on sidewalks. City police were also responsible for inspecting tenements for both overcrowding and illegal activity, often invading the privacy of apartment dwellers through forced entry.

Historical analysis of urban police practices suggests that police forces develop a particularly geographic set of preconceived ideas regarding which areas are inhabited by "criminal elements." As David Thale writes of policing in the early twentieth century in New York, "as the police developed, their respect for the rights of the working class was often limited; there were notable abridgements of the liberties of radical dissenters and strikers, while the privacy of many tenement dwellers was frequently violated."[44] This geographically based attitude toward working-class districts, in combination with factors like the Red Scare and the attitudes of their superiors in the police department, led many officers to view ethnic communities as outside of the realm of proper citizenship, and to view the residents of these areas as people whose rights could be violated with impunity.

Because the challenge of managing public demonstrations often implicates directly the basic function of policing, to maintain control of public space, they are often the sternest test of police attitudes and "impartiality." When these types of actions are taken by groups considered as less than full citizens, police officers often respond by reasserting their control of space by using undue force. In the case of public demonstrations over eviction and rent increases, tenant organizations presented a direct threat to the police department's monopoly over the control of public space. During the Red Scare, rent strikers utilized their numbers to block entryways, sidewalks, and streets to prevent landlords and their hired agents from physically removing tenants. Police authority was directly challenged, whether the officers were sympathetic to the plight of the renters or not.

The attitudes and perceptions of community members also affect community-police relations. Community members base their actions in public, whether as individuals, in groups, or as part of an organized demonstration, based on their own preconceived notions of the police officers and department. In the public perception, these attitudes are often framed around issues of justice and fairness, and often stem from past incidents where police acted with impunity.[45] For New York's Jewish community, memories of the 1902 Hoe Riots, as well as other incidents in which the NYPD were referred to as "Cossacks," surely affected attitudes toward the police.[46] When members of a community believe that police officers treated them in an arbitrary manner, they are often less likely to challenge police authority. But this is not always the case. In the incident involving the arrest of Louis Goldberg, the organizers of the meeting and Goldberg himself were well aware of both the recent police directive prohibiting the use of non-English languages in public meetings and the attitudes of the police toward the Jewish community, particularly its more radical element.[47] Evidence from the case indicates that Goldberg purposefully addressed the crowd in Yiddish, even though the rally until then had been conducted in English, and most of his audience certainly understood English.[48] Goldberg's action was a purposeful challenge to the order based on his position as a community leader, a lawyer of some standing, and on past police department abuses directed at members of his community.

The final two elements conditioning police actions, the stated and interpreted goal of policing, and the local interpretation of public order statutes, are closely intertwined. Organized urban police forces like the NYPD were formed mainly in the mid–nineteenth century, modeled on the city of London's force, to maintain public order.[49] Urban police patrols maintained order by controlling and defining the proper and improper use of public space. Their primary function was to make certain that urban environments were both livable for the upper and middle class, and conducive to the interests of commerce.[50] The mission of effective policing was to contain the activities of the "dangerous" classes to certain geographic locales while protecting the property of "proper" citizens. Police officers carry out this mission through enforcement of penal and statutory laws that are often applied, particularly in the case of minor or non-felony statutes, according to the definition of their superiors and their own discretion. Most statutes and ordinances pertaining to disorderly conduct and public order are notoriously vague, allowing for a considerable degree of subjective discretion in their enforcement. As a result "the enterprise of order maintenance seems to consist of aimless, random arrests."[51] Consequently, order maintenance was and is a "source of discomfort and alienation" for both police and citizens.[52]

While police forces were organized to maintain order in urban space, they are also charged with protecting the welfare of urban populations, regardless of class, ethnicity, gender, or race, generally charged with responding to calls for assistance, and other public service functions.[53] The balance maintained between these potentially incompatible impulses is often skewed by the relative power of competing interests. In the case of rent strikers and tenant organizations, it was a common practice for building owners as well as business owners to pay bribes to precinct captains to favor the interests of property ownership over renters and free speech and assembly rights.[54] So while police officers may have at times been sympathetic to the cause of renters or strikers, their superiors were often in the pay of their opponents, and the mission of policing and the interpretation of ordinances would thus be skewed to favor order and property owners over the interests of non-property-owning populations.

On the crucial question of local interpretation of statutes, the broad language of New York's Penal Law Section 43 illuminates its susceptibility to claims of vagueness and unfair interpretation. It reads, in part, "A person is guilty of disorderly conduct, when with the intent to cause public inconvenience, annoyance or alarm, or recklessly creating a risk thereof, he disturbs vehicular or pedestrian traffic or he congregates with other persons in a public place and refuses to comply with a lawful police order." The wording of this, and most disorderly conduct laws, leaves the time and place of enforcement open to the interpretation of the officer. The flexibility and possibility of discretionary judgment that such a law allowed were also the source of its potential vagueness. For this reason police officers often searched for additional justification or added legitimacy when they acted as supposed objective enforcers of law and maintainers of public order.[55] Thus the importance of the English-only order cannot be overstated in the Goldberg case. The order limited the breadth of Penal Law Section 43, narrowing the focus to a question of language, whereas in other situations, the police may have based their use of the disorderly conduct statute on a belief or assumption that the organizers of a public rally were "agitators" or consisted of individuals perceived to be a threat, such as anarchists or radical socialists. In issuing the English-only directive, Commissioner Enright in fact eliminated in advance the need for discretionary judgment that officers usually exercised in public-order maintenance, forcing the officers on the scene to arrest Goldberg the moment he commenced speaking in Yiddish.

At the same time, Enright's order was ultimately found to be without justification and thus did not supply any legitimacy to the arrest. As the Appellate Division in Goldberg's false imprisonment claim would later declare, the arrest was "an oppressive violation of the rights of Jewish citizens."[56] Although the court did not identify the source of these "rights," its use of the language of rights underscored that the authority of the police, even in order maintenance, was not without limits. Yet it is ironic that had the police arrested Goldberg and charged him with violation of Penal Law Section 43, based upon their own discretionary assessment that his speech would cause public inconvenience or a risk of such disruption, the arrest might have withstood challenge, given the tendency of courts to defer to such on-the-spot judgments. It was because the arrest was based on Enright's categorical order prohibiting speech without pointing to any basis for concluding that the speech threatened public order, that Goldberg succeeded on appeal in reinstating his false imprisonment lawsuit.

Thus, the enforcement of public-order laws occurs within a matrix of factors, some structural and continuous, and others contingent. Officers always have available the ability to disrupt public gatherings under the authority of public-order statutes, but the decision on how and when to use this power to control public space is affected by contingent circumstances. In the Goldberg case, the actions of the arresting officers were clearly structured by a general feeling of crisis as a result of world and national events that stimulated fear of both leftist political ideologies and "foreigners." The actions of the department were shaped by the attitudes and political positions of city leaders like Mayor Hylan, split between appeasing a large electoral bloc and protecting property ownership, and Commissioner Enright, with his misunderstanding and suspicion of ethnic communities. Tensions between the police and ethnic communities, based on both historical misunderstandings and contentions and contemporary conditions, were another crucial determinant of when and how police exercised authority to maintain public order. The influence of powerful factions further guided how city leaders, rank-and-file officers, and members of the public viewed the historic mission of the police department. All of these factors informed the Police Commissioner's issuance of the English-only directive and, in turn, determined how a public-order statute like Penal Law Section 43 would be interpreted and enforced in the Goldberg case.

The interplay of locally specific conditions with these structural factors shaped the officers' response here. The arresting officers were, in fact, only following orders, albeit a legally unjustified order, the English-only proscription. This order was based upon the fear that dangerous messages could be conveyed by dangerous speakers without the knowledge of authorities. The fear was stoked by the overall perception of crisis during the Red Scare and the association of radicalism with non-English-speaking populations. The fear was further informed by the proproperty, proorder attitudes and political positions of city and police management, existing community-police relations, and the perceived order-maintaining mission of the police department. By taking account of structural and contingent factors, and their dynamic interaction, the analytic framework I have modeled here offers a nuanced explanation of outcomes in situationally complex police interactions with the public.

Conclusion

Urban police forces have long used public-order statutes such as New York's Penal Law Section 43, often in conjunction with preemptive arrests, to maintain control over public space during mass assemblies and other public protests. While courts have moved steadily toward recognizing First Amendment rights to engage in public protest since the Red Scare period,[57] they still tend to give considerable deference to the on-the-street judgments of police officers. As well, police departments like the NYPD continue to utilize preemptive arrest as an order-maintenance tactic, particularly during times of increased public tension, as demonstrated during the 2004 Republican National Convention. The August 31, 2004, preemptive arrest of members of the War Resisters League (WRL) during a peaceful march at the Republican National Convention is one recent example, suggesting both structural similarities to the Goldberg case and contingent differences. The heightened security situation brought on by the threat of terrorism had increased tensions as the convention commenced. The administration of Mayor Bloomberg and Police Chief Raymond Kelly were publicly and privately committed to insuring that the convention went off as planned and that conventioneers were to be isolated from the planned protests.[58] Concerns over civil liberties and over the overt police brutality associated with the previous New York City mayoral administration had also contributed to erosion in police–community relations. Further, anecdotal evidence suggests that the NYPD had very little respect for antiwar protestors, considering them a nuisance during a period of heightened alert and tension.[59] While it remains to be revealed to what extent police officers were using their on-the-spot discretion, or acting on orders, the WRL protestors were, in fact, arrested before they broke the law.[60]

Comparison of the two incidents reveals interesting questions for further study concerning the explanatory force of the interplay between structural and contingent factors. The structural conditions that framed the actions of the police were continuous: a heightened sense of crisis, police-community tensions, a proenforcement mayoral and police administration, and official emphasis of the importance of order-maintenance. Yet the existence of historically specific conditions also informed the outcomes. In the Goldberg incident, ethnic tensions between police and the Brooklyn Jewish community were part of a longstanding history of confrontation. The arrest of Goldberg and other incidents involving "radicals" reveal not only an ideological element but a class element, as well. By contrast, the RNC arrests are difficult to link to ethnic tensions, as neither the WRL nor the NYPD was dominated by any one, or several, ethnic groups. But in each case, police used the powers inherent in their role as maintainers of public-order, as well as the vague definition of what constitutes a violation of order, in situations of perceived crisis to suppress speech and public assembly. Here, the structural conditions that framed the actions of the police in both cases and resulted in violations of basic rights seemed determinative, despite differing contingent conditions. To better assess the interplay of structural and contingent factors, a more wideranging, comparative study of incidents of police violations of basic rights under similar structural conditions would yield valuable information regarding the primacy of contingent and structural conditions as determinants of police action.

In closing, I suggest that in the fields of both history and the social sciences, more attention needs to be paid to the tension between structural continuity and historical contingency in assessing the value of each to explain social phenomena. Such an endeavor requires breaking down artificial barriers that exist between the studies of discrete ideographic events and structural explanations and focusing attention on how each can serve the other. The situated analysis of the case study, here the arrest of Louis Goldberg in 1919, offers a nuanced analytic approach that can illuminate the explanatory potential of the relation between the structurally continuous and the historically contingent in the complex politics, economics, and demographics involved in policing public order.

Notes

1. See, e.g., Daniel A. Farber, William N. Eskridge Jr., and Philip P. Frickey, *Constitutional Law: Themes for the Constitution's Third Century 631–644*, 3rd ed. (St. Paul, MN: West, 2003).
2. See *Gitlow v. New York*, 268 US 652 (1925).
3. *Report of the Mayor's Committee on Taxation and Investigation of Mortgage Loans and the Mayor's Committee on Rent Profiteering* (New York, 1919), pp. 39–41. A legally sanctioned program of yearly, signed leases was not achieved until the mid-1920s, and only after many legal battles.
4. *New York Herald*, October 1, 1919.
5. Much of the background on tenant organizing for this chapter is taken from Joseph A. Spencer, "The Post–World War I Housing Crisis," in Ronald Lawson and Mark Naison, eds., *The Tenant Movement in New York City, 1904–1984* (New Brunswick: Rutgers University Press, 1986).
6. Mayor's Committee on Rent Profiteering.
7. Works Progress Administration Historical Records Survey (New York City Municipal Archives).
8. Spencer, "The Post–World War I Housing Crisis," p. 51.
9. Spencer charts the radical roots of many such organizations, like the Bronx Tenant League, that were originally organized by Socialist Party members and affiliates.
10. Union roles increased in nonagricultural sectors by 19% between 1917 and 1920, due largely to the combination of increases in the overall numbers of factory workers and the wage increases that organized labor was able to obtain. The housing shortage can be traced, in part, to the overall rise in the price of building materials as part of a general increase in prices, and to the overall increase in urban populations, as workers migrated to cities seeking employment

in war industries. See Paul Le Blanc, *A Short History of the U.S. Working Class: From Colonial Times to the Twenty-first Century* (New York: Humanity Books, 1999), pp. 68–70.

11. Katherine Meyer, "A Study of Tenant Associations in New York City," Master's Thesis, Columbia University Department of Sociology, 1928, pp. 6–15.

12. Paul LeBlanc, *A Short History of the US Working Class.* (New York: Humanity Books, 1999), pp. 69–71.

13. *New York Times*, October 3, 4, 1919. The dispute concerned which privately owned lines had the right to use tracks at what time, and whether transfers between systems would be honored.

14. *New York Times*, October 1, 1919; *New York Herald*, October 1, 1919.

15. *New York Call*, October 3, 1919.

16. *New York Herald*, October 2, 1919.

17. The working relationship between members of the Socialist Party and organizations like the Greater New York Tenants League and the Brooklyn Tenants Union can be seen in the daily reports in Socialist-leaning papers such as the *New York Call* and *the Daily Forward*.

18. Women were often at the forefront of organizing tenant activity, as well as boycotts of local businesses. The Socialist Women's Consumer League was responsible for organizing the Bronx Tenant Union in 1917, one of the largest, most militant, and effective of the various tenant associations operating in the city during the World War I period.

19. *Brooklyn Eagle*, September 28, 1919.

20. New York City Police Department, *Special Orders, 1905–1930* (New York Public Library).

21. *Brooklyn Daily Forward*, October 2, 1919.

22. *New York Times*, October 3, 1919.

23. *Goldberg v. Kletz*, 191 N.Y.S. 452 (A. D. 2d Dep't 1921).

24. Ibid. at 454.

25. Ibid. at 455.

26. Ibid.

27. The Appellate Court ruling noted that the NYPD had not even established the fact that a public meeting was taking place. Ibid. at 453.

28. On the interaction of structure and historically contingent events see George Steinmetz, "Critical Realism and Historical Sociology" *Comparative Studies in Society and History*, 38(4), pp. 170–186, Steinmetz, "Odious Comparisons: Incommensurability, the Case Study and Small n's in Sociology" *Sociological Theory*, 22(3), pp. 371–400. William Sewell "Three Temporalities towards an Eventful Sociology" in T. J. McDonald, ed., *The Historic Turn in the Human Sciences* (Michigan: University of Michigan Press, 1996).

29. Under the authority of the Espionage Act of 1917, federal agents carried out numerous raids of IWW offices arresting several hundred members, including Bill Haywood, charging them with obstructing the war effort for their opposition to the wartime draft. Debs was arrested in 1918 for denouncing these and other prosecutions, and charged with sedition. He ran for President in 1920 as

the Socialist Party candidate from his prison cell. see Melvin Dubufsky and Foster Rhea Dulles, *Labor in America: A History*, 7th ed. (Wheeling, IL: Harlan Davidson, 2004), pp. 195–209 and Nick Salvatoré, *Eugene V. Debs: Citizen and Socialist* (Urbana, IL: University of Illinois Press, 1982), pp. 355–358.

30. *New York Tribune*, November 23, 1919.
31. Melvin Urofsky, "A Note on the Expulsion of the Five Socialists," *New York History*, 47 (1966), pp. 41–51.
32. David Thale, *Civilizing New York City: Police Patrol, 1880–1935*, Ph.D. Dissertation, University of Chicago, 1995.
33. Enright's lawyers referred to two cases, *People of the State of New York v. Nesin*, 179 A.D. 869, 167 N.Y.S. 49.(2d Dep't 1917) and *People of the State of New York v. Glison*, 100 Misc. 354, 166 N.Y.S. 711 (N.Y.Gen.Sess. 1917), in which the courts upheld convictions for, respectively, acts endangering the public peace, and disorderly conduct, based on the content of the public pronouncements of both defendants. In the *Nesin* case, Nesin urged a crowd to "not obey the laws of Congress" regarding conscription. *Nesin, 167 N.Y.S. at 49.* In *Glison*, the defendant "caused a breach of the peace" by distributing inflammatory antiwar pamphlets to marchers at a prowar rally. *Glison, 166 N.Y.S. at 711.*
34. Dennis Baron, *The English-Only Question* (New Haven: Yale University Press, 1990), pp. 126–127.
35. Kenneth T. Jackson, *The Encyclopedia of New York City* (New Haven: Yale University Press, 1995).
36. *New York Times*, August 10, 1919.
37. Spencer, "The Post–World War I Housing Crisis," p. 65.
38. *New York Herald*, September 27, 1919.
39. Thomas Reppetto, *The Blue Parade* (New York: Free Press 1978), p. 68.
40. *New York Times*, October 1, 1919. The most serious complaints were leveled against Enright by the Citizens Union, which alleged that Enright's favoritism toward certain officers had "demoralized" the entire force.
41. *New York Times*, October 1, 1919.
42. Thale, *Civilizing New York City*, p. 13.
43. Ibid., p. 15.
44. Ibid., p. 415.
45. Thale, *Civilizing New York City*, p. 415.
46. The *Daily Forward*, July 1, 2, 1902. During a funeral procession in New York City's Lower East Side, Jewish mourners were pelted with thrown objects by a largely Irish crowd inside a factory. When the mourners fought back, police arrested only Jewish rioters.
47. *Brooklyn Eagle*, October 4, 1919.
48. *New York Times*, October 3, 1919.
49. James Richardson, *The New York Police* (New York: Oxford University Press, 1970).
50. Marilynn S. Johnson, *Street Justice: A History of Police Violence in New York City* (Boston: Beacon Press, 2003), pp. 14–16. James Richardson, *The New York Police* (New York: Oxford University Press, 1970).

51. Thale, *Civilizing New York City*, p. 14.
52. Thale, *Civilizing New York City*, p. ix.
53. The police functioned as a social welfare service in many areas until other city agencies slowly relieved them of these functions. See, for instance, the police role in managing the support of homeless juveniles in Stephen Robertson's *Crimes Against Children: Sexual Violence and Legal Culture in New York City, 1880–1960* (Chapel Hill: University of North Carolina Press, 2003).
54. Mark Naison, "From Eviction Resistance to Rent Control," in Ronald Lawson and Mark Naison, eds., *The Tenant Movement in New York City, 1904–1984* (New Brunswick, NJ: Rutgers University Press).
55. Thale, *Civilizing New York City*, pp. 354–359. Thale cites instances in which officers seeking to "break up" congregating youths on street corners cited regulations regarding the blocking of sidewalk access, which were more often enforced against street vendors.
56. *Goldberg v. Kletz*,199 A.D. 188, 191 N.Y.S., 453–454.
57. David Cole, *The New McCarthyism: Repeating History in the War on Terror*, 38 Harv. C.R.-C.L. Rev., 1, 7 (2003).
58. *New York Times*, August 24, 2004.
59. Accounts of police confrontations with protestors are drawn from *The Villager*, 74(19), pp. 1–4, a local weekly serving lower Manhattan, accounts in *The Village Voice*, and first-hand experience.
60. *New York Times*, September 3, 2004, March 23, 2005, April 12, 2005, May 11, 2005. Members of the WRL were set to engage in a permitted march up 5th Avenue on August 31, 2004, and had stated in advance that some marchers would engage in acts of civil disobedience. They were arrested before the march commenced. The police dismissed charges against over 90% of the arrested protestors from the convention, including those from the WRL, citing a lack of evidence of wrongdoing. Civil suits have been filed against the city and the NYPD as a result.

4

Challenging Police Repression: Federal Activism and Local Reform in New York City

Marilynn S. Johnson

During the 1990s, New York City witnessed a wave of police brutality cases—involving Abner Louima, Amadou Diallo, and many others—that made police misconduct front-page news. Under the Clinton administration, the federal government responded to local complaints by filing lawsuits against the city and conducting a high-profile civil rights investigation in 2000 that helped expose some of the abusive practices of the New York City Police Department (NYPD). Just five years later, however, police brutality has seemingly disappeared from public debate. In fact, the events of September 11 reoriented police priorities almost overnight. Under the PATRIOT Act and other federal antiterrorism measures, the NYPD joined a national antiterrorism effort that has changed the face of local policing and introduced new, less visible forms of repression.

This sudden shift in the temper of policing, however, is part of a larger historical pattern. As historians of policing have noted, the federal government has played an important role in the fight against police violence and repression. Since the 1930s, the Justice Department, Congress, and the federal courts have repeatedly spoken out on local police practices, implementing critical legal safeguards and spurring reform efforts that changed the dynamics of local police-community relations. During times of heightened national security, however, the federal government has taken on a more sinister role, encouraging local police departments to become allies in countersubversion campaigns involving surveillance, intimidation, and racial profiling. In many cases, then, federal activism that reduced overt forms of police brutality gave way to more clandestine forms of repression that were more difficult to combat. In both cases, national and international events originating outside city limits shaped the practices of urban law enforcement.

This chapter will explore the federal impact on police practices in New York City over the past seventy-five years, focusing specifically on issues of violence and repression. On the one hand, federal intervention on behalf of free speech and due process in the 1930s, 1960s, and 1990s provided leverage for local civil rights activists and legal reformers working to curb police abuses and increase citizen oversight of the police. On the other hand, these advances were often followed by periods of retrenchment, when concern for national security prompted federal-local cooperation in less visible forms of surveillance and repression. Over the years, city officials have taken an increasingly forceful role in this federal-local partnership, sometimes influencing and competing with federal intelligence agencies. During these periods, federal and local authorities have worked assiduously to curtail constitutional rights in the name of national security. In the longer term, then, federal intervention has followed a pendulum-like pattern, periodically advancing the struggle against police violence and misconduct but at other times encouraging political surveillance, provocation, and repression.

The Depression and World War II Years

In nearly every area of social and political life, the 1930s saw a vast expansion of federal power. The legal arena was no exception. Much of the change grew out of reform efforts associated with the New Deal, as both the legislature and the courts defended the rights of organized labor and political dissidents. But the first sign of change came even earlier when a nationwide investigation of law enforcement put the federal government on record against abusive police practices.

Like other big city police departments in the 1920s, the NYPD confronted an explosion of vice, bootlegging, and racketeering as a result of Prohibition. The rise in illicit activities created more opportunities for police corruption, which, in turn, increased. Rising crime also encouraged law enforcement to resort to more aggressive and violent methods to control it. By far the most controversial crime-fighting tactic of the 1920s was the so-called third degree—a variety of questionable interrogation practices that involved physical violence and torture, prolonged grilling, food and sleep deprivation, and psychological coercion. Journalists and defense lawyers had challenged police use of third-degree tactics for some

time, but it was not until a federal commission investigated police misconduct in New York and other cities that meaningful reform ensued.[1]

In 1929, President Herbert Hoover created the National Commission
on Law Observance and Enforcement in response to law enforcement
problems created by Prohibition. Headed by former federal judge George
Wickersham, the Wickersham Commission—as it came to be known—
issued fourteen reports in 1931 providing a comprehensive national survey
of criminal justice. Interestingly, the report that had the greatest impact
was Number 11, *Lawlessness in Law Enforcement*, a devastating indictment
of police brutality and the third degree. Canvassing the country from
Boston to Los Angeles, the Wickersham investigation provided a survey of
police interrogation tactics in fifteen cities. Using statistics from the
Voluntary Defenders Committee—a New York legal aid society that
defended indigent suspects—the report ranked the NYPD as one of the
nation's worst offenders. While most cases involved beatings administered
with rubber hoses, fists, or blackjacks, other suspects reported being
choked with a necktie, dragged by the hair, wrenched by the testicles, or
hung out an upper story window. Similar atrocities occurred in several
other cities. Exposing the third degree in extensive and excruciating detail,
the Wickersham report forced the issue to the center of criminal justice
debates.[2]

Although the report proposed numerous judicial and legislative
remedies, it was the newly invigorated Federal Bureau of Investigation
(FBI) that was most instrumental in reducing police reliance on the third
degree. At a 1938 meeting of the New York State Police Chiefs Association,
for example, FBI Inspector W.H. Drane Lester urged local chiefs to take
every action necessary to eliminate the third-degree in their jurisdictions
and thus undercut pending anti–third-degree legislation. Likewise, FBI
Director J. Edgar Hoover denounced brutal third degree methods in favor
of scientific investigation and interrogation, and FBI agents did their best
to disseminate this message to local law enforcement. In a 1936 issue of the
FBI journal, *The Investigator*, Special Agent E.J. Chayfitz called the third
degree a "barbarity" that "constitutes an admission of failure." The FBI's
National Police Academy also discouraged brutal practices and promoted
police professionalism to its own agents and selected local officers. Before
long, police training manuals reflected this new approach. Ultimately, the
Wickersham report strengthened the position of reform-minded police
and reinforced trends toward police professionalism that frowned on such
abusive practices.[3]

The Supreme Court confirmed the growing disapproval of third-degree
methods. Although federal courts had long followed the rule on the inadmis-
sibility of coerced confessions (requiring that they be free and voluntary),

they had made no effort to extend this rule to the states. In the landmark *Brown v. Mississippi* case in 1936, however, the Supreme Court excluded the confessions of three black murder suspects who had been tortured by Mississippi police. In ruling the confessions inadmissible, the court extended the ban on use of coerced confessions that applied in federal courts to state and local cases under the due process clause of the Fourteenth Amendment. The *Brown* decision was a clear deterrent to the overt use of violent third-degree methods. In the 1940s, the Supreme Court expanded this precedent to cases involving prolonged police grilling and psychological coercion as well. In New York and other cities, charges of third-degree treatment noticeably declined as both prosecutors and police were persuaded that it often produced false information and was thus counterproductive. By the 1940s and 1950s, most interrogation cases coming before federal and state appellate courts involved psychological rather than physical coercion.[4]

Federal action was equally important in transforming policing of mass action, a critical area of conflict during the Depression years. In the early 1930s, New York experienced a bloody cycle of street battles between the NYPD and a growing movement of Communists and unemployed protesters. With the growing size and intensity of protests in Union Square, Harlem, and City Hall Park, the police responded with special riot squads armed with tear gas and rifles. By 1935, dozens of violent clashes had left three Communists dead and produced hundreds of injuries among protesters, police, and bystanders alike. The Communist Party as well as the American Civil Liberties Union (ACLU) and other liberal groups repeatedly denounced the administration for sanctioning such brutality and repression. Taking office in 1934, Mayor Fiorello La Guardia promised to bring a new era of tolerance and restraint in policing, but his directives initially fell on deaf ears as police commanders and officers continued their customary practices.[5]

Before long, however, two critical events would help make La Guardia's policy of tolerance more feasible. First, in July 1935, President Franklin Roosevelt signed the National Labor Relations Act guaranteeing workers the right to organize and providing federal oversight through the newly created National Labor Relations Board (NLRB). The Wagner Act, as it became known, explicitly protected workers' right to free speech in advocating unions and the right to protest unfair labor practices. Moreover, the act empowered the NLRB—rather than local police authorities—to determine the legitimate representatives of labor and to protect their right to strike and picket. The leftward shift of the New Deal in 1935—together with the growing threat of fascism abroad—also precipitated a major change in the Communist Party line. By the fall of 1935, Communists had abandoned their strident and isolationist stand and began to build alliances with Socialists, New Deal Democrats, and other progressive forces in a Popular Front against fascism. Communists would now work alongside other Progressives to build strong unions inside the new Committee of Industrial Organizations (CIO) and to fight for workers' rights within New Deal agencies.[6] Together, these measures helped defuse some of the long-standing hostilities between the NYPD and the city's Communist-led organizations.

Hoping to capitalize on these developments, La Guardia appointed a new police commissioner, Lewis Valentine, who affirmed the mayor's commitment to tolerance. From the beginning, the commissioner worked to reduce police violence through tighter supervision and the development of explicit procedures and regulations for handling crowds. Valentine emphasized advance consultation, careful planning, and close supervision via the department's new Bureau of Operations. Under this new system, precinct commanders no longer handled strikes and demonstrations on their own, but consulted with the Bureau in advance to determine acceptable conditions for picketing, parading, and other activities. In dealing with labor disputes, Valentine ordered police to act with "vigilance, good judgment, tact, diplomacy, restraint, self-control, fairness and a liberal, flexible policy." The use of "warnings and sympathetic advice," he noted, was preferable to arrest or the use of "oppressive methods."[7]

Although the Commissioner had little sympathy for Communists and other "agitators" in the new CIO unions, he expressed a firm belief in the New Deal labor formula. In time, he said, "disorder and unrest will fade away, and in a cordial spirit of confidence, good will and mutual understanding, capital and labor will march side by side to heights of success and prosperity never before seen."[8] Both Valentine and La Guardia maintained that labor disputes should be settled not by police nightsticks but by "tribunals set up by the federal government." And indeed by 1937 the NLRB and the federal courts were actively defining the parameters of acceptable labor-management relations. The Supreme Court upheld the Wagner Act in 1937 and proceeded to rule on several cases affirming the rights of labor, including the right to picket. The Supreme Court also handed down two significant decisions in 1937 upholding the rights of Communists and other political dissenters. In *De Jonge v. Oregon* and *Herndon v. Lowry*, the Court affirmed the first amendment rights of Communist organizers, thus increasing pressure on local government and police to exercise tolerance.[9]

Federal intervention, coupled with local administrative reform efforts, helped to ease conflict between radicals and police and resulted in a dramatic improvement in the NYPD's record of public-order policing. The New York

ACLU noted in its 1937–1938 annual report that "The Committee rarely has occasion to criticize the conduct of police in strikes." Police repression of Communist political activities also dropped dramatically in 1937, both in New York and around the country. The NYPD's improved record is evident from the reports of the Criminal Alien Squad (CAS), the department's countersubversion unit. These reports, filed by members of the squad assigned to hundreds of radical meetings from 1939 to 1941, contain few comments other than "no disorder or arrests." The most telling evidence of the department's change in policy, though, comes from a 1941 Civil Liberties Union (CLU) report on police action at street meetings. Based on reports by CLU observers at more than thirty strikes and street meetings that summer, the report found that "police follow a general hands-off policy toward the speakers, and generally try to make themselves fairly unobtrusive." Although most police were unsympathetic to labor and considered radicals to be "crackpots," the report said, their biases were passive and did not generally affect their work. In fact, police often took extra measures to protect the rights of speakers by dealing aggressively with hecklers and temporarily stopping traffic to allow pedestrians to pass around sidewalk crowds.[10]

As these reports indicate, the transformation in public-order policing in New York was truly significant. But the new style of policing also had some drawbacks. As evidenced by the extensive (CAS) reports, the NYPD came to rely increasingly on surveillance and intelligence by plainclothes detectives. In the late 1930s and 1940s, the CAS usually acted as a passive surveillance unit and took little or no action against demonstrators. In isolated cases, however, detectives from the CAS and other units made arrests and used third-degree tactics against suspects out of public view. The CLU reported a number of such cases, including the beatings of two CIO members in a Brooklyn shipyard strike in 1937 and a teachers' union leader protesting Works Progress Administration cuts in 1941.[11] At the same time that La Guardia and Valentine liberalized police policy toward public strikes and demonstrations, they increased reliance on the undercover red squad. Although behind-the-scenes repression was relatively rare during this period, the beatings of these labor radicals suggest that detectives sometimes resorted to old-fashioned red bashing in the confines of the stationhouse. Greater police tolerance of public protest was thus accompanied by more invasive and sophisticated forms of covert surveillance.

The federal government accelerated this trend as the nation moved toward war in the late 1930s. Like the FBI, the CAS in this period concentrated its spying efforts on anti-Semitic and pro-fascist organizations. The Christian Front, anti-Semitic followers of Father Charles Coughlin, was closely monitored as was the German-American Bund. With the outbreak of war in Europe in 1939, the Roosevelt administration appealed to local police agencies to cooperate with the FBI in fighting espionage, sabotage, violations of the Neutrality Acts, and other subversive activities. Over the next year, the FBI began issuing intelligence reports to the NYPD requesting assistance in ferreting out pro-fascist groups and activities. Local police officers were also sent to the National Police Academy for special training in antisabotage and counterespionage techniques. Four months after the attack on Pearl Harbor, the NYPD announced that it was combining the Criminal Alien, Sabotage, and Bomb Squads into a single wartime intelligence unit that would function "as a municipal arm of the FBI." Comprising 150 college-educated officers, the new NYPD unit worked undercover along the waterfront and in defense facilities to collect intelligence on sabotage and fifth-column activity. Thereafter, the *New York Times* regularly reported on joint FBI-NYPD antisabotage operations and intelligence sharing.[12] While the war emergency seemed to justify such heightened vigilance in the short term, the federal-local partnership deepened the NYPD's expertise in and commitment to clandestine intelligence operations that would become a permanent feature of urban policing. The potential abuses arising out of such a system, however, would not become evident until later.

The Postwar Years

Following World War II, the federal government blazed a new path in the area of civil rights enforcement. A major federal investigation of civil rights in 1947 exposed police brutality as a racial issue and strengthened the role of the Justice Department in overseeing local enforcement. Ultimately, however, these efforts—targeted toward the segregationist South—had only indirect effects on police practices in New York City. Moreover, what little progress did occur was overshadowed by cold war anti-Communist campaigns by the federal government, which divided and crippled the local antibrutality movement.

Building on the democratic rhetoric of the World War II years, civil rights activists drew attention to the abuse of black soldiers by military and civilian authorities as well as the continuing police mistreatment of black veterans in the late 1940s. President Harry Truman responded to these appeals by appointing a special executive committee to investigate civil rights violations. In 1947, the committee issued its report, *To Secure These Rights*, which exposed a wide variety of civil rights abuses including wrongful shootings and the use of "improper police practices" against black suspects. Although most of the report's proposals were never implemented, Congress did act on the committee's recommendation to strengthen federal authority in civil rights cases where state and local authorities had failed to act. Revising a section of the U.S. Criminal Code in 1948, Congress bolstered the power of the Civil Rights Division of the Justice Department (first established in 1939) by creating new federal penalties—a one-thousand dollar fine and/or a year in prison—for civil rights violations by law enforcement officers. Hereafter, citizens could appeal to federal prosecutors with some hope of getting a hearing outside the highly politicized local courts. In the South especially, federal intervention was often the only hope for black victims of official violence.[13]

Over the next four years, civil rights activists in New York referred numerous NYPD brutality cases to the Justice Department when local authorities refused to take action. Congressman Adam Clayton Powell, Jr., and City Councilmember Benjamin Davis—both from Harlem—spearheaded local antibrutality efforts, working with groups such as the National Association for the Advancement of Colored People (NAACP) and the Communist-led Civil Rights Congress. Among the many cases they pursued were those of Samuel Symonette, a Harlem candy store owner who was beaten when he protested a warrantless search of his store; Lloyd Curtis Jones, a disabled black veteran who was shot by police after refusing a move-on order; and Herman Newton, a Brooklyn motorist who was fatally shot as he fled from a traffic-related argument with an off-duty officer. The activists' efforts led to two municipal investigations of police brutality in 1947 and 1949, both of which exonerated police or maintained there was insufficient evidence to prosecute. Disappointingly, local activists got no encouragement when they forwarded these cases to the Justice Department.[14]

The feds' indifference frustrated and perplexed New York civil rights activists until February 1953, when the *World Telegram and Sun* made a startling revelation. For the past seven months, the Justice Department had deferred its investigations of civil rights complaints against the NYPD and had instead allowed the department to conduct its own inquiries. This secret agreement came to light following a 1952 brutality case involving Jacob Jackson, a black truck driver from Hell's Kitchen. Jackson and another black man were allegedly beaten by police while handcuffed together in the West 54th Street stationhouse. Both were hospitalized for their injuries, and Jackson underwent two operations in which metal plates were inserted in his skull. As in most brutality cases, the criminal case against the officer was unsuccessful, so the NAACP filed a civil rights complaint with the Justice Department. What the NAACP did not know, however, was that NYPD Commissioner George Monaghan, whose department was reeling from a massive corruption investigation, had made a quiet agreement with the Assistant U.S. Attorney General. According to the latter, the Justice Department agreed to give the NYPD "an opportunity to conduct its own investigations and launder its own linen without loss of morale." When a newly appointed U.S. attorney (who was unaware of the earlier agreement) sent FBI officers to interview NYPD officers about the Jackson case, Monaghan refused to cooperate with the investigation. Federal civil rights statutes, he maintained, were intended "for that section of the country south of the Mason-Dixon Line."[15]

Monaghan's attempts to stymie federal oversight, and the Justice Department's complicity therein, triggered a firestorm of criticism and demands for a citywide investigation of police practices. On the federal level, Congressman Adam Clayton Powell convinced the House Judiciary Committee to establish a subcommittee to investigate the situation. The subsequent hearings confirmed the existence of a secret FBI-NYPD agreement, but the Committee's final report was a tepid document, reducing the whole affair to one of administrative misjudgment and misunderstanding. Meanwhile, a federal grand jury (under the effective control of federal prosecutors) refused to indict the officer accused of beating Jacob Jackson. It likewise declined to investigate other recent cases of alleged NYPD brutality. Clearly, the federal government was treading lightly around the problem, hoping to stanch criticism of any perceived overzealousness. The loss of northern support for the new civil rights procedures would have seriously endangered what was the only line of defense against Klan terror and police violence in the South.[16]

The 1953 scandal did, however, have some indirect consequences in that it encouraged city leaders to introduce significant administrative reforms. First, the NYPD agreed to institute officer training in human relations. Within two months of the subcommittee's hearings, the New York police academy began offering training to all recruits on intergroup relations and the problems of minority groups. Around the same time, the department also appointed its first black deputy commissioner, George Redding. Equally significant was the department's creation of a Civilian Complaint Review Board (CCRB) in May 1953. This original board had no civilian members and was staffed by three police officials who reported directly to the commissioner. An internal body that continued to protect the department from outside scrutiny, the CCRB did not noticeably improve the department's disciplinary record in brutality cases. It did, however, institutionalize and standardize the complaint process and create an administrative entity that civil rights reformers could work to reformulate in later years.[17]

Beyond these indirect benefits, the federal government did little to abet the civil rights cause in postwar New York. In fact, the pervasive climate of Cold War antiCommunism led to federal legislation and prosecutions that ultimately decimated the local civil rights movement. On the left especially, continuing antiCommunist repression took its toll on the antibrutality movement. Ben Davis, the Communist city councilmember who had long played a leading role in the Harlem antibrutality campaign, was convicted of violating the Smith Act in 1949 and was sentenced to five years in prison. William Patterson and other Communist leaders of the Civil Rights Congress were also convicted for refusing to cooperate with antiCommunist investigators and were jailed in the early 1950s. In 1956, when the Justice Department used the Internal Security Act to force the CRC to register as a Communist front group, the organization collapsed. This repressive climate also had a devastating impact on the NAACP, which purged Communists from its local affiliates in New York and Brooklyn, including many antibrutality activists. Fearing association with left-wing groups, the NAACP abandoned its mass action tactics and retreated to a narrower strategy of courtroom litigation and negotiation with political elites.[18] The question of police violence would thus lay dormant until the ferment of the 1960s reignited the issue once again.

The 1960s

Under the liberal administrations of the early 1960s, the federal government once again expanded the safeguards of due process and endorsed political and social reforms to protect civil rights. Some of the strongest federal initiatives came from the Supreme Court, which under Chief Justice Earl Warren issued a series of rulings expanding the rights of criminal defendants. The 1961 *Mapp v. Ohio* decision, for example, extended to the states the Fourth Amendment right to be secure against unreasonable searches and seizures, a ruling which had the practical effect of helping to protect suspects from police beatings administered during illegal raids. More significantly, the Court's 1966 decision in *Miranda v. Arizona* resulted in critical new safeguards against psychologically coercive interrogations by requiring police to issue "Miranda warnings" prior to questioning. In New York, which had been experiencing a resurgence of violent third-degree cases against minority suspects in the early 1960s, the decision strengthened legal protections against physical abuse as well. Although the Court would later circumscribe the *Mapp* and *Miranda* rulings, the basic legal principles remained intact and helped to curb more overt forms of police misconduct.

In other areas, New York City took the lead in developing innovative police reforms that were subsequently promoted by federal policymakers. Because of the city's experience on the frontlines of racial activism and unrest, city leaders became pioneers in efforts to reduce social tensions. Following the 1964 Harlem uprising, for instance, the NYPD met with local community and civil rights leaders who demanded far-reaching changes in police operations. Soon after, the department appointed Lloyd Sealey as captain of Harlem's Twenty-Eighth Precinct, making him the city's first black precinct commander. The NYPD also created a new Community Affairs program to open lines of communication with local minority communities. To increase the representation of blacks and Latinos in the force, the NYPD announced the formation of a new cadet training program for 1,500 minority youth under one of the city's federally funded antipoverty programs.[19]

With the election of Mayor John Lindsay in 1965, the department underwent further reform. First, Lindsay reorganized the CCRB to include three police and four civilian appointees and a separate investigative staff under a civilian director. Though not fully independent of the NYPD, the new CCRB increased citizen representation and oversight and became one of a handful of civilian review boards operating in the country at the time. To prevent a resumption of ghetto violence, Lindsay then organized a sixteen-member Urban Action Task Force to monitor potential trouble spots in thirteen different neighborhoods. Urban Task Force members also served as official monitors at protest marches and demonstrations in an effort to mediate disputes and prevent violence. At the same time, the NYPD issued new orders governing police protocols and the use of force in controlling crowds. In printed instructions issued to all officers assigned to riot areas, the commissioner ordered police to refrain from using racial slurs and provocative language or actions, and to avoid unnecessary drawing or discharge of weapons. In practice, this meant containment rather than dispersal of rioters and less aggressive pursuit of looters in a manner that "traded goods and appliances for human lives." In both riots and demonstrations, then, top police officials emphasized containment and restraint in lieu of violence.[20]

This liberal approach to urban policing was endorsed by the federal government in some of its major policy statements of the 1960s. The most detailed proposals were put forth by the National Advisory Commission on Civil Disorders (known as the Kerner Commission), which issued its report in 1968. In a section titled "The Police and the Community," the Kerner Commission recommended many of the liberal reforms already enacted in New York: better training and operating procedures for handling violent conflicts, the recruitment and promotion of minority officers, and the establishment of citizen review boards and community relations programs. Mayor Lindsay's role as vice-chairman of the commission no doubt helped to promote the city's efforts, but the commission's stamp of approval likewise served to reinforce many of these reform ideas among police managers around the country.[21]

But even as NYPD reforms were gaining national recognition, they were meeting growing resistance back home as rank-and-file police officers and their unions grew increasingly frustrated with escalating crime and social unrest. The new CCRB was the first major casualty of this emerging backlash. Led by the powerful Patrolmen's Benevolent Association (PBA), a grassroots campaign against the new review board won a resounding victory with the approval of an anticivilian review referendum in November 1966. In a campaign saturated with racial innuendo, the police union highlighted the problems of crime and disorder and appealed to New Yorkers to free the NYPD of unnecessary bureaucratic restraints. The PBA also amplified its criticism of Lindsay's restraint policies for handling civil disorder, a sentiment shared by many white rank-and-file officers. Angered by the growing hostility and violence of young militants, some police rebelled against Lindsay's policy of restraint and unleashed their wrath indiscriminately against young protesters. Indeed, in 1967–1968, there was a series of violent clashes between police and black and latino youth, antiwar demonstrators, Yippies, and other dissident groups.

The best-known and most serious conflict occurred at Columbia University in the spring of 1968. In a convergence of civil rights and antiwar activism, students in the Columbia chapter of Students for a Democratic Society joined with black students protesting the university's plans to construct a gymnasium in nearby Morningside Park. Organizing a campus-wide strike in late April, the students occupied several university buildings for more than a week until the university called on the NYPD to clear the occupied buildings. In the police action that ensued, dozens of students were roughed up as they were dragged from the buildings. The most serious violence, however, occurred later when police were preparing to leave campus. Responding to taunts from the nearby students, police charged the crowd, swinging their batons and pummeling demonstrators and bystanders alike as they tried to flee. All told, 148 people were injured and 162 later filed complaints of excessive force—the most complaints ever filed in a single NYPD action. In the weeks that followed, both the NYCLU and the CCRB issued reports on the incident that scored the department for excessive force, poor planning, and weak discipline.[22]

The Columbia episode was the brutal culmination of growing tensions between police and demonstrators over the past year, but it also marked the beginning of a change in the tenor of policing of mass action. Concerned that overt police repression was stirring sympathy for student protests, both federal and local authorities stepped up their counterintelligence operations in an effort to "neutralize" militants. Within days of the Columbia strike, the FBI launched a new counterintelligence offensive,

COINTELPRO New Left, which targeted SDS and other radical campus groups.

Founded a decade earlier, COINTEL programs had first been developed in the late 1950s as aggressive counterintelligence campaigns designed to "expose, disrupt, misdirect, discredit or otherwise neutralize" the activities of the Communist Party. In the 1960s, the FBI expanded COINTEL's range of targets to include the Socialist Workers Party, White Hate Groups, Black Nationalist/Hate Groups, and the New Left. During these years, the FBI's New York field office employed around a hundred agents, roughly a quarter of whom focused on subversive activities. By necessity, then, the FBI worked very closely with the NYPD's own "red squad," called the Bureau of Special Services (BOSS). A successor to the old CAS, BOSS underwent significant expansion and revitalization in response to rising political activism in the 1960s. During this period, it employed more than a hundred detectives and supervisors who provided a steady stream of confidential intelligence data to the NYPD, the FBI, the CIA, Army Intelligence, and numerous urban red squads around the country. Indeed, BOSS was a key player in the national intelligence community, and its targets, operations, and goals paralleled those of federal agencies with whom it cooperated.[23]

BOSS detectives relied on both overt and covert operations, both of which led to periodic abuses. As in the past, BOSS gathered personal and political information on thousands of individuals and organizations. By the late 1960s, BOSS maintained over a million entries in its files and, when requested, transmitted this data to seven different federal agencies. As it turned out, BOSS also shared this data with city employers, bar examiners, and even private employers (who bribed or cajoled detectives to share information). Prospective teachers, lawyers, and other city workers thus found their employment options closed when damaging information surfaced about their political affiliations. BOSS intelligence gathering thus had a chilling effect on lawful political activities, as did some of the more visible work of its detectives. During antiwar demonstrations in the late 1960s, for example, undercover BOSS officers made highly visible efforts to film and photograph participants, took down their license plate numbers, and sometimes tried to incite violence through verbal or physical threats.[24]

The most egregious abuses, however, resulted from the squad's covert operations designed to infiltrate and disrupt radical groups, particularly the Black Panthers and other black militant groups in the late 1960s. Beginning in the mid-1960s, undercover BOSS detectives provided intelligence that led to the arrest of numerous black militant leaders. In their zeal to make cases, however, BOSS resorted to questionable wiretapping and eavesdropping practices while detectives sometimes acted as agent-provocateurs. As court testimony later revealed, BOSS officers proposed targets for bombings or assassinations, egged on reluctant comrades, and provided essential resources such as cars and guns to effect a "conspiracy." The FBI's COINTELPRO against Black Nationalist/Hate Groups, launched in 1967, used similar tactics against many of the same groups. Soon, BOSS and other urban red squads were working closely with the FBI in a campaign against the Black Panthers, whom J. Edgar Hoover labeled "the greatest threat to the internal security of the country." Federal and local agents infiltrated dozens of Panther groups, resulting in numerous raids, shootings, arrests, and trials around the country. In New York, BOSS detectives made several attempts to infiltrate and prosecute the Panthers in 1968–1969, but subsequent trials revealed little concrete evidence of the alleged robberies, assassinations, and bombings that BOSS attributed to them. Although many Panthers were later acquitted or booked on lesser charges of possession of weapons, the protracted trials and incarcerations destroyed the Panthers' organization permanently.[25]

The unsubstantiated cases against the Panthers, together with BOSS's ongoing harassment of New Left groups, raised public awareness of intelligence abuses. By the 1970s, it was clear that these clandestine forms of police repression were more common and more devastating than police batons and tear gas. The growing tide of criticism resulted in a wave of lawsuits against urban police departments in the 1970s. The prosecution of these cases was no doubt aided by the Watergate scandal, which exposed a score of illegal intelligence practices by federal agencies and officeholders. In New York, a diverse group of local activists—ranging from pacifists to Black Panthers—filed a class action suit against BOSS, charging that its intelligence abuses had infringed on their First Amendment rights. The 1971 case, *Handschu v. Special Services Division*, took years to litigate and revealed reams of information on BOSS operations in the process. The final settlement issued in 1985 resulted in new guidelines limiting police intelligence activities and the creation of a three-member authority to oversee BOSS investigations. Specifically, it prohibited police from starting files, photographing demonstrators, planting undercover agents, and other intrusive practices unless there was an indication of criminal activity involved. While some of the plaintiffs did not believe the consent decree went far enough, it introduced some critical safeguards and oversight mechanisms for BOSS. It also reflected federal reform efforts of the 1970s that established Congressional oversight and increased accountability in the nation's intelligence programs.[26]

In the 1960s, as in the 1930s, the impact of the federal government on local police practices was significant and multifaceted. In the first half of the decade, liberal federal and local initiatives for civilian review, community relations, affirmative action, and tactical restraint served to reinforce each other. Such reforms, along with key Warren Court decisions, strengthened the hand of antibrutality lawyers and reformers. But as social unrest intensified in the late 1960s, both federal and local authorities turned to more repressive and clandestine tactics to combat militants whom they viewed as a threat to national security. Quieter and more effective than violent police actions, counterintelligence campaigns also trampled on New Yorkers' constitutional rights and were eventually reined in by the federal court—at least for a while.

The 1990s and Beyond

Public concern with police violence crested once again in the 1990s, resulting in the most recent wave in the city's history of antibrutality activism. Although local protests over police misconduct had continued in the 1970s and 1980s, it was the brutal beating of Rodney King in Los Angeles—captured on videotape—that refocused attention on the issue in 1991. The following year, a predominantly white jury exonerated the five Los Angeles Police Department (LAPD) officers who administered the beating, and Los Angeles erupted in five days of deadly rioting. As in other cities, New York witnessed antibrutality protests and violent disturbances in the wake of the verdict, as local activists drew parallels between King and local brutality cases. A few weeks later, New York entered into its own crisis as a drug scandal triggered a major investigation by the Mollen Commission. Over the next year and a half, the Commission uncovered a shocking network of drug-related corruption and police violence in the South Bronx and other high-crime precincts. In the meantime, Mayor David Dinkins had finally convinced the City Council to establish an independent civilian review board with its own budget and investigative staff.

With the election of Mayor Rudolph Giuliani in 1993, however, the prospects for reform dimmed. A former federal prosecutor and strong police advocate, Giuliani dismissed the Mollen Commission's recommendations for improving police accountability and moved to cut the staff and funding of the new CCRB. In addition, he and his new police commissioner, William Bratton, instituted a new, more aggressive style of policing known as "zero tolerance." Under this approach, police undertook massive arrests for minor "quality of life" offenses (public drinking, panhandling, squeegee washing, etc.), sending a message that the streets were under control. These arrests locked up large numbers of people and allowed police to apprehend those with illegal weapons, drugs, or outstanding warrants. At the same time, the Street Crime Unit, a mobile plainclothes operation, was expanded and dispatched to make sweeps of drug and crime-infested areas identified by COMPSTAT, a computerized crime-tracking system. The Street Crime Unit thus swept through the city's poor neighborhoods with the quality-of-life strategy providing a thin legal pretext for stopping, frisking, and arresting large numbers of people in poor, nonwhite neighborhoods. Predictably, such methods sparked allegations of racial profiling and increased complaints of brutality and harassment.[27]

From 1994 to 1999, the city witnessed a slew of high-profile police shootings and brutality cases that galvanized a mass antibrutality movement. Responding to a series of controversial police killings of young Latinos in the Bronx in 1994, parents and other supporters of the victims formed Parents Against Police Brutality, a group that staged public protests and pressed for official redress. In 1997, the city was jolted by news that a Haitian immigrant, Abner Louima, had been arrested, beaten, and sodomized with a broomstick in the bathroom of Brooklyn's Seventieth Precinct. And in 1999, public outrage exploded again when officers with the Street Crime Unit fired forty-one shots at Amadou Diallo, an unarmed African immigrant, in the doorway of his South Bronx home. In the weeks that followed, antibrutality activists rallied thousands of protesters who launched an extended campaign of protests and civil disobedience outside Police Plaza.[28]

Local protests and investigations were bolstered by federal action under the Clinton administration. In 1997, the Brooklyn District Attorney's office turned the Louima case over to the FBI and federal prosecutors in hopes of winning stiffer sentences under federal civil rights laws. Louima's attacker, Officer Justin Volpe, subsequently pleaded guilty in federal court and was sentenced to thirty years in prison while three other officers implicated in the attack were convicted of lesser charges. Moreover, the U.S. Attorney in Brooklyn initiated a federal inquiry into whether there was a broader pattern of police cover-ups of brutality in the city. It was the first stage in a federal investigation of the NYPD made possible under the Violent Crime and Control Act. The Act, passed in 1994 in the wake of the Rodney King case, empowered the Justice Department to file civil lawsuits against state and local law-enforcement agencies that engaged in "patterns or practices" that violated civil rights. When successful, the Justice Department could seek injunctive relief by mandating law-enforcement agencies to make necessary changes to end abuses. Following the shooting of Amadou Diallo, Attorney General Janet Reno agreed to expand the pattern-or-practice investigation to include a study of the NYPD's stop-and-frisk policy as well.[29]

These federal initiatives culminated in a major investigation of police practices by the U.S. Commission on Civil Rights. Beginning in 1999, the commission conducted a year-long investigation in which it collected and analyzed data and heard testimony from both police and aggrieved citizens. The final report, issued in 2000, offered a detailed critique and recommendations on everything from recruitment and training to policing policies and discipline. For starters, the report underscored the failure of the department's affirmative action programs and recommended more aggressive recruiting to make the NYPD more representative of the city. Analyzing the department's stop-and-frisk reports, the commission found a dramatic racial disparity among those stopped by the NYPD. Blacks and Latinos made up 84 percent of people stopped by police, while comprising only 52 percent of the city's population. "The NYPD's data," the commission concluded, "strongly suggest that racial profiling plays some role in the stop and frisk practices of the overall department, and particularly in the Street Crime Unit." To correct such abusive practices and improve discipline and accountability, the commission urged that an independent monitor be appointed to provide permanent oversight of the department and the CCRB.[30]

Federal investigations, together with state and local efforts, seemed to augur promising changes in police and CCRB practices. The increased scrutiny to which the department was subject in the late 1990s, for example, prompted Mayor Giuliani to increase the staff and funding of the CCRB. The CCRB was thus able to process and substantiate more cases, and the police commissioner began disciplining more officers accused of misconduct. Moreover, the prospect of a federal pattern-or-practice lawsuit against the department increased the likelihood that further reforms would follow or that the court would impose a federal monitor. By 2000, the Justice Department had instituted lawsuits against four other state or local police departments; New York and Los Angeles appeared to be next. The election of Republican President George W. Bush later that year, however, effectively precluded that litigation. Convinced that further concessions were unnecessary, Mayor Giuliani refused to cooperate in the ongoing federal investigation of stop-and-frisk practices, dismissing any pattern-or-practice lawsuit as baseless.[31] As with so much federal legislation, the effectiveness of the pattern-or-practice provision of the 1994 Act was only as good as the commitment of the executive branch officials appointed to carry it out.

Concern over NYPD abuses was further obliterated by the terrorist attack on the World Trade Center on September 11, 2001. Killing nearly three thousand people, including twenty-three New York City police officers, the attack was the worst in the nation's history and affected New Yorkers most acutely. As the city suffered through the prolonged search efforts, daily funerals, and ongoing fears of air disasters and anthrax infection, the problem of police violence was dropped off the city's agenda.

Police officers had become heroes, and few were inclined to vilify the NYPD over past offenses.

The city's somber mood was also accompanied by a radical shift in the priorities of law enforcement in response to terrorism. Soon after September 11, the NYPD reconfigured its personnel and resources to provide maximum protection against attack. While thousands of police were deployed to seal off Lower Manhattan, the NYPD also dispatched large numbers of officers to guard bridges, tunnels, ports, and other sensitive areas. This visible antiterrorist response continued after the immediate crisis receded. Over the next year and a half, the NYPD organized Operation Atlas, an assortment of specially armed and often highly visible antiterrorist teams. These included Hercules (special forces-type units armed with sub–machine guns and deployed to potential terrorist targets); COBRA (special units dealing with chemical, biological, or radiological actions); an expanded and revamped Harbor Squad (which now works twenty-four hours checking bridges, tunnels, ports, the Statue of Liberty, and other potential targets); and police with bomb-sniffing dogs on the Staten Island ferries. This forceful presence grew at the expense of earlier anti-street crime efforts of the Giuliani era. In fact, as he struggled to reallocate resources in the spring of 2002, new Police Commissioner Raymond Kelly disbanded the notorious Street Crime Unit. As of 2005, there are more than a thousand NYPD officers assigned to fulltime antiterrorist duty, and the visible forces of Operation Atlas are only the tip of the iceberg—a growing number of these officers work in the more clandestine realm of intelligence and threat assessment.[32]

Much of the support for new antiterrorism programs has come from the federal government. From 2002 to 2005, the NYPD received roughly $490 million in federal grant money for special equipment and training to combat terrorism. The federal government has also promoted antiterrorism efforts by granting new and dangerous police powers to spy on and arrest potential terrorists under the PATRIOT ACT. While the act is theoretically limited to federal police agencies, it also encourages federal-local cooperation by requiring the FBI and CIA to train local police in handling national security information. Not surprisingly, municipal police departments around the country subsequently expanded their intelligence units to monitor terrorist activity. Since the allocation of federal antiterrorism dollars is based on the number of potential local threats, intelligence data not only helps prevent attacks but helps subsidize the continuing expansion of NYPD counterterrorism operations. As the nation's number one target, New York has developed the most sophisticated, hi-tech program in the country—a two-pronged operation that some have called "the city's own FBI and CIA."[33]

The Counter Terrorism Bureau is one pillar of this program. Founded in February 2002, the bureau employs roughly 250 officers headquartered in an undisclosed location in Coney Island. According to one reporter who visited the site, the building is chock full of hi-tech equipment providing international news broadcasts, lead news tickers, electronic maps, and computer systems with access to scores of databases. In the unit's Global Intelligence Room, bureau employees monitor foreign broadcasts in Arabic, Pashto, Urdu, and other languages. According to Commissioner Kelly, there are forty-five Arabic-speaking analysts whose services are sometimes shared with federal agencies. Around 125 of the Bureau's officers are assigned to the Joint Terrorism Task Force, where they work with other federal and state agents investigating terrorist threats in the New York area. The bureau has also posted liaison officers in Tel Aviv, London, Lyon, Singapore, and other overseas cities where they work with foreign police to share information and intelligence. The heads of the Counter Terrorism Bureau—Frank Libutti (2002–2003) and currently Michael Sheehan—are both former U.S. military commanders with backgrounds in terrorism and homeland security. Libutti, the original commanding officer, in fact resigned to become undersecretary of Homeland Security, reflecting the fluidity of personnel between federal and local antiterrorism agencies. Both the FBI and the NYPD acknowledge the periodic conflicts and competition between the two agencies; the Counter Terrorism Bureau's broad reach and bureaucratic independence have sometimes made the feds uncomfortable. Ultimately, though, federal-local cooperation is key, and local police have become in the words of FBI Director Robert Mueller "important force multipliers" for federal law enforcement and intelligence efforts.[34]

The second pillar of the NYPD's antiterrorism campaign is the newly invigorated Intelligence Bureau. Formerly the Bureau of Special Services, the city's old red squad had shrunken its operations following the Handschu Agreement to become a glorified "escort service" for visiting dignitaries. In the wake of September 11, however, the NYPD hired David Cohen, a top-level CIA director and covert operations specialist, to revamp the city's intelligence operations. One of Cohen's first priorities was the rescinding of the Handschu guidelines, which he claimed "hamper our efforts every day." In December 2002, Cohen presented his case before a federal judge who subsequently ruled to modify the consent decree. Under the new agreement, the NYPD is no longer required to have evidence of any criminal activity before opening an investigation. Any intelligence it collects can be retained in the Bureau's files and shared with other agencies. In lieu of the oversight of the Handschu Authority, the NYPD agreed to adopt the FBI's surveillance guidelines that were overhauled after September 11 to provide maximum latitude for investigators.[35]

Since this 2003 ruling, the NYPD Intelligence Bureau—whose current operations and staffing is highly secretive—has been busy collecting data, investigating tips, and planting undercover officers in suspect groups. The impact of such surveillance has fallen heaviest on Muslims and other immigrant groups, and as Andrea McArdle notes in chapter 8, immigrant communities have faced increased arrests and deportations on immigration violations, lengthy secret detentions, and other abuses. But the new intelligence apparatus is not targeted solely at foreign terrorists. Within days of the modification of the Handschu Agreement, the NYPD arrested hundreds of protesters at an antiwar rally and interrogated them about their political views and activities. Police have also resumed the practice of videotaping demonstrations, with the resulting tapes retained by the NYPD for at least a year. The NYCLU has objected to these practices, fearing a return to the red squad abuses of earlier years and their chilling effect on lawful dissent. Nor is it clear how the reinvigorated Intelligence Bureau is operating. Some intelligence experts insist that the coupling of intelligence operations with arrest-driven agencies like the NYPD sharply increases the likelihood that information will be misused.[36]

What is clear, though, is that the temper of policing in New York has changed dramatically in the past ten years and that the federal government has played an important role in this evolution. As law-enforcement priorities shifted from fighting more conventional crime in the 1990s to combating terrorism since September 11, the nature of police repression has shifted accordingly—from overt forms of harassment and brutality to more clandestine forms of surveillance and intelligence gathering. In the 1990s, as in the 1930s and 1960s, the federal government reinforced local reform efforts to combat brutality and racial profiling. A few years later, however, national security concerns and a changing political climate eclipsed those earlier efforts. Federal-local cooperation in the war on terror has helped spawn a new hi-tech, intelligence-oriented campaign by the NYPD that poses equally dangerous threats to civil liberties and due process. This turnaround is hardly new. The earlier periods of police reform were also followed by national security crises—World War II, the Cold War, and Vietnam—that promoted similar obsessions with spying and counterintelligence. Today the NYPD plays a stronger role in this federal-local partnership, competing with federal agencies for personnel, contacts, and strategies.

Over the years, Congress, the federal courts, presidential commissions, the Justice Department, and the Civil Rights Commission have all helped to safeguard citizens' rights, promote police professionalism, and improve police-community relations. But we tend to overlook the more repressive initiatives that have emanated from the federal government, enticing local police agencies to become partners in spying, infiltrating, and disrupting law-abiding political groups. Knowing the history of this cycle, we would do well to rethink our current enthusiasm for intelligence-oriented policing and remember its potential for eroding civil rights and liberties in the past. If we continue down this path, we will no doubt find ourselves turning back to the federal courts in a few years to restrain the autocratic police agencies that were unleashed to protect us.

Notes

1. For journalists' account of the third degree, see, Charles J.V. Murphy, "The Third Degree: Another Side of Our Crime Problem," *Outlook and Independent*, 151 (April 3, 1929), pp. 523–526; Oswald Garrison Villard, "Official Lawlessness: The Third Degree and the Crime Wave," *Harpers Monthly Magazine*, 160 (October 27, 1927), 605–614; A.C. Sedgwick, "The Third Degree and Crime," *Nation*, 124 (June 15, 1927), pp. 666–667; Emanuel H. Lavine, *The Third Degree: A Detailed and Appalling Expose of Police Brutality* (New York: Vanguard Press, 1930).

2. Zechariah Chafee Jr. et al., *The Third Degree* (New York: Arno Press, 1969; rep. 1931)—Note: this is a reprint of the Wickersham Commission's 1931 *Report on Lawlessness in Law Enforcement*.

3. Samuel Walker, *A Critical History of Police Reform* (Lexington, Massachussetts: Lexington Books, 1977), pp. 159–160; Samuel Walker, *In Defense of American Liberties: A History of the ACLU* (New York: Oxford University Press, 1990), p. 88; *New York Post*, March 23, 1936; *Times*, July 28, 1938; W.R. Kidd, *Police Interrogation* (New York: R.V. Basuino, 1940), pp. 48.

4. *Brown v. Mississippi*, 297 U.S. 278; 56 S. Ct. 461 (1936); Richard A. Leo, " 'From Coercion to Deception': The Changing Nature of Police Interrogation in America," in Richard A. and George C. Thomas III Leo, eds., *The Miranda Debate: Law, Justice, and Policing* (Boston: Northeastern University Press, 1998), pp. 65–74, 71; Lawrence Herman, "The Supreme Court, the Attorney General, and the Good Old days of Police Interrogation" in Richard A. and George C. Thomas III Leo, eds., *The Miranda Debate: Law, Justice, and Policing* (Boston: Northeastern University Press, 1998), pp. 132–141, 132; Jerome H. Skolnick and James J. Fyfe, *Above the Law: Police and the Excessive Use of Force* (New York: Free Press, 1993), pp. 48–49.

5. For a more detailed discussion of these conflicts, see, Marilynn S. Johnson, *Street Justice: A History of Police Violence in New York City* (Boston: Beacon Press, 2003), pp. 149–164.

6. James Green, *The World of the Worker* (New York: Hill and Wang, 1980), pp. 150, 162–163; Mark Naison, *Communists in Harlem During the Depression* (Urbana: University of Illinois Press, 1983), pp. 169–171.

7. "Proposed Police Regulations Relating to Crowds," vol. 2252A, ACLU Papers, Mudd Library, Princeton University; Lewis Valentine, "Our Police Policy Concerning Labor Disturbances," *Spring 3100* (December 1937) pp. 1–3.

8. Valentine, "Our Police Policy Concerning Labor Disturbances," pp. 1–3.

9. *New York Times*, June 3, 1937; Samuel Walker, *In Defense of American Liberties: A History of the ACLU* (New York: Oxford University Press, 1990), pp. 106, 111; *De Jonge v. Oregon*, 299 U.S. 353 (1937); *Herndon v. Lowry*, 301 U.S. 242 (1937).

10. ACLU Annual Report, 1937–1938, 23; *Civil Liberties Quarterly*, March 1938; Bernard G. Walpin, "Report on Police Attitudes and Actions at Street Assemblages," October 1941, reel 215, frames 126–141, ACLU Papers (Wilmington, DE: Scholarly Resources, 1996). For Criminal Alien Squad reports, see Subject Files for "Organizations, Communist Party," reel 150, frames 213–584, and reel 212, frames 1859–1904, Fiorello La Guardia Papers, Municipal Archives of the City of New York.

11. The Brooklyn shipyard strike violence seriously concerned La Guardia, who bypassed the usual police disciplinary channels and ordered an independent investigation by the Commissioner of Accounts. See, *Times*, August 5, 11, 1937; *Herald Tribune*, July 21, August 8, 10, 1937; *Post*, August 17, 1937; *Sun* August 16, 1937. Paul Blanshard, Commissioner of Accounts, "Report to the Mayor on Alleged Police Brutality in Shipyard Strike," August 9, 1937; letter to La Guardia from Osmund K. Fraenkel, August 11, 1937, reel 117, frame 290, La Guardia Papers; letter to Valentine from Florina Lasker, July 21, 1937; Herbert A. Fierst, "Investigation of Police Brutality," July 27, 1937; letter to Paul Blanshard from Herbert D. David, August 6, 1937; and Herbert D. David and Herbert A. Fierst, "Final Report to Mayor: Inquiry into Police Brutality in Brooklyn," n.d., all on reel 146, vol. 998, ACLU Papers. On the WPA protest, see *Times*, July 19, October 3, 20, 1941; *Daily Worker*, July 19, 23, 28, October 3, November 18, 21, 1941; WPA Teachers Union, "Statement of the Facts in the Case of Herbert Newton," November 1, 1941, reel 195, frame 91, ACLU Papers.

12. *Times*, September 7, 1939; June 14, August 4, 1940; April 8, 1942.

13. Martha Biondi, "The Struggle for Black Equality in New York City," Ph.D. Dissertation, Columbia University, 1997, pp. 240–242; President's Commission on Civil Rights, *To Secure These Rights* (New York: Simon and Schuster, 1947), pp. 25, 114, 155–157.

14. For a more detailed account of the postwar antibrutality campaign, see Marilynn S. Johnson, *Street Justice*, pp. 203–222.

15. *World Telegram and Sun*, February 16, 1953; *Times*, February 17, 18, 21, 25, 28, March 7, 1953; editorial in *Crisis*, 60 (March 1953); Lardner and Reppetto, *NYPD: A City and Its Police* (New York: Henry Holt, 2000), pp. 263–264.

16. *Times*, February 27, March 3; *World Telegram and Sun*, July 6, 1953.

17. *Times*, May 2, 23, October 17, 1953, May 16, 1955; Edith M. Alexander, *Ten Years along the Path of Unity in New York City*, July 12, 1954, Subject files, Mayor's Committee on Unity folder, Reel 40102, frame 1199, Robert F. Wagner, Jr. Papers, MACNY; Andrew Darien, "Patrolling the Borders," Ph.D. Dissertation, New York University, 2000, 65; ACLU Annual Report, 1951–1953, pp. 94–95; New York Civil Liberties Union, Recommendations to Police Department for Investigating Complaints of Civil Rights Violations, NYC Police Brutality 1953–1954 folder, Box 456, Part IIA, NAACP Papers,

Library of Congress; NYPD, Press Release No. 44, May 16, 1955, in Police-Civilian Complaint Review Board—Pre-1960 folder, vertical files, MACNY; Biondi, "The Struggle for Black Equality," pp. 291.

18. Gerald Horne, *Black Liberation/Red Scare* (Newark, DE: University of Delaware Press, 1994), pp. 208, 244; Gerald Horne, *Communist Front?* (Rutherford, NJ: Farleigh Dickenson University Press, 1988), pp. 354–358.

19. *Times*, July 21, August 1, 1964; Darien, "Patrolling the Borders," pp. 157–158; Lardner and Repetto, *NYPD*, pp. 252–253.

20. *Times*, October 2, 1967, April 12, 17, 1968; Vincent Cannato, *The Ungovernable City* (New York: Basic Books, 2001), pp. 129–130; Paul Chevigny, *Police Power* (New York: Vintage, 1969), pp. 176–178; "Guidelines for Arrest at Scene of Mass Demonstrations," Confidential Subject Files, Reel 8, Box 14, Folder 174: Police Department (4), John Lindsay Papers; MACNY; "The Law and Public Demonstrations," *Spring 3100* (March 1969), pp. 8–19.

21. National Advisory Commission on Civil Disorders (Kerner Commission), *Report* (New York: New York Times Company, 1968), pp. 299–322.

22. *Times*, April 30, May 1, 1968; Jerry L. Avorn, *Up Against the Ivy Wall* (New York: Atheneum, 1970), pp. 186–195; Roger Kahn, *The Battle for Morningside Heights* (New York: William Morrow, 1970), pp. 200–213; Fact Finding Commission Appointed to Investigate the Disturbances at Columbia University in April and May 1968, *Crisis at Columbia* (New York: Vintage, 1968), pp. 140–142; Cannato, *The Ungovernable City*, pp. 253–254; Louis Stutman, R. Harcourt Dodds, Joseph T. McDonough, and Benjamin Ward, "CCRB Report on the Disposition of Complaints Arising from the Columbia University Incidents in April and May 1968," March 26, 1970, Subject files, reel 11, box 21, folder 364, Civilian Review Board 1966–1970, Lindsay Papers.

23. David Cunningham, *There's Something Happening Here: the New Left, The Klan, and FBI Counterintelligence* (Berkeley: University of California Press, 2004), pp. 6, 50, 83; Anthony Bouza, *Police Intelligence* (New York: AMS Press, 1976), pp. 24, 27–28, 34; Frank Donner, *Protectors of Privilege* (Berkeley: University of California Press, 1990), pp. 56–58.

24. Donner, *Protectors of Privilege*, pp. 162–165.

25. Ibid., pp. 172–191.

26. *Handschu v. Special Services Division*, 605 F. SUPP. 1384 (S.D.N.Y. 1985); Donner, *Protectors of Privilege*, pp. 356–357; Chisun Lee, "The Force Multipliers: NYPD to Bring Nationwide Spying Effort Home," *Village Voice* (February 26–March 4, 2003), www.villagevoice.com/news/0309, lee,42140,5.html (accessed online, May 30, 2005).

27. For a more detailed account of the brutality crisis on the 1990s, see Johnson, *Street Justice*, pp. 285–302. The impact of zero-tolerance policing is examined in Andrea McArdle and Tanya Erzen, eds., *Zero Tolerance* (New York: New York University Press, 2001).

28. Andrew Hsiao, "Mother of Invention," in McArdle and Erzen, eds., *Zero Tolerance*, 179–186, 189–190; *Times*, August 13, 14, 15, 16, 19, 22, 24, September 9, 1997, February 27, 1998, February 5, 6, March 4, 26, 1999; Human Rights Watch, Shielded From Justice, (New York, 1998), pp. 286–295; Norman Siegel, Michael

Meyers, and Margaret Fung, *Deflecting the Blame* (New York Civil Liberties Union: March 1998).

29. *Times*, September 9, 1997, February 27, 1998, December 10, 1999; U.S. Civil Rights Commission, *Police Practices and Civil Rights in New York City* (August 2000), Chapter 1: 6–7.

30. USCRC, *Police Practices and Civil Rights*, Executive Summary 1, 2, Chapter Two, pp. 4–20, Chapter Five, pp. 9–12. The Commission's findings of racially skewed stop-and-frisk practices confirmed similar findings by the New York State Attorney General and the CCRB. See, Eliot Spitzer, *The New York City Police Department's Stop and Frisk Practices* (New York, December 1, 1999); and CCRB, *Street Stop Encounter Report* (June 2001). Spitzer's report noted that even when the statistics were adjusted to reflect the different arrest rates among racial groups, Latinos were still stopped 39% more often than whites, and blacks were stopped 23% more often.

31. *Times*, January 27, March 27, April 13, July 14, 2001; CCRB, *Status Reports* (1994–2001) at www.nyc.gov/html/ccrb/html/reports.html) (accessed May 2005).

32. *Times*, April 10, September 7, 2002, February 14, March 31, May 14, 2003; Ray Kelly, "May the Force Be with You," GothamGazette.com, May 4, 2004, at www.gothamgazette.com/article//20040510/202/973 (accessed on May 31, 2005); Craig Horowitz, "The NYPD's War on Terror," *New York Magazine* February 3, 2003) www.newyorkmetro.com/nymetro/news/features/n_8286/index.html (accessed May 31, 2005).

33. *Times*, December 22, 2004, March 19, 2005; Craig Horowitz, "The NYPD's War on Terror"; Robert Dreyfuss, "The Cops are Watching You," *Nation*, June 3, 2003, www.thenation.com/doc.mhtml?i = 20020603&s = dreyfuss (accessed June 1, 2005).

34. Horowitz, "The NYPD's War on Terror"; *Times*, May 20, 2003, May 15, 2005; Chisun Lee, "The Force Multipliers: NYPD to Bring Nationwide Spying Effort Home," *Village Voice*, February 26–March 4, 2003, www.villagevoice.com/news/0309,lee,42140,5.html (accessed on, May 30, 2005). Police Commissioner Kelly, who headed the department during the 1993 bombing of the World Trade Center, has been particularly aggressive in building NYPD intelligence-gathering capabilities because of his belief that federal agencies did not do enough to prevent another attack.

35. *Times*, February 12, March 13, 2003; Horowitz, "The NYPD's War on Terror." Henceforth, the Handschu Authority will act as an appeals body for intelligence subjects who feel their rights have been unfairly violated.

36. *Times*, August 8, 2003, December 27, 2004; Chisun Lee, "The Force Multipliers."

5

The Failure of Force: Policing Terrorism in Northern Ireland

Joanne Klein

In the 1960s, Northern Irish Catholics began a civil rights movement demanding their rights as citizens and an end to Protestant abuses of political power. While the British government considered their appeals for reform, the Protestant-controlled Northern Irish government banned civil rights marches and insisted that Catholics had no cause for complaint. This provoked violent clashes between Catholic marchers and the predominantly Protestant Royal Ulster Constabulary (RUC). Protestant extremists began setting off bombs in Catholic neighborhoods and Catholic extremists retaliated; both sides launched into campaigns of bombing, assassination, and assault hoping to drive each other out of the region. In 1969, the British sent in the army to end the chaos since the partisan RUC was clearly part of the problem. However, the presence of the army instead intensified the climate of civil war. A British attempt in 1974 to create a government where Protestants and Catholics shared power failed, and by 1975 the British had to abandon the militarization policy.

The British government decided to treat terrorism as a criminal problem, not a political one, even though the law defined terrorism as violence with political intentions. This criminalization strategy, adopted in 1975, hoped to stigmatize terrorists as common criminals rather than political fighters. However, the RUC almost exclusively targeted Catholics, portraying them as disloyal to Britain. Police measures became more extreme and increasingly counterproductive. Emergency powers of arrest, interrogation, and detention undermined due process and escalated the violence. In 1981, hunger strikes by Irish Republican Army (IRA) prisoners forced the conflict back into the political arena, overturning the British criminalization strategy. Catholics stopped boycotting elections, and Sinn Fein, the political arm of the IRA, became difficult to ignore. Despite Protestant fury, Great Britain and the Irish Republic began to work together to find a political solution. In the 1990s, tortuous negotiations resulted in the 1998 Good Friday Accords, the first attempt at a Northern Irish government that shared power since 1974. Whether or not this opportunity for compromise will succeed depends on whether the British and Northern Irish have learned that ignoring the political roots of terrorism could not end the conflict.

The failure of the British strategy of criminalizing terrorism originated in confusing the straightforward need to respond to specific criminal conduct associated with terrorism with the complicated but crucial issue of remedying the political conditions creating the terrorism. Furthermore, their strategy was based on the erroneous assumption that the traditional British system of policing by consent existed in Northern Ireland and ignored that the progressive militarization of RUC practices was exacerbating the political tension. The British continued to insist that terrorism could be handled as a conventional crime at the same time that the RUC was using increasingly unconventional and violent practices to fight terrorism. Standard police methods for solving conventional crimes, particularly basic information gathering, could be effective in dealing with particular terrorist offenses in a community that considered the police to be legitimate. But Catholics in Northern Ireland identified the RUC as an oppressive outsider. Rather than solving crime and maintaining order, the RUC used arrests and interrogations, often arbitrary and inhumane, to gather political information on extremist groups. These extreme police measures undermined RUC legitimacy in the eyes of Catholics and drove them into terrorism. These measures also corrupted RUC officers into thinking that all Catholics were enemies unless proven otherwise, perpetuating the problems.

The British criminalization strategy tried to ignore the political crisis between Catholics and Protestants, but its implementation reinforced Northern Ireland's entrenched political polarization. The British insisted that terrorism would fade away once the Catholic community realized that terrorists were simply criminals and stopped supporting the small number of Catholic terrorists. But at the same time, the RUC was treating all Catholics as potential terrorists and therefore as criminals, enraging Catholics. While many Catholics did not support terrorism, RUC actions confirmed Catholic fears that a Protestant-dominated Northern Ireland would never treat them as fellow citizens. Emergency powers of search, arrest, and detention designed by the British Parliament to help the police cope with terrorism often weakened basic human and civil rights. The powers had an alarming tendency to become permanent and to be used against conventional criminals for whom they were never intended, further eroding the criminal justice system and basic rights. While these problems were recognized, the criminalization of terrorism was too convenient a way for the British to avoid confronting the central problem that the Northern Irish government favored Protestants over Catholics, dating back to 1921. What the British ultimately concluded is that policing could not solve terrorism and, in the case of Northern Ireland, it almost certainly made the political situation worse.[1]

The roots of the Troubles, the Northern Irish political violence that began in the 1960s, can be traced to the partition of Ireland in 1921, which created a Northern Ireland dominated by Protestants who denied Catholics shared governance out of fear of a united Catholic Ireland. The Civil Authorities (Special Powers) Act of 1922 gave the Protestant government based at Stormont the power to maintain law and order with whatever steps were necessary, including arrest and detention without warrant or trial.[2] Stormont interpreted this to mean keeping the roughly 40 percent of the population that was Catholic under constant watch due to their suspect loyalties. The RUC, formed in 1920 to replace the Royal Irish Constabulary, was 90 percent Protestant and routinely gathered intelligence on Catholic political activities unrelated to any criminal endeavors. The exclusively Protestant Ulster Special Constabulary (USC) was "notoriously anti-Catholic and prone to indiscipline," particularly the B-Specials corps that patrolled local neighborhoods.[3] Catholics considered the USC to be an excuse to grant Protestants gun licenses, normally difficult to obtain due to rigorous British firearm restrictions.[4] From the beginning, criminal justice in Northern Ireland meant Protestants controlling Catholics rather than policing by consent as existed in Great Britain. Property qualifications for jury eligibility guaranteed that juries were largely Protestant. Inevitably, Catholics facing criminal charges were denied impartial trials. In addition to problems with policing, Catholics were infuriated by the gerrymandering of electoral districts that silenced their political voice, by the unfair allocation of jobs and housing, and by Protestant insistence that they lived in an ideal democracy. Instead of developing a functioning multiparty democratic political system, Northern Ireland became split into Protestants, often referred to as Loyalists or Unionists, and Catholics, referred to as Nationalists or Republicans.[5] For fifty years, Northern Ireland experienced a tyranny of the majority rather than a democracy that guaranteed equal protection under the law for all citizens.[6]

In the 1960s, predominantly middle-class Catholics found parallels to their own situation in the civil rights movement in the United States and formed the Northern Ireland Civil Rights Association (NICRA). Their goals included guarantees of freedom of speech, assembly, and association, the protection of the rights of individuals, the end of abuses of power, and basic freedoms for all.[7] The abuse of special powers by the Stormont government was also central to Catholic grievances.[8] At first, NICRA concentrated on letter writing but found this ineffective because elements within Stormont "refused to accept the existence, much less the legitimacy, of Catholic grievances."[9] In 1968, the civil rights movements copied U.S. tactics and organized marches. But when Catholics tried to get permission to march, Protestant groups would schedule their own marches for the same locations. Stormont then banned all marches out of concern for public order, incensing Catholics who considered the bans yet another way to suppress dissent.[10] Civil rights activists staged marches anyway, leading to inevitable violence with Protestants, the RUC, and the B-Specials. In some cases, Protestant crowds cheered on the RUC as they charged into Catholic crowds, batons drawn.

Protestants responded to the civil rights movement violently, assuming that the IRA must be behind the demonstrations. In reality, the IRA at this time was not interested in civil rights for Northern Irish Catholics; they wanted the end of both Northern Ireland, and the creation of the Republic of Ireland, and the creation of a new Marxist Irish state.[11] Convinced that the IRA was using the movement as a way to destabilize the state, the RUC and B-Specials attacked civil rights marchers and collaborated with Loyalist attacks on Catholic neighborhoods.[12] The Ulster Defence Association (UDA) appeared, joining the already existing Ulster Volunteer Force (UVF), a group comparable to the IRA.[13] Protestant fundamentalism began to gain supporters, personified by Ian Paisley and his Democratic Unionist Party who regarded any changes to Protestant Ulster to be a betrayal of the union with Britain. All of these Protestant groups, together with the USC and RUC, had overlapping membership. The worst Protestant violence in 1969 was the Battle of Bogside. In August, Protestant Loyalists held parades through Catholic neighborhoods in Londonderry, sparking riots that spread to Belfast and elsewhere. Arson attacks burned hundreds of Catholic homes, leaving thousands of families homeless. Stormont sent in the B-Specials who only aggravated the situation. A total of 10 people died and 154 were shot. Many Catholics blamed the IRA for not defending them against the Protestant attacks. Ironically, given the IRA's earlier lack of involvement, Protestant violence provoked the IRA into organizing in defense of Catholics. The violence escalated.[14]

The British government, hoping to defuse the situation, promised reforms and a parliamentary committee to investigate the actions of the RUC and B-Specials. Many Catholics were willing at least to see what the British had to offer, but the British failed to comprehend the deep Protestant animosity toward compromise with Catholics. The Hunt committee, formed to investigate policing, soon concluded that the RUC and B-Specials supported the Protestant side against the Catholics regardless of law and order, undermining the legitimacy of the government. Until this problem was solved, government reform would be difficult. The committee recommended a fundamental overhaul of the RUC in an attempt to transform it from a partisan into a neutral force modeled on the London Metropolitan-type of policing by consent. They were even disarmed, though this proposal had to be withdrawn when violence continued. The B-Specials were disbanded and replaced with the Ulster Defence Regiment (UDR) in an attempt to give them a new identity. However, the committee's recommendations proved to be ineffective because they expected the RUC and UDR to ignore fifty years of history protecting the Protestant state from Catholic inroads and to take on a new character of political neutrality during a period of growing political violence between Catholics and Protestants. Committee recommendations could not change the traditional police culture. The rank-and-file did not support Metropolitan-type reforms and many continued "to embrace a sectarian approach to law enforcement."[15] Many B-Specials simply joined the new UDR, undermining the committee's goal of creating a new force. The failure of the Hunt Committee jeopardized political reform since the RUC and UDR remained partisan, supporting a Protestant Northern Ireland.

In 1969, with political reform faltering, violence intensifying, and policing becoming unreliable, the British government adopted a policy of militarization to solve the Northern Ireland problem. The idea was that a neutral outside force could restore order. The British sent in the British army to replace the RUC after Protestants bombed a Catholic neighborhood and Stormont seemed unable or unwilling to cope. However, soldiers were rarely trained to be effective police officers and military leadership was trained in colonial tactics aimed at winning over hostile populations through "inducement, persuasion and, if necessary, coercion."[16] At first, Catholics welcomed the army meant to protect them from Protestant violence. But Protestant hardliners reinforced the army's natural tendency to view anyone attacking the British government, including Catholic nationalists and the IRA, as the enemy.[17] Since the British government gave Stormont influence over the operations of the army, any opportunity to create a neutral force was lost. Army tactics alienated Catholics from the British government, driving many into the nationalist camp. Now facing both hostile Protestants and the British army, the old IRA leadership was replaced by a more aggressive group that launched bombings against Protestants, the army, and London.[18] Rather than restoring order, the presence of soldiers changed the image of the Troubles from rioting between Protestants and Catholics into civil war. While never as skeptical about compromise as Protestants, Catholics now saw themselves at war with the British government, making political solutions seem unattainable.

The army increasingly relied on strongarm tactics legitimized by temporary or emergency legal provisions in an attempt to control Catholic neighborhoods, actions viewed by Catholics as military repression of their basic rights. New limits on freedoms began in 1970 with a curfew. Soon, roadblocks were set up in Catholic areas to screen pedestrians and occupants of vehicles. In 1971, 17,262 houses were searched, increasing to 75,000 houses by 1973, "one-fifth of all houses in Northern Ireland."[19] Considering that Catholics made up forty percent of the population, nearly half of Catholic homes were most likely searched by the army. Searches were frightening experiences for families, especially children, and frequently left homes in shambles. In 1971, internment without trial was adopted by the British in a desperate move as the numbers of deaths from terrorism continued to grow. Unfortunately, the army used out-of-date Stormont lists of Catholic extremists to make their initial arrests, leading to the internment of many innocent Catholics. This led to widespread rioting throughout Catholic areas in Northern Ireland and reinforced Catholic perceptions that the British army was a tool of the Protestants.

The purpose of internment by the British army became gathering intelligence on Catholic extremist groups, rather than to solve terrorist crimes. Many arrests were arbitrary and any Catholic was vulnerable. Most of those arrested were men between the ages of fifteen and thirty-five who were assumed to be extremists unless proven otherwise. Amnesty International quickly condemned internment and demanded government intervention to halt the use of the "five techniques" of interrogation—"wall-standing, hooding, continuous noise, deprivation of food and deprivation of sleep."[20] The government promised to end their use but the army kept using them anyway. In 1978, the European Court of Human Rights found the British guilty of "inhuman and degrading treatment" of detainees at internment centers in 1971. Ironically, the army did not initially realize that the official IRA had been replaced by a more aggressive variant carrying out much of the violence. The new IRA group responded to internment by changing their organization, adopting a cell structure, usually of four, that limited damage if anyone talked under interrogation. Internment both convinced many Catholics that the British army was even worse than the RUC and led to the IRA becoming harder to track down.

The year after internment began, more people died than in any other year of the Troubles. In January 1972, fourteen Catholics were killed by soldiers who opened fire on a civil rights march in Londonderry in what became known as Bloody Sunday. The soldiers were all exonerated in a quick inquiry, provoking Catholic arson and bombings attacks on the British.[21] "The perception that soldiers carried out unjustified killings, and escaped prosecution for them, [was] one of the deepest well-springs of the troubles."[22] Hatred of the British grew. When it became clear to the British that Stormont could not resolve the crisis, they disbanded the government and assumed direct rule of Northern Ireland in March. In July, the IRA set off twenty bombs in seventy-five minutes in Belfast on Bloody Friday, killing 9 and injuring 130 people, over half women and children in town shopping. Even though warnings of the bombs had been telephoned in by the IRA, the number of bombs and civilians overwhelmed British army and RUC attempts to prevent the disaster.[23] Ten days later, the British army moved into and occupied Catholic neighborhoods. By December, 496 people had died during the year, over half of them civilians.

In the midst of the mayhem that the army seemed unable to prevent, the British government held a series of conferences in an attempt to address Catholic political grievances without upsetting the Protestant majority. Illustrating how difficult this balancing act was to achieve, in a belated effort at being evenhanded, the government extended internment to Protestants. They also granted "special-category" status to convicted political prisoners, such as republicans and nationalists, which allowed them to wear their own clothes and receive more visits and mail, rather like prisoner-of-war status.[24] While mollifying Catholics at least a little, these moves simply infuriated Protestants against the British. Finally, in December 1973, at a conference at Sunningdale including Protestant and Catholic representatives, the British set up a power-sharing scheme. Within six months, this arrangement was overthrown by an Ulster Workers Council strike that was openly supported by the RUC. On the evening of November 21, 1974, IRA bombings at two pubs in Birmingham, England, killed 21 and injured 182. This attack was so abhorrent that it triggered English attacks on Irish community centers, pubs, and businesses in Britain. Some Irish workers were attacked at English factories and airport workers refused to handle flights heading for Belfast or Dublin.[25] Within a week, the bombings led to a new Prevention of Terrorism (Temporary Provisions) Act that expanded police powers. A list of proscribed terrorist organizations was created, making membership or support of them a crime.[26] Police could detain without a warrant anyone suspected of ties to proscribed groups and the government could exclude from living in Great Britain or Northern Ireland anyone suspected of being part of them.[27] The year had begun with an attempt at shared government but ended with tensions between Protestants and Catholics worse than ever.

In 1975, after the failed attempt at a political solution and with terrorism continuing unabated, the British adopted a criminalization strategy against Northern Irish terrorism to replace the disappointing militarization policy. The British plan was to replace the army with the RUC and begin treating terrorism as ordinary criminal activity rather than as a political offense.[28]

Internment was phased out and in 1976 the "special-category" status that had been granted to convicted political prisoners in 1972 was terminated for new offenders.[29] Since terrorists were now common criminals rather than fighting for a political cause, the British halted attempts to resolve the crisis through diplomacy and instead adopted a policy of no negotiations with anyone or any organizations considered to be supporting terrorism.[30] Put simply, the hope was that Catholic republican and nationalist groups would lose popular backing if identified as criminal organizations and terrorism would die out from lack of community support.

However, criminalization assumed that conventional British-type policing could be carried out in Northern Ireland by the RUC. But the RUC had not transformed into the "policing-by-consent" force that the Hunt committee had recommended and instead became even more militarized when it took over the army's policing duties. The atmosphere of war persisted. Their tactics toward Catholics were aggressive, defining them as the enemy, at the same time that RUC members colluded with Protestant groups engaged in violence against Catholics.[31] Making use of special powers of arrest and detention granted by Parliament, they continued the arbitrary arrests begun by the army and set up two interrogation centers that prompted European Court of Human Rights cases. RUC efforts at public order sometimes transformed into police riots against Catholic civilians.[32] The RUC was even involved in Belfast city planning changes, such as building Catholic housing estates with limited entrances and constructing businesses to act as barriers around them, designed to confine "problem populations" to specific areas, "deliberately creating ghettos in which dissident populations may be contained."[33] Rather than calming the situation after the army left, the actions of the RUC magnified Catholic support for fighting back against the Protestants.

Criminalization was based on the rule of law but failed to acknowledge that Catholics might perceive the laws themselves as illegitimate. Simon Crawshaw of the Anti-Terrorist Branch of the Metropolitan Police stated the official position that terrorism "must be fought within the law, for if we go outside the law we run the grave risk of failure and condemnation,"[34] but ignored the reality that the laws themselves were open to challenge. Historian Matthew Lippman wrote in 1982, "the inflammatory political rhetoric in the House of Commons was translated into the neutral language of [law] . . . The abrogation of civil liberties thus has been codified into statutes that are accorded the respect and authority of The Law. As a result, political acts, such as demonstrating support for the IRA, have been labeled as criminal acts for which an individual can be fined and jailed."[35] Various temporary and emergency acts rushed into law allowed for, among other things, proscribing organizations tied to terrorism, excluding British citizens tied to such organizations from Great Britain or Northern Ireland, giving the police the power to search or arrest without a warrant anyone suspected of connections to a proscribed organization, making it illegal to support a proscribed organization in any way, and eroding the right to remain silent.[36] The IRA and the Irish National Liberation Army (INLA) were proscribed immediately. The UVF was also proscribed but taken off the list for eighteen months in 1974–1975. However, the UDA was not proscribed until 1992 during negotiations to find a peaceful solution for Northern Ireland. That proscription was not handled evenly added to the anger of Catholics.

Resembling the internment policy under militarization, the primary use the RUC made of British legislation was the arbitrary arrests of Catholics for the purpose of intelligence gathering rather than solving crimes. The RUC targeted Catholics legally since any Catholic could be suspected of ties to the IRA, INLA, or other proscribed organizations. Using their discretionary powers, the RUC was able to pay less attention to Protestants even though they, too, could have ties to proscribed groups. Requirements for arrests were so loose that the police could arrest anyone living in a neighborhood if they suspected that the neighborhood harbored terrorists.[37] Many of those arrested were not asked about specific events but instead about details of their personal lives and neighbors, part of RUC tactics to create personal files on as many people and communities as possible.[38] In 1980, only eleven percent of those arrested in Northern Ireland were charged with crimes while in England at the time, eighty to ninety percent of those arrested were charged.[39] Clearly, these arrests had little to do with their supposed purpose of resolving actual crimes, illustrating a basic flaw in the criminalization policy. Leading British criminologists, Mario Matassa and Tim Newburn, noted this central contradiction: "On the one hand there was the official desire to 'normalise' political violence while, on the other, introducing special powers implicitly recognising the apparent 'abnormality' of the situation."[40] Catholics were not slow to point out that the RUC was indiscriminately arresting Catholics even more aggressively than the British army had done. However, since the RUC was not doing anything technically illegal, arbitrary arrests continued.

After the assassination of the British ambassador to the Republic of Ireland in 1976, the RUC Chief Constable changed existing interpretations of Judges Rules that were meant to protect suspects in custody and, in the process, eroded the rights of suspects. "Interviews" of criminal suspects were still protected by the Rules but "interrogations" used for intelligence gathering were not.[41] This change coincided with the opening of two interrogation centers at Castlereagh and Gough Barracks and underscored that the RUC considered policing terrorism to be an intelligence-gathering operation more than an effort to solve crimes. As a result of the abusive practices used at the centers, including the supposedly banned five techniques, nearly nine out of ten detainees made confessions. The RUC Chief Constable warned his men to protect prisoners from "self-inflicted injuries" at the same time that a Parliamentary Committee of Inquiry concluded that at least some injuries must have been inflicted by the RUC.[42] In 1977 Amnesty International called for investigations into the treatment of detainees and the Republic of Ireland filed complaints with the European Commission of Human Rights.[43] Parliament formed the Bennett Committee in 1978 to investigate and it made its report in 1979. Even though the RUC refused to acknowledge that any abuse had occurred, the report recommended that interviews be monitored by closed-circuit television and other safeguards were set up to prevent physical abuse. According to Paddy Hillyard, director of the University of Bristol Centre for Social Exclusion and Social Justice, the report did "little to curtail the extreme psychological pressures which are at the heart of the interrogation process,"[44] particularly after the RUC began relying on a law that allowed them to hold detainees for up to seven days without charging them.[45] Complaints against the RUC jumped from 414 in 1970 to 3,045 in 1984.[46] As recently as 1994, the RUC was still being criticized for its interrogation methods.[47]

Confessions of witnesses and suspected terrorists were crucial to the RUC, regardless of how they were extracted, since they led to convictions in "Diplock" courts, "a confession-based prosecution process centred around non-jury single-judge courts."[48] This new system was created in 1973 to handle terrorist cases out of concern that extremists from either side could intimidate juries and witnesses. While sounding reasonable in theory, these courts, developed into another arbitrary means of targeting mostly Catholics whose confessions had been acquired through dubious RUC interrogation methods. "The fact that 75 to 80 percent of convictions in Diplock courts were obtained on the basis of confessions . . . eroded their credibility."[49] Defendants who challenged the legitimacy of the courts received the longest sentences while defendants who pleaded guilty were treated leniently. The judges became case-hardened and cynical, rarely acquitting at the same time that regular jury trial acquittal rates increased.[50] The courts "undermined the traditional common law rule requiring trial judges to warn juries about the dangers of convicting on accomplice evidence without corroboration."[51] This departure from established practice became particularly critical in the 1980s when, due to the limits on interrogation methods imposed by the Bennett report, the RUC began to use supergrasses, prisoners promised immunity and lesser sentences if they testified against other prisoners. However, after initial spectacular results, many of the convictions obtained through supergrass testimony were thrown out on appeal.[52] To strengthen the courts, in 1988 and 1994 new acts eroded suspects' right to silence and protection against self-incrimination, giving the courts the right to draw inferences from suspects not answering questions or not testifying in their own defense.[53] This "abrogation of trial by jury . . . was one of the most fundamental inroads on the protection of due process rights" in Northern Ireland.[54] Meant to be a temporary measure adopted at the height of the Troubles, Diplock courts became a permanent part of the judicial system.

Frustrated by how the Bennett report limited interrogations and by the collapse of the supergrass system, as well as unsettled by the success of Sinn Fein in 1982 elections, new counterinsurgency units within the RUC began to rely on shooting suspects. In the early 1980s, the RUC created special undercover mobilized units that soon became involved in highly suspect killings. In a number of controversial cases, the units tracked down identified terrorists with the goal of liquidating them on sight rather than arresting them, apparently with the approval of senior officers. The units saw their duties as combat "in which 'known' insurgents are tracked by undercover officers and shot on the spot—something more akin to the rules of war than to criminal justice."[55] Made up of select officers, these units carried out summary justice to avoid the frustrations of creating strong legal cases against suspected terrorists.[56] While the RUC denied the existence of any "shoot to kill" policy, in a three-week period in 1982, six unarmed people were shot dead by undercover officers. The RUC released contradictory versions of the events, undermining their credibility.

In all the "shoot to kill" cases, the RUC claimed that their officers had killed in self-defense but blocked efforts by outside investigations to discover the truth behind the RUC official story. In the first case, RUC officers claimed that a car driven by suspected terrorists had crashed through a road barrier and that the officer had shot three men in self-defense when passengers in the car opened fire. However, no weapons were found on the victims and witnesses blamed the RUC for the shooting. Despite this, the officers involved were acquitted and commended by the judge for their courage. Two weeks later, two unarmed teenage boys were shot in a hail of bullets, one fatally, by officers at a shed being staked out by the RUC for weapons. Three weeks later, an RUC officer walked up to two suspected terrorists in a car, shot the passenger, reloaded his weapon, and shot the driver. The officer was acquitted. When Assistant Chief Constable of Manchester, John Stalker, was sent to investigate the six killings, he found that an RUC cover-up was in effect. He concluded, "The circumstances of those shootings pointed to a police inclination, if not a policy, to shoot suspects dead without warning rather than to arrest them."[57] When he persisted in trying to carry out his duties, he was removed and threatened with personal humiliation if he did not keep silent.[58] Suspect killings continued, though less frequently, and investigations continued to be obstructed by the RUC. Twenty-six of the fifty-two people killed by the RUC in the Troubles died in the 1980s, six more in 1991 and 1992, compared to twenty killed from 1969 to 1976 and no one killed from 1993 to 1999.[59] The RUC paid a high price for their strategy of shooting first and explaining later. They were viewed as legitimate targets by terrorists and suffered "the highest death and injury rates as any police in the world."[60] Between 1980 and 1990, ninety-one RUC officers were killed, the same number as between 1969 and 1979 at the height of the Troubles.[61] The shoot-to-kill policy reinforced the perception that the RUC was at war with extremists, rather than involved in ordinary policing.[62] The preponderance of young Catholic men among the victims of lethal force used by the RUC intensified the climate of war between Protestants and Catholics.[63]

While RUC techniques supported by emergency powers brought about a decline in the numbers of terrorist killings, they did not eliminate the violence and contributed to its persistence. The underlying political issues still festered. In the 1980s and 1990s, annual deaths from terrorism in Northern Ireland had dropped from the hundreds common in the 1970s to around 60–90 a year. However, even though terrorist outbreaks had decreased from their highest levels between 1971 and 1977, hundreds of incidents still occurred annually.[64] The curtailing of civil liberties by various Prevention of Terrorism Acts created the appearance of a criminal justice system biased against Catholics, adding to their distrust of the government. Simon Crawshaw of the Metropolitan Police Anti-Terrorist Branch admitted that "some erosion of democratic freedom may be inevitable" and labeled the 1974 Prevention of Terrorism Act "probably one of the most repressive pieces of legislation in a Western democracy."[65] But while police authorities considered such legislation to be necessary to fight terrorism, the attempt to restore law and order to Northern Ireland could not succeed when laws and the RUC eroded legal protections of citizens. Catholics had long condemned their denial of human rights under Northern Irish governments and the actions of the RUC and British parliament simply reinforced their position.

This criminalization strategy denied the political basis of terrorism while at the same time allowing the RUC to behave as if they were at war with terrorists whenever it served their purposes. The strategy backfired when the denial of special status for political prisoners provoked huge prisoner protests, forcing politics back into the limelight. In 1976, the

British government decided to cease granting special status to new prisoners as part of their campaign to treat terrorists as common criminals. In response, many republican prisoners housed at the Maze in H-Block, a new cellular prison, began a blanket protest, refusing to wear prison clothes issued to them, which continued for over a year. When prison authorities refused to budge, republicans shifted to a dirty protest in 1978, where they covered their cells in excreta to highlight poor prison conditions. They also lodged a complaint before the European Commission of Human Rights (ECHR), arguing that they were being forced to live in degrading circumstances. While the Commission decided that many of the problems were self-inflicted, it added, "The Commission must express its concern at the inflexible approach of the state authorities which has been concerned more to punish offenders against prison discipline than to explore ways of resolving such a serious deadlock."[66] This statement could describe the entire Northern Irish problem. In October 1980, seven prisoners began a hunger strike that ended in December when British authorities promised changes. However, when the promised reforms failed to meet expectations, another hunger strike began in March 1981. Prisoners staggered the timing of their strikes for maximum impact. Bobby Sands, an IRA member, was the first to die in May. Nine others died by October.[67] Each death led to rioting in Catholic neighborhoods. The RUC responded by firing thousands of plastic bullets and "the alienation of a new generation of Catholics from the police was assured."[68] The government finally granted concessions, including allowing prisoners to wear their own clothes.[69] But the more critical accomplishment was that the worldwide media attention treated the hunger strikes as political protests.

The sympathetic attention garnered by the hunger strikes energized Catholics and convinced them that political action, including the effective use of protests and media, could be successful in forcing the British government to respond to their demands for political rights. The strikes also compelled the IRA and Sinn Fein to consider a major shift in their strategies toward political participation. Neither group had supported the hunger strikes for fear their failure would demoralize supporters but suddenly found themselves with a public relations windfall. Since the 1921 partition of Ireland, ardent nationalists had followed a policy of abstentionism, refusing to participate in either the Northern Irish or Irish Republican governments since this would betray the "one Ireland" cause. However, this practice allowed Northern Irish authorities to deny that the IRA and other proscribed groups had popular support from the Catholic community. The publicity around the strikes united Catholics, who elected Bobby Sands to Parliament in April, and other strikers to local councils in May and to the Irish Republic's Parliament in June.[70]

Around the same time, Sinn Fein was taken over by a new generation who had survived internment in the 1970s. Led by Gerry Adams, Danny Morrison, and other internees, the party abandoned abstentionism and began to focus on grassroots political mobilization to take advantage of the hunger strike support. They adopted the Armalite-Ballot Box strategy, defined by Morrison as "taking power in Ireland with a ballot paper in one hand and an Armalite [rifle] in the other."[71] Sinn Fein candidates began to run for the European Parliament, the British Parliament, and the Northern Ireland Assembly. It became much harder for Protestants to deny that Sinn Fein had popular support when the party received around 20 percent of the Catholic vote for the Northern Ireland Assembly in 1982 and Gerry Adams was elected to the British Parliament in 1983. Their success "shook the Dublin government out of its political torpor regarding the North, and it gave the lie to the assertion that republicanism had no significant support."[72] In 1985, British Prime Minister Thatcher and Irish Prime Minister FitzGerald signed the Anglo-Irish Agreement, promising to work together in a "joint, co-operative and peaceful effort to tackle the continuing political problems of Northern Ireland."[73] The ultimate goal was to revive the power sharing idea attempted in 1974 at the Sunningdale conference. News of the agreement led to massive demonstrations against it by Protestants in November.

The combination of successful Sinn Fein politics and the negotiations toward the Anglo-Irish Agreement gave the 1985 Orange Order parade season a sharper significance as Protestants felt that their lock-hold on Northern Ireland's government was slipping. Suddenly, the British government support that Protestants enjoyed was no longer certain. The passionately Unionist and Protestant Order, with strong ties to the UDA, UDR, and RUC, expanded their war on Catholics to include the British government.[74] Every year, Orangemen held parades on July 12 to celebrate the victory of Protestants over Catholics at the Battle of the Boyne (1695), and they expected to march through Catholic neighborhoods based on rather dubious traditions. The parades often became excuses for violence against Catholics, with homes broken into and occupants assaulted. In 1985, under pressure from Britain during negotiations for the Accord, the government ruled that the parades should avoid Catholic areas. Due to the heavy publicity around the parades that year, the RUC had to enforce the ruling, comparable to halting the Fourth of July or Bastille Day. Deeply resentful, Protestant fundamentalist leader "Ian Paisley declared that it was time for the RUC to choose whether to be 'for Northern Ireland or against it.' "[75] Protestant extremists began to attack the homes of RUC officers, already a target of Catholic extremists.[76] Protestant extremists saw the RUC's willingness to protect Catholics as another sign that Protestant

Ireland was in danger. When, in 1987, the IRA bombed a Remembrance Sunday ceremony at Enniskillen, killing eleven mostly older people in the Poppy Day Bombing, Protestant hatred for any compromise with Catholics intensified.[77]

During the 1980s, confidence in the RUC's ability to provide fair law and order deteriorated rapidly, debilitating the criminalization strategy. Attitudes toward the RUC reflected views on all sides of the Northern Ireland situation. Most Protestants supported the RUC as "the 'thin green line' protecting them from the Armageddon of a united Ireland and the end of their way of life." At the same time, they were angry at the RUC for blocking the Orange parades. Most Catholics saw "the police as an instrument of state repression"[78] and felt that the RUC was simply unacceptable, a force that regularly killed Catholics without legal consequences for officers whom many viewed as murderers. They not only had no confidence in the RUC, but they also questioned the legitimacy of the state that supported it.[79] The most extreme Protestants joined Catholics in considering the RUC to be agents of the British government determined to undermine their goals, either a unified Ireland or a Protestant Northern Ireland.

The RUC remained a military force rather than a "policing by consent" organization due to the political battlefield in which it operated and the tactics it used. It continued to arrest individuals based on their potential as sources of intelligence or as terrorists rather than on ordinary suspicion of committing a specific crime.[80] The danger for the RUC was that "the paramilitary style will have a brutalizing effect on officers, and that its institutionalization will undermine progress towards normalization," according to sociologist Ronald Weitzer.[81] The organization itself encouraged arbitrary arrests, inhumane interrogation techniques, and shoot-to-kill policies while insisting that the RUC was a conventional police force. These practices damaged the integrity of the force and of the officers themselves. With every commission sent to investigate some possible RUC outrage, the need for genuine oversight and accountability was clear, but efforts to set up outside oversight failed to produce results. As Graham Ellison and Jim Smyth, the leading historians of the RUC, observed, "policing can only operate properly by consent allied with strong structures to ensure accountability. The practice of policing in Northern Ireland has been lacking in both these areas."[82] Unfortunately, both police authorities and the government were reluctant to admit to these deficiencies.

Not only did the extraordinary powers of the RUC contribute to the conflict, those powers also seeped into conventional policing both in Northern Ireland and in Great Britain. Their quick-fix qualities, particularly for public order, blinded authorities to their long-term problems and made emergency powers tempting to use in situations not related to the policing of terrorism.[83] The line between conventional and militarized policing blurred, even though studies demonstrated that "the long-term disbenefits of overly repressive tactics far outweigh any short-term advantages."[84] Supposedly temporary powers were regularly renewed until the Terrorism Act of 2000 made many temporary provisions permanent and applicable to all of the United Kingdom. This completed a gradual adaptation of Northern Irish legislation to Great Britain, including broad powers of "stop, question, and search," arrest, and detention.[85] There was even talk of curtailing the right to jury trials despite the obvious problems with justice as carried out by Diplock courts. The adoption of repressive measures, often rushed into law in reaction to specific terrorist outrages, was a tempting way to show that governments were taking a strong stance against terrorism but counterproductive as a solution for terrorism. As shown in Northern Ireland, repressive tactics could contain the violence, but could not resolve it. That required addressing the political causes of the conflict.

Earlier attempts at a political resolution for Northern Ireland had been consistently undermined by both Protestants and Catholics. Ironically, "extremists on both sides had common cause in heightening tension between Protestant and Roman Catholic communities and undermining efforts at nonsectarian reform."[86] Each side had a sense of superiority, Unionists as true Protestants loyal to the crown and Nationalists as true Irishmen loyal to a united Ireland. Compromise would require both to betray central ideologies and many feared the new directions required by political solutions. "Political strategies [were]... more susceptible to risk and failure than traditional guerrilla methods,"[87] basically the same dilemma facing the government tempted to rely on repressive policing regardless of its failures. Any effort at political remedy, such as Sunningdale, failed "either because it did not offer the minority nationalist community a sufficiently certain role in the decision-making process, or because it qualified the principle of simple majority rule to an extent unacceptable to the unionist community."[88] Any signs of compromise provoked violent demonstrations and often led to the creation of small but extremely violent spin-off groups on both sides.

Political compromise proved to be especially difficult for Protestants who considered it a betrayal of their unswerving loyalty to the United Kingdom. However, their perception of being British tended to be narrow, "based on the Protestant monarchy of the late 17th century, rather than a realistic appraisal of the late 20th century conditions of a modern democracy."[89] They could not let go of their long-standing siege mentality or image of Catholics as enemies of the state; they viewed compromise as a first step to being subsumed by the Irish Republic.[90] It was Protestants who staged huge protests against the 1985 Anglo-Irish Accords, viewing the inclusion of the Irish Republic as treachery. In the 1980s, to their dismay, came the British "government realization that it cannot afford to appear too susceptible to direct Loyalist influence . . . [finding] many of the Protestant proposals as retrogressive and counterproductive."[91] The crackdown on the 1985 Orange Order parade season seemed to confirm their worst fears, that their deeply cherished heritage was being destroyed. The Orange Order became one of the leaders in fighting any settlement with Catholics. For the overwhelmingly Protestant RUC, on the front lines of the battle against terrorism, compromise could be equated with surrender to the enemy.

Catholics found compromise less objectionable since they had more to gain than Protestants from any power-sharing agreement. Many considered that a peaceful settlement now meant more than the dream of a united Ireland. The newfound political effectiveness of Sinn Fein convinced many that abandoning abstentionism was not a betrayal of their cause, so, unlike Protestants, they had already begun adjusting to changes in long-held beliefs. By the 1980s, the IRA realized that it could not defeat the British through military tactics even though it continued its violent campaign. The IRA also recognized that the RUC, despite official statements to the contrary, were "under no illusion that they can defeat the Republican insurgents until a political solution can be achieved."[92] The British government was becoming impatient to resolve the conflict, tired of the spilling over of terrorist violence into Britain. "Irish terrorism, despite the massive efforts to beat it head on, . . . could not be completely eliminated by counterterrorist measures. At best, it was contained within limits, a development that made political negotiations a profitable option for the nationalists."[93] Protestant hesitation to compromise put Catholics willing to consider power sharing in a better position with the British.

By the 1990s, the frightening number of people killed convinced enough politicians and leaders on both sides that negotiating a political compromise had to be attempted. Between 1966 and 1999, over 3,600 people died in the Troubles. Civilians suffered more than anyone, 698 Protestants and 1,232 Catholics. The British army killed 138 Catholic civilians and 20 Protestants civilians. The RUC killed twenty-six Catholic civilians but only fifteen members of the IRA and INLA; they killed three Protestant civilians and five members of the UDA and UVF.[94] The rest were killed by paramilitary groups. The IRA was responsible for over half of the deaths, with republican paramilitary groups killing 2,139 people in all. The UDA and UVF, along with a handful of other loyalist paramilitary groups, killed 1,050 people.[95] Both sides killed their own people, including those killed by accident, for being suspected informers, or supporting compromise at the wrong time. Too many times, people became unintended victims caught in crossfires, mistaken for someone else, or as a result of tragic accidents. Too often, the victims were children, killed in bombings, in arson attacks, by stray bullets and by plastic bullets. Continuing as before was unthinkable to many except the most extreme.

Negotiations including the British, Irish Republic, Protestants, and Catholics dragged on against a background of continued violence by terrorists and repressive measures by the British government, no one comfortable with what seemed to be admissions of defeat for their causes but at least willing to talk to each other. Meetings took place in Germany in 1988 setting the stage for a 1991 agreement for talks between Northern Ireland's legally recognized political parties. After several deadlocks, the IRA announced a ceasefire in August 1994 and the Loyalist Military Command announced a ceasefire in October. However, growing conflicts developed over the decommissioning of IRA weapons, a condition for Sinn Fein to be allowed to join the talks. Unhappy with what they perceived to be unfair concessions on their side without comparable sacrifices by Protestants, the IRA broke their ceasefire in 1996. In 1996 and 1997, Orange Order parade season violence hit new highs with Protestants apprehensive about radical changes in their way of life. Within a week of the 1997 parades, Gerry Adams convinced the IRA to resume their ceasefire after Sinn Fein polled sixteen percent of the vote in elections for the British parliament. In reaction to the ceasefires but also to encourage acceptance of the talks, the British relaxed security measures and reined in the RUC.[96] This move toward more conventional policing in an attempt to garner public support acknowledged that the previous military tactics had contributed to worsening tensions.

Finally acknowledging that the solution to Northern Ireland's terrorist problems had to include the resolution of the political inequities between Protestants and Catholics, the Good Friday Accords were signed in 1998, setting up a power-sharing government for Northern Ireland.[97] The Accords were endorsed by 71 percent of Northern Irish voters. This translated into support from most Catholics and about half of Protestants, reflecting how much more Catholics had to gain from an agreement than Protestants, who lost their monopoly on power. Nevertheless, half of the Protestants voted to support a peace that required sharing power. The official British policy finally admitted that Irish terrorism could be "contained but not defeated militarily; there [was] no purely military solution."[98] The Accords "recognized the legitimacy of whatever choice is freely exercised by a majority of the people of Northern Ireland with regard to its status, whether they prefer to continue to support the Union with Great Britain or a sovereign united Ireland."[99] They created a new Northern Ireland

Assembly, elected by proportional representation and safeguarded by the European Convention of Human Rights. The Accords included a section affirming human rights, including free political thought, freedom of expression and religion, freedom from sectarian harassment, freedom to choose place of residence, and the right of women to full and equal participation.[100] The trickier issue of decommissioning paramilitary organizations was left rather vague, with promises of commitment to see it through. This issue proved to be so explosive that it led to a suspension of the Northern Ireland government for four months in 2000.

The Accords provoked violent responses from extremists on both sides hoping to derail a power-sharing government that they considered to be a betrayal of their fundamental convictions. The Accords were brittle, arrived at more out of desperation than necessarily out of any support for religious harmony, making it critical to destroy them before the new government had a chance to establish a successful record of cooperation. Orange Order parades in 1998 nearly smashed the fragile peace. Despite a ban on marching down a Catholic street in Drumcree, the Order was determined to push through. Protestant extremists launched arson attacks and drove nearly three hundred families from their homes. On July 12, three Catholic boys, aged ten, nine, and eight, were burned to death when a UVF group threw a petrol bomb into their home.[101] This tragedy convinced many Orange supporters to go home. Pro-Accord Protestants began to oppose the Orange parades openly, taking advantage of public outrage at the deaths.[102] A month later, the "Real" IRA, an extremist splinter group, set off a bomb in Omagh that killed twenty-nine Protestant and Catholic shoppers. Victims included two infants and ten school children.[103] Sinn Fein reacted quickly, stating, "We see our job to be one of stopping the activities of these people."[104] Similar to the Orange parades, the maliciousness of the violence ultimately acted against the extremists. The "Real" IRA declared a ceasefire days later. Killings by fringe groups continued but for now the people of Northern Ireland seemed committed to supporting the government they had created.

The Accords left the future of the RUC to the Patten commission, an independent body charged with reviewing and proposing changes to the criminal justice system in Northern Ireland. The Accords made it clear that fundamental changes had to be made in the entire fabric of the RUC so that it was suitable for "a normal peaceful society."[105] This phrase, agreed to during negotiations, undermined any lingering pretensions that the RUC was a "normal" police force. The commission's daunting charge was to make recommendations "designed to ensure that policing arrangements, including composition, recruitment, training, culture, ethos and symbols, are such that in a new approach Northern Ireland has a police service that can enjoy widespread support from, and is seen as an integral part of, the community as a whole."[106] The RUC had no reputation of policing by consent by the entire community, so beginning from scratch became the best option. The Patten commission recommended that the force be replaced by a new police service with new uniforms and symbols, new structures, and independent oversight. "While nationalists and republicans have broadly welcomed the report, unionists have denounced it in no uncertain terms."[107] This reaction is not surprising given the history of the RUC as the defenders of the Protestant community.

In 2001 the Police Service for Northern Ireland (PSNI) replaced the RUC. The green RUC uniform and the crowned harp symbol were replaced by uniforms so dark green that they appeared black, and by a sunburst-style badge. According to the PSNI web site, the sunburst "represents a new beginning or new dawn for the new Police Service. The shape is echoed in the central star that provides six areas between its rays for a series of symbols. . . . scales of justice; a harp; a torch; an olive branch; a shamrock and a crown. The centre-piece houses the Cross of Saint Patrick which places all six symbols in the context of Northern Ireland."[108] The plethora of symbols suggested an intense effort to try to please everyone. Overall, the new uniforms and badge resembled those of British police, the police culture that the PSNI was trying to emulate. Trainees were to be half Protestant and half Catholic. An independent agency, the Consensia Partnership, handled recruiting. An independent Police Ombudsman was created to ensure accountability.[109] In 2005, the PSNI began recruiting for a History Enquiry Team (HET) "to examine unresolved deaths in Northern Ireland attributable to the security situation during the period from 1968 to 1998, known as 'The Troubles'."[110] Whether or not this new police service can create policing by consent in Northern Ireland or will become the RUC in a new form remains to be seen. A new generation of Protestants and Catholics will need to create a new police culture that is not tainted by sectarianism. The RUC's strategy of ignoring the politics driving terrorism in favor of the criminalization of terrorism in reality too often meant ignoring legitimate Catholic political grievances in favor of maintaining the Protestant status quo. While the PSNI obviously will continue to handle crimes associated with terrorism, the hope is that the politics of power sharing will be reflected in the mentality of the new police force.

The long conflict in Northern Ireland can be traced back to the violence of the partition of Ireland in 1921 and the political inequities of Stormont. Protestants feared including Catholics in the government, creating fifty years of rule that excluded forty percent of the population, and Catholics saw a united Ireland as their only option for political equality. The civil rights that Catholics marched for in 1968 and the reforms the British attempted to implement at Sunningdale were only realized thirty years later. Between 1975 and 1998, the British and the RUC adopted a policy of criminalization that denied the political roots of terrorism. At the same time the British government authorized repressive emergency police powers that were far removed from policing by consent. The RUC lost sight of basic human rights and professional ethics in the cause of national security. Arbitrary arrests, interrogation centers, Diplock courts, and shoot-to-kill policies gave Catholics no reason to support the RUC or the British government. Repressive tactics did not acknowledge the underlying problems creating terrorism, they undermined public support of policing and government, and ultimately they did not stop terrorism. If anything, RUC actions inflamed the political conflicts that led to its creation. Only when Northern Ireland's problems began to be addressed in the political sphere did the region make progress toward peace.

In the end, drafting the Accords could prove to be easier than implementing them. "Northern Ireland has never functioned as an active, pluralistic and participatory democracy.... its political life has been defined by an entrenched emergency."[111] The peace achieved with the Good Friday Accords thus far has been tenuous. To make the new government work, its people will have to put decades of anger aside and give up the mentality of war. The temptation to revert to more straightforward violence and repression remains.

Acknowledgment

Thanks are due to my graduate assistant, Joshua Haskett, and to the Boise State University Interlibrary Loan staff for their assistance in finding sources for this chapter.

Notes

1. For a comprehensive study of conflict in Northern Ireland, see Brendan O'Leary and John McGarry, *The Politics of Antagonism: Understanding Northern Ireland* (London: The Athlone Press, 1996).
2. Graham Ellison and Jim Smyth, *The Crowned Harp: Policing Northern Ireland* (London: Pluto Press, 2000), p. 31.
3. Ronald Weitzer, "Policing a Divided Society: Obstacles to Normalization in Northern Ireland," *Social Problems*, 33 (1) (October 1985), p. 42.
4. Paddy Hillyard, "The Normalization of Special Powers," in Nicola Lacey, ed., *A Reader on Criminal Justice* (Oxford: Oxford University Press, 1994), p. 64.

5. "Northern Ireland: An Anglo-Irish Dilemma? An ISC Report," *Conflict Studies: The Institute for the Study of Conflict*, No. 185 (1986), p. 10. For the purposes of this chapter, the terms Protestants and Catholics will be used. Neither group was monolithic and where practical, specific groups will be designated. The use of either term should not be interpreted as meaning everyone in either group but as a convenient shorthand.

6. The situation in Northern Ireland under Stormont shared traits with the U.S. South under Jim Crow laws where the rights of minorities were undermined by the "separate but equal" decision in the *Plessy v. Ferguson* U.S. Supreme Court case (1896).

7. Ellison and Jim Smyth, *The Crowned Harp*, pp. 54–55.

8. See Laura K. Donohue, *Counter-Terrorist Law and Emergency Powers in the United Kingdom 1922–2000* (Dublin: Irish Academic Press, 2001), chapters one and two, for a detailed analysis of the use and abuse of Special Powers Acts from 1922 to 1972.

9. Ellison and Smyth, *The Crowned Harp*, p. 72.

10. Terence Taylor, "United Kingdom," in Yonah Alexander, ed., *Combating Terrorism: Strategies of Ten Countries* (Ann Arbor: University Michigan Press, 2002), p. 216.

11. For comprehensive histories of the IRA, see Tim Pat Coogan, *The IRA* (New York: Palgrave, 2002); and J. Bowyer Bell, *The IRA 1968–2000: Analysis of a Secret Army* (London: Frank Cass, 2000).

12. Donohue, *Counter-Terrorist Law*, p. 58; Paul Wilkinson, *Terrorism versus Democracy: The Liberal State Response* (London: Frank Cass, 2002), p. 31. Even today, the RUC web page, in its section on the history of the B-Specials, implies that the civil rights movement had ties to the IRA. Royal Ulster Constabulary: the George Cross <http://www.royalulsterconstabulary.org/history3.htm> (accessed May 28, 2005).

13. For further information on Protestant groups, see Steve Bruce, *The Red Hand: Protestant Paramilitaries in Northern Ireland* (Oxford: Oxford University Press, 1992).

14. David McKittrick, Seamus Kelters, Brian Feeney, and Chris Thornton, *Lost Lives: The Stories of the Men, Women and Children who Died as a Result of the Northern Ireland Troubles* (Edinburgh: Mainstream Publishing, 2000), pp. 30–31.

15. Weitzer, "Policing a Divided Society," p. 46.

16. Ellison and Smyth, *The Crowned Harp*, p. 74.

17. Ibid., pp. 74–75; also Walter Laqueur, *The Age of Terrorism* (Boston: Little, Brown and Company, 1987), pp. 208–215.

18. This new group called itself the Provisional Irish Republican Army (PIRA) and quickly replaced the official "IRA" as the main Catholic extremist group. Most people began calling the "PIRA" the IRA, and actions associated with PIRA were described as IRA actions. Nevertheless, the official IRA continued to exist as a very small organization. This chapter will follow the convention of using the term "IRA" rather than the less familiar "PIRA." For a history of the first twenty years of the PIRA, see Patrick Bishop and Eamonn Mallie, *The Provisional IRA* (London: Heinemann, 1987).

19. Hillyard, "The Normalization of Special Powers," p. 72.
20. Tom Hadden, Kevin Boyle, and Colm Campbell, "Emergency Law in Northern Ireland: The Context," in Anthony Jennings, ed., *Justice Under Fire: The Abuse of Civil Liberties in Northern Ireland* (London: Pluto Press, 1988), p. 6; also Donohue, *Counter-Terrorist Law*, p. 120.
21. See McKittrick, et al, *Lost Lives*, pp. 143–149, for an account of Bloody Sunday and a list of victims. In 2000, new inquiries into Bloody Sunday began, to replace the initial investigation.
22. Ibid., p. 14.
23. See Ibid., pp. 229–233.
24. Michel Von Tangen Page, "A 'Most difficult and Unpalatable Part'—the Release of Politically Motivated Violent Offenders," in Michael Cox, Adrian Guelke, and Fiona Stephens, eds., *A Farewell to Arms? From "Long War" to Long Peace in Northern Ireland* (Manchester: Manchester University Press, 2000), p. 94.
25. McKittrick, et al., *Lost Lives*, pp. 496–500; P. Taylor, Brits: The War Against the IRA (London: Bloomsbury 2001): pp. 173–175.
26. A proscribed organization or group was legally condemned and prohibited; connections to proscribed organizations were therefore illegal.
27. Mario Matassa and Tim Newburn, "Policing and Terrorism," in Tim Newburn, ed., *The Handbook of Policing*, (Devon: Willan Publishing, 2003), pp. 481–482.
28. The army continued to play a role in policing the areas on the border with the Republic of Ireland. For the purposes of this chapter, the army's ongoing role there will not be explored.
29. Von Tangen Page, "A 'most difficult and unpalatable part' " pp. 94–95.
30. Paddy Hillyard, "Lessons from Ireland," in Bob Fine and Robert Miller, eds., *Policing the Miners' Strike* (London: Lawrence and Wishart, 1985), p. 178.
31. See Ellison and Smyth, *The Crowned Harp*, chapter 8, for full discussion of collusion.
32. Weitzer, "Policing a Divided Society," p. 44.
33. Hillyard, "The Normalization of Special Powers," pp. 77–78. The army was also involved in Belfast city planning.
34. Simon Crawshaw, "Countering Terrorism: The British Model," in R.H. Ward and H.E. Smith, eds., *International Terrorism: The Domestic Response* (Chicago: Office of International Criminal Justice, 1987), p. 21.
35. Matthew Lippman, "TheAbrogation of Domestic Human Rights: Northern Ireland and the Rule of British Law," in Yonah Alexander and Kenneth A. Myers, eds., *Terrorism in Europe* (New York: St. Martin's Press, 1982), p. 195. See also Peter Hall, "The Prevention of Terrorism Acts," in Anthony Jennings, ed., *Justice Under Fire: The Abuse of Civil Liberties in Northern Ireland* (London: Pluto Press, 1988), pp. 144–190.
36. See Donohue, *Counter-Terrorist Law*, pp. xi–xvi; Matassa and Newburn, "Policing and Terrorism," pp. 477–478, for lists of antiterrorist legislation. Exclusion was rendered nonoperational by parliament in 1998 but it is still on the books. See David Bonner, "The United Kingdom's Response to Terrorism: The Impact of Decisions of European Judicial Institutions and of the Northern Ireland 'Peace Process'," in Fernando Reinares, ed., *European Democracies Against*

Terrorism: Governmental Policies and Intergovernmental Cooperation (Aldershot: Ashgate, 2000), p. 47. For a full analysis of exclusion, see Paddy Hillyard, *Suspect Community: People's Experience of the Prevention of Terrorism Acts in Britain* (London: Pluto Press, 1993), chapters 9–10.

37. Dermont P.J. Walsh, "Arrest and Interrogation," in Anthony Jennings, ed., *Justice Under Fire: The Abuse of Civil Liberties in Northern Ireland* (London: Pluto Press, 1988), p. 32.

38. Ibid., p. 35.

39. Hillyard, "The Normalization of Special Powers," pp. 75–76; Weitzer, "Policing a Divided Society," p. 44.

40. Matassa and Newburn, "Policing and Terrorism," p. 482.

41. Ibid., p. 483.

42. Hillyard, "Lessons from Ireland," p. 183.

43. Hillyard, "The Normalization of Special Powers," pp. 71, 79; Donohue, *Counter-Terrorist Law*, p. 178.

44. Hillyard, "The Normalization of Special Powers," p. 80.

45. Walsh, "Arrest and Interrogation," p. 39.

46. Weitzer, "Policing a Divided Society," p. 45.

47. Bonner, "The United Kingdom's Response to Terrorism," p. 44.

48. Steven Greer, "Where the Grass is Greener? Supergrasses in Comparative Perspective," in R. Billingsley, et al. eds., *Informers: Policing, Policy, Practice* (Devon: Willan Publishing, 2001), p. 129.

49. T. Taylor, "United Kingdom," p. 219.

50. Hillyard, "The Normalization of Special Powers," pp. 81–82; Steven Greer and Antony White, "A Return to Trial by Jury," in Anthony Jennings, ed., *Justice Under Fire: The Abuse of Civil Liberties in Northern Ireland* (London: Pluto Press, 1988), p. 54.

51. Greer, "Where the Grass is Greener?" p. 129.

52. See Ibid.; also Steven Greer, "The Supergrass System," in Anthony Jennings, ed., *Justice Under Fire: The Abuse of Civil Liberties in Northern Ireland* (London: Pluto Press, 1988), p. 73–103; James Morton, *Supergrasses and Informers: An Informal History of Undercover Police Work* (London: Little, Brown and Company, 1995).

53. Bonner, "The United Kingdom's Response to Terrorism," pp. 46–47.

54. Fionnuala Ní Aoláin, *The Politics of Force: Conflict Management and State Violence in Northern Ireland* (Belfast: The Blackstaff Press, 2000), p. 49.

55. Weitzer, "Policing a Divided Society," p. 44. See also Ní Aoláin, *The Politics of Force*, pp. 59–61.

56. Ronald Weitzer, *Policing Under Fire: Ethnic Conflict and Police-Community Relations in Northern Ireland* (Albany, New York: State University of New York Press, 1995), pp. 178–180.

57. John Stalker, *Stalker* (London: Harrap, 1988), p. 253 as quoted in Ellison and Smyth, *The Crowned Harp*, p. 130. See Anthony Jennings, "Shoot to Kill: The Final Courts of Justice," in Anthony Jennings, ed., *Justice Under Fire: The Abuse of Civil Liberties in Northern Ireland* (London: Pluto Press, 1988), pp. 117–121.

58. Hillyard, "The Normalization of Special Powers," p. 90.

59. McKittrick, et al., *Lost Lives*, p. 1475.

60. Weitzer, "Arrest and Interrogation," p. 47.

61. McKittrick, et al., *Lost Lives*, p. 1475.

62. Information in this paragraph drawn from Ellison and Smyth, *The Crowned Harp*, pp. 116–133. The "shoot to kill" policy and arbitrary arrests made their way into Irish popular culture, a clear example found in the lyrics of the song, "Birmingham Six" (1987), by Shane MacGowan of the Pogues. Lyrics include, "God help you if ever you're caught on these shores And the coppers need someone And they walk through that door" and "over in Ireland eight more men lie dead Kicked down and shot in the back of the head." The lyrics, "But they're still doing time For being Irish in the wrong place And at the wrong time," refer to the Birmingham Six and Guildford Four cases where ten were wrongly convicted for IRA bombings. All were eventually released, the Four in 1989 and the Six in 1991. See P. Taylor, *Brits*, pp. 174–175.

63. Ní Aoláin, *The Politics of Force*, p. 95. During the Troubles, the army and RUC killed 135 republican paramilitary members compared to 16 loyalist paramilitary members; while partially a result of the higher activity of republicans, the numbers also show that security forces used lethal force against Catholic paramilitaries at a higher rate than against Protestants (McKittrick, et al., *Lost Lives*, p. 1483).

64. T. Taylor, "United Kingdom," p. 202.

65. Crawshaw, "Countering Terrorism," pp. 19–20.

66. Hillyard, "The Normalization of Special Powers," 1994, p. 85. See Bonner, "The United Kingdom's Response to Terrorism," pp. 51–61, for discussion of cases brought before the ECHR relating to Northern Ireland.

67. McKittrick, et al., *Lost Lives*, pp. 857–859.

68. Ellison and Smyth, *The Crowned Harp*, p. xvii. For lethality of plastic bullets as a form of crowd control, see Anthony Jennings, "Bullets above the Law," in Jennings, pp. 131–143.

69. Hillyard, "The Normalization of Special Powers," pp. 83–85; Ellison and Smyth, *The Crowned Harp*, pp. 99–104.

70. None was allowed to serve since they were convicted felons.

71. John A. Hannigan, "The Armalite and the Ballot Box: Dilemmas of Strategy and Ideology in the Provisional IRA," *Social Problems*, 33(1) (October 1985), p. 34.

72. Ellison and Smyth, *The Crowned Harp*, p. xvii.

73. ISC Report, p. 1.

74. The Orange Order took its name from the victory of Protestant William III of Orange over Catholic James II in the Glorious Revolution (1689).

75. Weitzer, "Policing a Divided Society," 1985, pp. 51–52.

76. ISC Report, p. 20. In 1985, 415 RUC officers were injured compared to 18 British soldiers (ISC Report, p. 24)

77. McKittrick, et al., *Lost Lives*, pp. 1094–1099. A group of UDA men drinking at a pub went out to shoot Catholics in retaliation. They killed a nineteen-year-old Protestant man whom they mistook for a Catholic.

78. Ellison and Smyth, *The Crowned Harp*, p. 177.

79. Hillyard, "Lessons from Ireland," p. 186; Wilkinson, *Terrorism versus Democracy*, p. 33.

80. This is similar to the U.S. problem of police officers arresting individuals for "driving while black" or other blatant racial profiling.

81. Weitzer, "Policing a Divided Society," 1985, p. 49.

82. Ellison and Smyth, *The Crowned Harp*, p. xix.

83. Hillyard, "The Normalization of Special Powers,", p. 96.

84. Matassa and Newburn, "Policing and Terrorism," p. 481.

85. Bonner, "The United Kingdom's Response to Terrorism," p. 34. For further information on the 2000 Terrorism Act, see Clive Walker, "Policy Options and Priorities: British Perspectives," in Marianne van Leeuwen, ed. *Confronting Terrorism: European Experiences, Threat Perceptions and Policies* (The Hague: Kluwer Law International, 2003), pp. 11–35.

86. T. Taylor, "United Kingdom," p. 200.

87. Hannigan, "The Armalite and the Ballot Box," p. 36.

88. ISC Report, p. 1.

89. Ibid., p. 4. This attitude is eerily similar to Irish Americans with unrealistically rosy visions of a golden age of Ireland who donate money to the IRA without comprehending the real situation.

90. ISC Report, p. 27.

91. Weitzer, "Policing a Divided Society," 1985, p. 52.

92. Ibid., p. 50.

93. T. Taylor, "United Kingdom," p. 214.

94. McKittrick, et al., *Lost Lives*, p. 1483.

95. Ibid., pp. 1474–1475.

96. Only eighteen RUC officers died in the 1990s during the negotiations, compared to nearly a hundred in each of the previous decades (McKittrick, et al., *Lost Lives*, p. 1474).

97. See Cox, et al., *A Farewell to Arms?* pp. 301–322, for the text of the Good Friday Accords, as well as other documents connected to the agreement.

98. Bonner, "The United Kingdom's Response to Terrorism," p. 36.

99. Cox, et al., *A Farewell to Arms?* p. 302.

100. Ibid., p. 314.

101. McKittrick, et al., *Lost Lives*, pp. 1434–1436.

102. John Darby, "The Effect of Violence on the Irish Peace Process," in Cox, et al., *A Farewell to Arms?* pp. 266–267.

103. McKittrick, et al., *Lost Lives*, pp. 1437–1461.

104. Darby, "The Effect of Violence on the Irish Peace Process," p. 267.

105. Cox, et al., *A Farewell to Arms?* p. 320.

106. Ibid., p. 319.

107. Ellison and Smyth, *The Crowned Harp*, p. 150.

108. "The New Crest Explained," The Police Service for Northern Ireland (PSNI). <www.psni.police.uk/index/about_psni/pg_our_crest.htm> (May 28, 2005).

109. The Police Ombudsman. <www.policeombudsman.org> (May 28, 2005).

110. The Consensia Partnership. <www.selectnip.org> (28 May 2005).
111. Ní Aoláin, *The Politics of Force*, p. 224.

Bibliography

Bell, J. Bowyer. *The IRA 1968–2000: Analysis of a Secret Army*. London: Frank Cass, 2000.

Bishop, Patrick and Eamonn Mallie. *The Provisional IRA*. London: Heinemann, 1987.

Bonner, David. "The United Kingdom's Response to Terrorism: The Impact of Decisions of European Judicial Institutions and of the Northern Ireland 'Peace Process'." In *European Democracies Against Terrorism: Governmental Policies and Intergovernmental Cooperation*, edited by Fernando Reinares. Aldershot: Ashgate, 2000, pp. 31–72.

Bruce, Steve. *The Red Hand: Protestant Paramilitaries in Northern Ireland*. Oxford: Oxford University Press, 1992.

The Consensia Partnership. <www.selectnip.org> (accessed May 28, 2005).

Coogan, Tim Pat. *The IRA*. New York: Palgrave, 2002.

Cox, Michael, Adrian Guelke, and Fiona Stephens, eds. *A Farewell to Arms? From "Long War" to Long Peace in Northern Ireland*. Manchester: Manchester University Press, 2000.

Crawshaw, Simon. "Countering Terrorism: The British Model." In *International Terrorism: The Domestic Response*, edited by R.H. Ward and H.E. Smith. Chicago: Office of International Criminal Justice, 1987, pp. 11–21.

Darby, John. "The Effect of Violence on the Irish Peace Process." In *A Farewell to Arms? From "Long War" to Long Peace in Northern Ireland*, edited by Michael Cox, Adrian Guelke, and Fiona Stephens. Manchester: Manchester University Press, 2000, pp. 263–274.

Dickson, Brice. "Policing and Human Rights after the Conflict." In *A Farewell to Arms? From 'Long War' to Long Peace in Northern Ireland*, edited by Michael Cox, Adrian Guelke, and Fiona Stephens. Manchester: Manchester University Press, 2000, pp. 104–115.

Donohue, Laura K. *Counter-Terrorist Law and Emergency Powers in the United Kingdom 1922–2000*. Dublin: Irish Academic Press, 2001.

Ellison, Graham and Jim Smyth. *The Crowned Harp: Policing Northern Ireland*. London: Pluto Press, 2000.

Greer, Steven. "The Supergrass System." In *Justice Under Fire: The Abuse of Civil Liberties in Northern Ireland*, edited by Anthony Jennings. London: Pluto Press, 1988, pp. 73–103.

Greer, Steven. "Where the Grass is Greener? Supergrasses in Comparative Perspective." In *Informers: Policing, Policy, Practice*, edited by R. Billingsley et al. Devon: Willan Publishing, 2001, pp. 123–140.

Greer, Steven and Antony White. "A Return to Trial by Jury." In *Justice Under Fire: The Abuse of Civil Liberties in Northern Ireland*, edited by Anthony Jennings. London: Pluto Press, 1988, pp. 47–72.

Hadden, Tom, Kevin Boyle, and Colm Campbell. "Emergency Law in Northern Ireland: The Context." In *Justice Under Fire: The Abuse of Civil Liberties in Northern Ireland*, edited by Anthony Jennings. London: Pluto Press, 1988, pp. 1–26.

Hall, Peter. "The Prevention of Terrorism Acts." In *Justice Under Fire: The Abuse of Civil Liberties in Northern Ireland*, edited by Anthony Jennings. London: Pluto Press, 1988, pp. 144–190.

Hannigan, John A. "The Armalite and the Ballot Box: Dilemmas of Strategy and Ideology in the Provisional IRA." *Social Problems*, Vol. 33, No. 1, October 1985, pp. 31–40.

Hillyard, Paddy. "Lessons from Ireland." In *Policing the Miners' Strike*, edited by Bob Fine and Robert Miller. London: Lawrence and Wishart, 1985, pp. 177–187.

Hillyard, Paddy. "The Normalization of Special Powers." In *A Reader on Criminal Justice*, edited by Nicola Lacey. Oxford: Oxford University Press, 1994, pp. 63–102.

Hillyard, Paddy. *Suspect Community: People's Experience of the Prevention of Terrorism Acts in Britain*. London: Pluto Press, 1993.

Jennings, Anthony. "Shoot to Kill: The Final Courts of Justice." In *Justice Under Fire: The Abuse of Civil Liberties in Northern Ireland*, edited by Anthony Jennings. London: Pluto Press, 1988, pp. 104–130.

Jennings, Anthony. "Bullets above the Law." In *Justice Under Fire: The Abuse of Civil Liberties in Northern Ireland*, edited by Anthony Jennings. London: Pluto Press, 1988, pp. 131–143.

Laqueur, Walter. *The Age of Terrorism*. Boston: Little, Brown and Company, 1987.

Lippman, Matthew. "The Abrogation of Domestic Human Rights: Northern Ireland and the Rule of British Law." In *Terrorism in Europe*, edited by Yonah Alexander and Kenneth A. Myers. New York: St. Martin's Press, 1982.

Matassa, Mario and Tim Newburn. "Policing and Terrorism." In *The Handbook of Policing*, edited by Tim Newburn. Devon: Willan Publishing, 2003, pp. 467–500.

McKittrick, David, Seamus Kelters, Brian Feeney, and Chris Thornton. *Lost Lives: The Stories of the Men, Women and Children who Died as a Result of the Northern Ireland Troubles*. Edinburgh: Mainstream Publishing, 2000.

Morton, James. *Supergrasses and Informers: An Informal History of Undercover Police Work*. London: Little, Brown and Company, 1995.

Ní Aoláin, Fionnuala. *The Politics of Force: Conflict Management and State Violence in Northern Ireland*. Belfast: The Blackstaff Press, 2000.

"Northern Ireland: An Anglo-Irish Dilemma? An ISC Report." *Conflict Studies: The Institute for the Study of Conflict*, No. 185, 1986.

O'Leary, Brendan and John McGarry. *The Politics of Antagonism: Understanding Northern Ireland*. London: The Athlone Press, 1996.

The Police Ombudsman. <www.policeombudsman.org> (accessed May 28, 2005).

Police Service for Northern Ireland (PSNI). <www.psni.police.uk> (accessed May 28, 2005).

Royal Ulster Constabulary. <www.royalulsterconstabulary.org> (accessed May 28, 2005).

Taylor, Peter. *Brits: The War Against the IRA*. London: Bloomsbury, 2001.

Taylor, Terence. "United Kingdom." In *Combating Terrorism: Strategies of Ten Countries*, edited by Yonah Alexander. Ann Arbor: University Michigan Press, 2002, pp. 187–223.

Von Tangen Page, Michael. "A 'Most Difficult and Unpalatable Part'—the Release of Politically Motivated Violent Offenders." In *A Farewell to Arms? From "Long War" to Long Peace in Northern Ireland*, edited by Michael Cox, Adrian Guelke, and Fiona Stephens. Manchester: Manchester University Press, 2000, pp. 93–103.

Walker, Clive. "Policy Options and Priorities: British Perspectives." In *Confronting Terrorism: European Experiences, Threat Perceptions and Policies*, edited by Marianne van Leeuwen. The Hague: Kluwer Law International, 2003, pp. 11–35.

Walsh, Dermont P.J. "Arrest and Interrogation." In *Justice Under Fire: The Abuse of Civil Liberties in Northern Ireland*, edited by Anthony Jennings. London: Pluto Press, 1988, pp. 27–46.

Weitzer, Ronald. "Policing a Divided Society: Obstacles to Normalization in Northern Ireland." *Social Problems*, Vol. 33, No. 1, October 1985, pp. 41–55.

Weitzer, Ronald. *Policing Under Fire: Ethnic Conflict and Police-Community Relations in Northern Ireland*. Albany, New York: State University of New York Press, 1995.

Wilkinson, Paul. *Terrorism Versus Democracy: The Liberal State Response*. London: Frank Cass, 2002.

6

Democracy, Citizenship, and Police Procedure in New Orleans: The Importance of the Local Context for Defining Rights

Anthony W. Pereira

Introduction

In the contemporary world, crime and terrorism raise the specter of chronic low-intensity conflict blurring the dividing line between peace and war in many countries (Davis and Pereira 2003; Mann 2002). Concerns about public security are becoming increasingly important to the organization of national and local politics. Tactical decisions about policing—how and where to deploy the state's array of coercive forces, military and civilian, how these interact with burgeoning private security agencies and irregular armed forces—have ever larger implications for individual civil, political, social, and human rights, and thus the functioning and quality of democracy (Ungar 2002; Zaverucha 2003). In a democracy, the police play an important role in defining the meaning of rights, because democracies hold out the promise of the rule of law, including a state bound by constitutional constraint, and coercive institutions that respect individuals' equality before the law and right to fair and transparent procedures in the investigation, adjudication, and punishment of crime. Thus, tactical decisions about policing also raise larger questions about the relationship between the police and other institutions, such as courts, charged with enforcing the rule of law (Carothers 1998; Kant de Lima 1995; Mendez, O'Donnell and Pinheiro 1999; O'Donnell 2000).

In this chapter, I examine how police authority, performance, and power operate in cities, and argue that the local context of policing is crucial for understanding the meaning of individual rights. I discuss several aspects of police roles and procedures in one city in the United States, New Orleans, Louisiana. Policing in New Orleans is done by a municipal force controlled by the mayor (the New Orleans Police Department, or NOPD). The NOPD only has jurisdiction within the city limits proper—Orleans Parish—and policing elsewhere in the greater metropolitan area is done by the separate police forces of Jefferson, Saint Tammany, Saint Bernard, Saint Charles, and other parishes (the equivalent of counties). In addition, policing in New Orleans and other cities in the post-September 11 United States is being restructured to emphasize preventive antiterrorism activity under the auspices of the newly created federal Homeland Security Agency. This restructuring involves heightened cooperation between the NOPD and Federal authorities, but thus far appears to have had little effect on NOPD operations.

New Orleans is a port city in an economically depressed region that relies heavily on agriculture, petroleum, and tourism. In addition to serving as a major convention site, the city hosts annual Carnival/Mardi Gras celebrations that attract thousands of visitors from outside the state. Political authorities are thus particularly concerned about crimes affecting tourism. The city has large numbers of poor, unemployed, and underemployed residents, and relatively high rates of violent crime, even by the standards of the United States, which has higher rates of crime than most other advanced industrial countries.[1] In addition, the NOPD has received unwanted attention for corruption, inefficiency, and the use of violent methods against criminal suspects. An international human rights organization claimed in 1994 that the NOPD "led the nation in citizen complaints of both policy brutality and corruption."[2]

In that same year, a major reform of the police began under then-Mayor Marc Morial (1994–2002). Morial hired a new police chief, Richard Pennington, a veteran of the Washington, D.C. police force. In 1995–1997, Pennington raised police salaries, fired some corrupt officers, and engaged in dialogue with leaders of community organizations. He also imported a new model of crime reporting from New York City, COMPSTAT, to make police performance in the city's districts easier to measure. These efforts somewhat enhanced the image of the force and were accompanied by decreases in some categories of crimes.[3]

However, in response to complaints, the civil rights division of the U.S. Department of Justice conducted an investigation of the NOPD from 1996 to 2004. The investigation ended on March 23, 2004, when the Justice Department concluded that the changes the NOPD made "will remedy past constitutional deficiencies, promote best practices and help protect the civil rights of those who come into contact with the NOPD."[4] Somewhat oddly, the six-year Justice Department investigation did not result in the establishment of an independent agency capable of investigating new allegations of NOPD corruption and violence; instead, such complaints are received and handled by the Public Integrity Division, a unit within the police department itself. The wisdom of that outcome may be questioned, given the continued evidence that the NOPD sometimes uses deadly force under questionable circumstances.[5] Recently, however, after facing a barrage of criticism following the deaths of eight people at the hands of the police in the first half of 2005, then-Police Commissioner Eddie Compass announced that he would move the force away from a zero-tolerance "arrest mode" and toward a friendlier, more community-oriented "service mode."[6]

This chapter examines four aspects of policing in New Orleans: criminal investigations; the roles of police officers and the internal dynamics of the force; police-prosecutor relations; and the process of criminal indictment and trial. The perspective that I keep in mind in my analysis is that of a person residing or working in New Orleans. At each stage of the process from arrest to trial, what can that individual expect of the police—what rights can she or he expect to be respected? Furthermore, how have post-September 11 developments in policing affected those rights? I argue that a lack of social rights for many New Orleans residents, combined with a police force with a relatively high repressive capacity, has created a city of sharp inequalities. The post-September 11 focus on terrorist threats has done little to alleviate these inequalities, which were dramatically exposed by the flood that followed Hurricane Katrina in 2005.

Police Investigations

The NOPD is a force of about 1,600 officers for a city of slightly under 500,000 people.[7] The department is divided into eight districts, each with its own commander. The second district has 120 officers;[8] the other districts have similar numbers, with the rest of the force allocated to specialized units. Investigations are conducted by detectives, who are under the authority of the same unit commander who manages the patrol officers. Criminal investigations in the 8th District, which includes the major tourist and business section of the city (the French Quarter and Central Business District) are given a high priority by the NOPD. A Major Case Homicide Unit with eight detectives and four supervisors—more than in the other districts—handles the investigation of murders there.[9]

This imbalance is an example of inequality in the enforcement of rights in the city—the allocation of resources suggests that, for political authorities and the business elite, the lives of tourists and conventioneers are more important than the lives of residents.

In New Orleans as in the rest of the United States, police investigations begin with the patrol officer who is first alerted to the occurrence of a crime. The report of the patrol officer is key to creating a sense that the department is responsive to the community within its jurisdiction. Moreover, the patrol officer's "proper observation, securing, and protection of the crime scene" and taking of testimony from victims and witnesses is vital to the subsequent investigation (Palmiotto 1998: 7, 18). One expert writes that the "single most important determinant of whether or not a case will be solved is the information the victim supplies to the immediate responding patrol officer" and that if the victim cannot identify the perpetrator when the crime is reported, the crime is unlikely to be solved (Palmiotto 1998: 17).[10]

Yet not all arrests or police reports lead to follow-up investigations. Limits on resources lead to a form of "triaging," and thus even many serious crimes are not investigated beyond the initial police report. In New Orleans, the police make approximately 90,000 arrests per year, a high number in a city of fewer than 500,000 people, reflecting the "zero tolerance" mode of policing that, as noted, the NOPD commissioner only recently has begun to move away from.[11] A recent study showed that of those arrests, roughly 20,000 resulted in cases sent to prosecutors in the District Attorney's (DA) office. Of those cases, roughly 9,000 were accepted for prosecution. A study of a random sample of 2,578 arrests for various crimes between June, 1999 and May, 2000 in New Orleans showed that roughly thirty-four percent of those arrested were prosecuted, with a conviction rate of those prosecuted of seventy-four percent.[12] This conviction rate appears to be close to the national average.[13]

In New Orleans, as in other cities, there is a gap between formal police procedure and actual practice. While the NOPD's written policy is that police reports should be filed with the DA's office within five days of arrests, on average, forty-one days elapse between the arrest and the submission of the police report.[14] Furthermore, reports are often incomplete, with patrol officers neglecting to fill in sections. These delays and omissions create problems in police-prosecutor relations, to be discussed more fully in the third section.

Detectives engage in follow-up investigations of some crimes, studying the initial police report to see if leads were overlooked, analyzing evidence, sifting through information, and interviewing suspects and witnesses. In New Orleans, follow-up investigations may involve police coordination with a number of other law enforcement agencies in the area, including the Federal Bureau of Investigation (FBI) and the U.S. Marshals Service, as well as specialized units within the police force itself, such as COPS (a squad financed by the Housing Authority of New Orleans that operates in public housing projects, and the Violent Offenders Warrant Squad (VOWS) a team that tries to serve arrest warrants on potentially violent criminal suspects). While the NOPD enjoys a good reputation in its handling of large crowds—it gets annual practice at this during Carnival—and has a high capacity for arresting people on the streets, it is sometimes criticized for its lack of follow-up investigatory capacity. This criticism was prominent in a seven-part study of murder in New Orleans by the city's main newspaper, the *Times-Picayune*, in February, 2004. In this series, Loyola Law School professor and defense attorney Dane Ciolino was quoted as saying, "NOPD is very good at picking up people on the street. They are less experienced in longer-term investigations . . . In a lot of cases . . . [murder suspects] are innocent people getting picked up, a person picked up on a rumor or a person who just happened to be around and was picked up because of proximity."[15]

An important component of police investigation is crime analysis—gathering information and evidence from units of the police department and outside agencies, collecting the data by case and recording and examining it. The NOPD does not enjoy a great reputation in this area. In 2003, the NOPD conducted a clean up of its Central Evidence and Property Room that led to the destruction or disappearance of hundreds of items relevant to an estimated 55 ongoing murder investigations and 2,500 rape cases. (In the latter, poor record keeping prevented any estimate of the number of these cases that were ongoing and that could have been prosecuted.) Evidence lost included sealed "rape kits" (doctors' notes and other evidence in rape cases) and DNA tests in murder investigations. Two police captains were eventually suspended for 105 and 80 days respectively for their responsibility for this embarrassing destruction of evidence.[16] Some observers even suggested that the destruction was deliberate, an effort to sabotage the prosecution of criminals who had somehow paid off members of the police department.

Another crucial element in the investigation of many crimes, particularly murder, is the willingness of witnesses to testify against perpetrators. In this area, the NOPD faces difficulties not entirely of its own making. Witnesses to New Orleans murders are generally reluctant to testify. Of the 275 documented murders in the city in 2003, arrests were made in 106 cases. By early 2004, about 30 percent of the latter had been thrown out of court or never brought to court due to witness problems, while roughly 60 percent were pending. Only one conviction for first-degree murder had been made up to that point, with two acquittals and six plea bargains in which defendants were charged with manslaughter or negligent homicide.[17] In terms of homicide convictions, this performance is significantly lower than in other parts of the United States.[18] NOPD police detective Jimmie Turner said, "It is almost like word on the street is: the easiest case to get away with is murder."[19]

While the NOPD clearly faces grave obstacles in the investigation of murder, the unreliability of data makes it difficult to assess its capacity in the investigation of other crimes. In 2003, a scandal erupted because of reports that the NOPD's First District systematically downgraded crimes in order to make the district's crime-fighting record look better than it was. For example, a shooting in which a victim was wounded was reclassified from attempted murder to a "miscellaneous incident." The department's COMPSTAT crime-reporting system, initiated in 1996 as a method of mapping the incidence of crime by district, apparently gave district commanders an incentive to underreport Uniform Crime Reports (UCR) crimes. These are crimes reported every quarter to the FBI under the UCR system, and include murder, rape, robbery, assault, burglary, theft, car theft, and arson. The NOPD Commissioner reassigned the First District Commander and fired five officers in the wake of the reporting scandal. However, subsequent journalistic investigation indicated that the downgrading had involved other districts of the NOPD as well.[20]

Overall, the NOPD's variable investigative capacity reflects the inequalities of New Orleans itself. A high priority is given to investigating crimes involving visitors to the city, since these crimes affect the city's principal industry, tourism. Murders in poor neighborhoods are much less effectively investigated, not only because of low priority and a lack of resources on the part of the police, but also because of fear and a lack of cooperation with the police on the part of residents. The force has handled criminal evidence in a slipshod manner, due to incompetence and, possibly, corrupt relationships between the police and criminals. COMPSTAT data, whose use was established to guarantee the accountability of district commanders and make police performance more transparent, have been manipulated by commanders eager to make a good impression with their superiors and reassure the public that crime was declining. And, as we shall see more clearly in the section on police-prosecutor relations, crimes of property are more vigorously investigated and prosecuted than crimes against persons. This picture of police performance suggests that the allocation of the police's investigatory capacity—like the distribution of other benefits such as education and health services—is highly unequal in New Orleans. There are gradations in residents' access to policing. Far from being a pure public good,[21] police services in New Orleans are extended on the basis of complicated networks of patronage, loyalty, and exchange.

Officers' Roles and the Internal Dynamics of the Police

Police officers in the NOPD, as in other U.S. police departments, are employed according to a hierarchical classification scheme. Newly hired officers start at the level of officer 1 after graduation from the police academy. With more experience, they have the chance to be promoted to officer 2, 3, and 4, depending on their performance on the job, and from there to sergeant, lieutenant, and captain.[22] While it is hierarchical, the NOPD, like most other U.S. police departments, is not as rigidly dualistic as other police forces in the world. In Latin America, for example, police departments are often divided by an insuperable barrier between the university-educated and well-paid higher officers and the less educated, poorly trained, and poorly paid lower ranks. In the United States, in contrast, advancement to the top is open to the lowest ranks of the force. In the NOPD, former Superintendent Eddie Compass started his career as an officer 1.[23] Salaries for the NOPD, while low in the past, have increased recently. Police officers with one year of experience are now paid $35,000 per year,[24] a lower-middle-class salary in the city and only slightly less than the median household income in the United States.[25]

The NOPD imposes a controversial residency requirement on its officers. All officers are supposed to live within the city limits. Unpopular among members of the police force, some critics blame this requirement for the department's failure to successfully hire enough recruits. (There has been a discussion in New Orleans about eliminating the residency requirement. Because the 2005 flood destroyed half the city's housing stock, the requirement will probably be lifted.) The present mayor, Ray Nagin, has pledged to boost the force to 2,000 from the current level of 1,600, but this figure has not yet been reached. A study of the department's personnel revealed that 20 percent of the police hired in 1999 subsequently left the force.[26] And a recent survey of about half of the department's commissioned officers, conducted by a consulting firm on behalf of the NOPD, found that 87 percent described morale as low, while 44 percent saw their next career move as leaving the NOPD. Poor working conditions, a lack of fairness and honesty in promotions, low-quality administration and leadership, and the politicization of the department were some of the reasons cited for this negative assessment.[27]

If inequalities characterize the distribution of police resources as seen from the outside, they also permeate the operations of the NOPD as seen from within. Despite the openness of the organization to promoting from the lower ranks, a great many police officers seem to regard their agency's management as ineffectual and unfair. Turnover is consequently high, the force is understaffed, and the city's political leaders cannot recruit up to full strength. This worsens police officers' working conditions and contributes to low morale. Such a vicious circle does not offer a strong foundation on which to build high-quality policing and relations of trust and confidence between the police and city residents.

Police-Prosecutor Relations

The police and prosecutors in New Orleans face a rate of violent crime that is high by U.S. standards. In 2002, New Orleans had 53.3 murders per 100,000 people, placing it higher than Washington D.C., Detroit, Baltimore, Atlanta, and Chicago in this category. [28] In 2003, the murder rate increased to 57.7 per 100,000, nearly ten times the national average.[29] Nearly half of these murders take place in a small, seven-square-mile zone in a city of 190 square miles. This "hot zone" contains four public housing projects, and many murders in the area are connected to drug trafficking or involve feuds between rival families and gangs. This zone is heavily monitored by the FBI and Drug Enforcement Agency (DEA), which work on drug trafficking, and by the NOPD's Special Weapons and Tactics (SWAT) unit and the Bureau of Alcohol, Tobacco, and Firearms (ATF), which attempt to monitor gun violations and gang activity.[30]

In the hot zone, policing can be heavy-handed. As in other aspects of policing, inequalities mark the application of violence by the police. In poor neighborhoods they use force with impunity; in middle class and affluent sections of the city, they are more careful. In the words of one resident of a New Orleans housing project, "In my project police set off an alarm of fear to the people who are supposed to be protected. It's like we're prisoners in our own community. I saw the police beat a boy once . . . I just hope the force gets better over time and I thank God for the good cops who truly protect and serve."[31]

In New Orleans, the Commissioner of the NOPD is appointed by and serves at the pleasure of the mayor, who is elected for a four-year term and can serve a maximum of two consecutive terms. In contrast to the NOPD Commissioner, the Orleans Parish DA is directly elected, and unlike the mayor, is not term-limited. New Orleans had the same DA, Harry Connick, from 1973 to 2003. Connick, then a Democrat, adroitly maneuvered between the city's black majority, with its various political machines, and the white elite.[32] The U.S. Attorney Jim Letten, responsible for the prosecution of federal crimes in the city, is appointed by the U.S. Attorney General, who runs the federal Justice Department.

In the United States, prosecutors maintain fairly close relations with the police. Since the 1960s, policing in the United States has changed as defendants' procedural due process rights were more strongly emphasized by the courts (a trend that has begun to turn the other way, against such rights, in recent years.) In some jurisdictions, prosecutors are even called in to crime scenes to assist in the gathering of evidence at the very beginning of the criminal investigation (Palmiotto 1998: 20, 529).

In New Orleans as in other U.S. cities, patrol officers arrest a person on probable cause that he or she committed a crime, collect the basic evidence, and turn it over to the prosecutor, who reviews it and decides whether it can become the basis for a prosecution. The DA's Office can request further investigation by the police, and also has its own staff investigators who conduct supplemental investigations.[33]

More than in most other U.S. cities, relations between the police and DA's Office in New Orleans have been strained. There are some signs of recent improvements, but complaints on both sides abound. Rafael Goyeneche, the president of the nonprofit watchdog group the Metropolitan Crime Commission (MCC), said, "There is not a lot of cooperation between the Police Department and the DA's office."[34] Complaints on the DA's side include police slowness in submitting reports, as well as sloppy and incomplete reports. Furthermore, the DA's office has complained that NOPD officers' failure to appear in court has resulted in their dismissal of criminal cases. From the police perspective, the DA's office is understaffed and has high turnover, resulting in delays and a backlog of cases. (When the current DA took office in early 2003, he announced that his office had 5,000–6,000 pending cases.)[35] In addition, the witness protection program is underfunded and inadequate, exacerbating the problem of reluctant witnesses in murder cases.

A further troubling aspect of police-prosecutor relations in New Orleans is the reliance of both agencies on private funding and assistance. For example, the New Orleans Police Foundation, a private entity funded largely by hotel owners and other companies in the tourist industry, pays the NOPD for extra patrolling in parts of the city used heavily by hotel guests.[36] For its part, the New Orleans DA recently established a group of private, volunteer lawyers to work as special prosecutors in his office.[37] While neither of these initiatives is inherently nefarious, and both probably improve the performance of both agencies in many respects, they raise complicated questions. The police and prosecutors are formally public bodies, ostensibly committed to the equality of all citizens before the law. When their performance of basic duties of patrolling and prosecuting depends on private donations, the potential for the even greater insertion of private agenda into the public sphere than is currently the norm in this neoliberal era becomes obvious. Whom do the police and prosecutors "protect and serve," and to whom are they accountable?

Despite problems in police-prosecutor relations in New Orleans, the U.S. system is one in which the police are more closely supervised by and accountable to prosecutors than in many other countries, such as those in Latin America. In New Orleans, as in other localities, all police are trained in the fundamentals of criminal offenses and search-and-seizure rules. The DA also conducts some in-service training for the police.[38] Since prosecutors tend to reflect the courts that they operate in, it seems fair to conclude that although most police officers in the United States are not law-school educated, they are forced, through the DA's office, to be accountable to the judiciary, and thus adhere more carefully to the rule of law than the police in many other countries.

At the same time, the police can only be as good as the judicial (and political) system they work in. In New Orleans, judges are elected, and raise thousands of dollars for their campaigns. Much of this money comes from individuals and companies that do business in the judges' courts. Although the bar association and other reformers talk of the desirability of moving to a judicial system based on merit-based appointments, judicial elections are deeply entrenched in Louisiana politics and are unlikely to be eliminated any time soon. Beyond the problems raised by elected judges, judicial corruption is common in New Orleans and Louisiana. In the past two decades, five Louisiana judges have been found guilty of criminal acts while in office, and a five- and-a-half-year federal investigation, Operation Wrinkled Robe, has charged twelve defendants, including two New Orleans-area judges, with various crimes.[39] Many of these crimes involve bail bondsmen bribing judges. Because judges can serve the bail bondsmen's business interests in their posting of bonds, they are often the target of illicit attempts at influence-peddling by the bondsmen.

In summary, police-prosecutor relations present some of the same characteristics that we have observed in the areas of police investigations and the internal dynamics of the police. The prosecution of crimes involves entrenched conflicts of interests and complicated networks of clientelism and patronage that exacerbate inequalities in the application of the law to New Orleans residents. Overwhelmed by the rate of violent crime, the DA's office prosecutes selectively, ineffectively, and often without the necessary cooperation of the police. Both the police and prosecutors receive private assistance that at least potentially distorts their provision of services, leading them to favor the protection of the interests that provide such assistance. And elected judges, enmeshed in political networks, encounter conflicts of interest in their treatment of defendants in court. There may be formal equality before the law in New Orleans, but in practice, there are more barriers to the realization of that equality than in many other U.S. cities.

Pretrial and Trial Procedures

Both the pretrial and trial processes in New Orleans are regulated by an elaborate body of criminal law that specifies exactly how such procedures are supposed to be conducted. This law is basically the same as that prevailing in the rest of the United States. While civil law in Louisiana is marked by the influence of the Napoleonic Code, and differs from common law, this is not true of criminal law.[40] This section reviews evidence of the pattern of prosecuting and judging criminal offenses in New Orleans.

A prosecutor deciding to pursue a case charges the suspect with a felony. The defendant is entitled to a preliminary examination to determine if probable cause exists to believe she or he has committed the offense— this is intended to safeguard against heavy-handed police procedures (Louisiana Constitution, article 1, section 14). The hearing is an oral and adversarial procedure, with presentations by the prosecutor and defense attorney, confrontation and cross-examinations of witnesses (Louisiana Code of Criminal Procedure, article 294). In the hearing, prosecutors often call police officers to testify about the facts of the case in order to avoid exposing the victim or witnesses to cross-examination by the defense attorney.

Because the preliminary hearing is not a trial, its standard of proof is lower, and hearings usually result in the judge finding probable cause for an indictment. When probable cause is not found, the accused is released from custody, but only the prosecutor has the authority to dismiss the charges against the accused (Louisiana Code of Criminal Procedure, article 296). For defendants whose hearings have resulted in a ruling of probable cause, the next step is an indictment before a grand jury. In Orleans Parish, the judge chooses 14 jurors to make up the grand jury, and also selects the jury foreman (Louisiana Code of Criminal Procedure, article 413). The DA, through the use of the grand jury, has broad and enforceable investigatory powers, including access to a subpoena for the appearance of a witness to testify or for the submission of documents (Louisiana Code of Criminal Procedure, article 439). The grand jurors are obliged to listen to any evidence that the DA presents, and may call for other information on their own. They are also required by law to indict an individual when they conclude that the evidence would justify a conviction, absent an alternative explanation of or direct contradiction of the facts of the case (Louisiana Code of Criminal Procedure, article 443). This is a more exacting standard than that governing ordinary police behavior—it is more demanding than the probable cause necessary for an arrest.

There are two basic types of indictment in Louisiana. One is for capital crimes (offenses that could receive the death penalty) or charges that could result in life imprisonment. Requiring "a plain, concise, and definite written statement of the essential facts constituting the offense charged" (Louisiana Code of Criminal Procedure, article 464), the informational requirements of this type of indictment are high, although the Louisiana Code of Criminal Procedure allows prosecutors considerable latitude to specify information later or to alter it. The second, a short-form indictment that applies to forty-six less serious offenses (Louisiana Code of Criminal Procedure, article 465), merely alerts the accused to the basic crime she or he is charged with committing. The accused must obtain other details by requesting a bill of particulars (Louisiana Code of Criminal Procedure, article 484). Louisiana law, like the law of other U.S. states, also specifies time limits for the prosecution and trial of particular crimes, with an exception for capital and life imprisonment crimes, which can be prosecuted and tried at any time (Louisiana Code of Criminal Procedure, article 571).

The number of jury trials in Orleans Parish fluctuates between 350 and 500 per year in the current period. The DA's Office in New Orleans, in comparison to DA's offices in other U.S. cities, has a reputation for being selective in the cases that it prosecutes, and in relying infrequently on plea bargains. When prosecutors resort to plea bargains, in which they and the accused agree to a particular charge, usually a reduced sentence, in lieu of going to trial, they do so to reduce their caseload. They may also use them to extract evidence useful for the prosecution of other crimes. Between 1988 and 1999 the Orleans Parish DA's Office dealt with 239,000 cases and 432,000 charges. The office rejected 52 percent of all cases recommended to it. Of the cases accepted, 65 percent were resolved when defendants pleaded guilty as charged, and 13 percent went to trial. Only 9 percent of cases involved plea bargains.[41]

This record was vigorously defended by the law professors who compiled the information. "There is plea bargaining in New Orleans, but there is less here of the worst kind," said Professor Ron Wright of Wake Forest University Law School. "You shouldn't file charges you're not able to win at trial. This is a significantly more honest system."[42] Others were more critical. The MCC reported that the DA's Office convicted only four of every ten people arrested on state charges—an unacceptably low percentage in their view. It issued a report accusing the NOPD of sloppy police reports and the DA of ineffective procedures, and charged that New Orleans "wastes" $1.5 million per year detaining criminal suspects who are later released when the DA's office does not charge them.[43]

Conviction rates in New Orleans actually vary by type of crime. If we calculate the conviction rate by taking the number of those convicted and comparing it to the number initially charged with a crime, we find that the conviction rate ranges from a low of 55 and 57 percent for rape (and other sex crimes) and homicide, respectively, to 100 percent for burglary.[44] If the conviction rate is calculated differently as the percentage of those arrested who are eventually convicted, the picture looks different.[45] While 27 percent of those arrested for burglary are convicted, only 12.5 percent of those arrested for murder are. A very large number—61 percent—of the successfully convicted crimes are drug cases, and drug offenders are convicted at a higher rate than all other crimes (36 percent of all arrests).[46] This has led critics of the NOPD to charge that the police spend more time arresting and investigating nonviolent drug crimes—easy but not very serious cases in which suspects are caught with the evidence of their crime—than they do homicide. These data are not typical of U.S. cities. In a major Justice Department study of felony cases in the seventy-five largest counties in the United States in 2000, researchers found conviction rates for drug offenses, murder, and burglary to be roughly equivalent (67, 64, and 59 percent respectively).[47]

These data on arrests and convictions are disturbing, because they suggest that policing in New Orleans prioritizes the interests of political authorities over those of local communities. Consistent with the priorities of the national "war on drugs," small-time drug users and dealers—usually those operating in poor and largely minority communities—are heavily targeted. These drug defendants are widely prosecuted, successfully convicted, and given tough terms in prisons full of more violent and dangerous criminals. The state responds to drug crimes with vigorous repression. Similarly, crimes against property are also prosecuted fairly effectively. But when it comes to homicides, especially homicides in poor neighborhoods, the record of investigation, prosecution, and sentencing is poor.

This apparent indifference or lack of capacity is sometimes justified with reference to the fact that many homicide victims have criminal records and appear to have been involved in drug trafficking and other illegal activities.[48] However, in a democratic society, justice for all segments of society, including the families of criminal suspects, is a formal goal. In practice, criminal justice is a scarce good allocated on an unequal basis. While the biases of the "war on drugs" noted above are national, they have a particularly harsh impact on poor and peripheral segments of the population such as the poor of New Orleans. Again, this breeds resentment of and a lack of trust in the police, fuelling a perception among residents of the city's hot zones that the police can repress but not protect their communities.

An analysis of the trial process, and its relation to policing and a conception of rights, would be incomplete without some mention of incarceration in New Orleans and Louisiana. Imprisonment is an important component of any criminal justice system, because the extent to which a society imprisons people is a reflection of how many residents lose rights in the name of the safety of the majority. Internationally, rates of imprisonment vary widely from 69 per 100,000 in southern Europe to over 600 per 100,000 in the United States and Russia.[49] In addition, the nature of the prison system can affect crime—prisons aimed at rehabilitation can, at least potentially, achieve the reintegration of criminals into society, whereas punitive and violent prisons may release people who are more, not less, likely to engage in crime again.

In this regard, the prison situation for those convicted in New Orleans reinforces the inequalities alluded to earlier, because Louisiana imprisons a large number of its residents, and it does so in a fairly repressive manner. Louisiana has the distinction of being the state with the highest incarceration rate in the country with the highest incarceration rate in the world. It has 799 prisoners per 100,000 people, about 17 percent higher than the overall U.S. rate of incarceration.[50] Louisiana's total prisoner population climbed from 17,268 in 1989 to 36,047 in 2001, more than doubling in 12 years. The Department of Corrections budget—resources spent to house and feed the increasing prison population—has jumped from $111.6 million in 1980–1981 to $648.7 million in 2000–2001, an increase of 481 percent, almost three times the rate of inflation.

Furthermore, Louisiana's state prison, Angola—the largest maximum-security prison in the United States—has an unenviable reputation for violence and corruption.[51] About 42 percent of its inmates come from greater New Orleans (Orleans and Jefferson parishes), three-quarters are black, and more than half are serving life sentences.[52] Louisiana is also more punitive toward its prisoners than other states. It is one of only a few U.S. states that forbid certain categories of convicted criminals from ever going before a parole board, meaning that life sentences are really for life. This means that the prison population is unlikely to diminish soon. Furthermore, mandatory minimum sentences often require nonviolent offenders such as those convicted of drug offenses to serve long sentences.[53] New Orleans itself, not just Angola prison, reflects these trends. The city houses the state's second-largest prison, the Orleans Parish

Prison, with more than 6,000 inmates. A separate law-enforcement agency, the Sheriff's Office, runs this institution. It has almost as many employees as the NOPD—1,100—and a budget half the size of the police department.[54]

These data confirm the picture of policing in New Orleans presented in this chapter. The NOPD is part of a criminal justice system that has a high capacity to imprison a large segment of the population. At the same time, many city residents suffer from a lack of social rights. The public school system is notoriously poor and corrupt, the public health facilities are overburdened, there is a lack of good jobs and housing, and New Orleans has one of the lowest rates of home ownership in the nation.[55] This combination of a lack of social rights and a high-capacity repressive apparatus has a perverse effect on state-society relations. Perhaps more than in any other city in the United States, the cliché that a poor black male has more chance of going to prison than to college applies to New Orleans.

Local Rights and Two Disasters: September 11 and Hurricane Katrina

Nationally, the terrorist attacks of September 11, 2001, triggered the biggest reorganization of the Federal government since the end of World War II. The new Department of Homeland Security (DHS) absorbed the Coast Guard, Secret Service, and Federal Emergency Management Agency, and incorporated and restructured the Customs Service, Immigration and Naturalization Service, and Border Patrol.[56] The creation of the DHS has potentially changed the rules of the game for municipal police forces throughout the United States. In the competition for scarce resources, police departments now tend to emphasize the prevention and investigation of terrorism as much as ordinary crime as a raison d'etre. New Orleans' officials have pointed to their port facilities to justify increased attention and aid, but the evidence suggests that unlike the situation in New York City, New Orleans has not experienced a major shift in the procedures and goals of its policing.

Colonel Terry Ebbert, the former Marine officer in charge of Homeland Security in New Orleans, has spoken about working with the NOPD to make the force more capable of preventing, rather than simply investigating, terrorist acts. Yet there has been no reorganization of the NOPD as a result of the "war on terror." (In New York City, in contrast, a special antiterrorist unit scours the subway system and other potential targets of terrorists on a daily basis. The NYPD also sent a representative to Madrid to gather information after the bombings there in 2004.[57]) Furthermore, one of the chief terrorism-related concerns in New Orleans is the port, which primarily involves the jurisdiction of Customs and the Coast Guard rather than the NOPD.

The most significant change in the NOPD in recent years has primarily involved public relations in response to complaints about the use of deadly force and concern for the NOPD's image among the police leadership, rather than procedures and organization. The promised shift to more service-oriented policing does not yet appear to have changed policing at the district level, and appears primarily to be an attempt to modify community-police relations in day-to-day patrolling and the prevention and investigation of ordinary crime.[58] It does not reflect an increased emphasis on counterterrorism, at least at the operational level.

As it relates to the theme of this chapter—the rights of residents of New Orleans vis-à-vis the police force and other coercive institutions of the state—September 11 pales in significance to another disaster, Hurricane Katrina, and the subsequent flooding of the city in late August and early September, 2005. The flood, one of the worst natural disasters in U.S. history, revealed some uncomfortable features of the security regime in New Orleans that deserve some attention here.

First, when it comes to the basic Hobbesian right of security against natural and human predators, the catastrophe showed that there were two categories of residents in New Orleans. The first consisted of the majority of the population that was able to respond to the mandatory evacuation order issued by Mayor Ray Nagin on August 27, 2005, in advance of the arrival of Hurricane Katrina. These people had private cars with which to evacuate, and some resources with which to deal with the other costs of evacuation. Some wealthy individuals within this group were even able to send mercenaries to guard their homes before the city was reopened.[59] A second, smaller group of people, around 10–15 percent of the population, were the old, the sick, and the very poor. These people lacked automobiles, mobility, or contacts, and remained in the city. They were ultimately dependent on public assistance during the disaster, first upon the city for shelter, food, and water, and later on the federal government for evacuation.

This two-tiered structure of the city's population, and the corresponding level of rights it implied, was exposed by Hurricane Katrina, revealing an emergency preparedness system that essentially relied on the market in order to function in the short term. Second-tier residents unable to evacuate on the basis of the market had to wait five days before the federal government began to respond effectively to their plight. Put another way, security can be reconceptualized as not only security against crime, but as "human security," security against a host of natural and human predations (King and Murray 2001/2002; Nelles 2003; Ogata and Cels 2003). The differential distribution of the right to human security put the lives of tens of thousands of the city's residents in danger during and after Hurricane Katrina.

Locally, the dividing line between the first-tier and second-tier residents was not race but class. While a majority of people in the second-tier was black, most black residents were able to evacuate, and city authorities such as Mayor Nagin and Police Chief Compass are black. However, on the national scene, race played a role in generating criticism of the federal government's response to the crisis. The perception was that New Orleans residents who suffered at the Superdome and Convention Center while waiting to be evacuated were not attended to promptly because of their race, as well as their poverty.[60]

A second noteworthy feature of the disaster is the emergence of armed gangs to take advantage of the breakdown of order. The looting that took place was not just of food and water, but of consumer goods, including electronic equipment and jewelry, and arms and ammunition. One NOPD officer was shot in the head and badly wounded by a looter during the flooding of the city. These and similar actions reveal the presence of small numbers of New Orleans residents committed to defying the NOPD, preying on commercial establishments and their fellow citizens, and forsaking the kind of solidarity called for by authorities, and engaged in by the majority of people, during natural disasters. It is probably the case that the relative numbers of these types of criminals is higher in New Orleans than in other U.S. cities; the crime statistics suggest this. However, similar groups exist in other cities such as Los Angeles, Chicago, Detroit, Washington D.C., and New York. The difference between New Orleans and these other cities is that the scope of the natural disaster in New Orleans exposed the opportunism of these criminal groups in a way that rarely occurs elsewhere. (The Los Angeles riots of spring 1992 might be comparable in that respect.)

In this sense I disagree with commentator Ken Serbin that Hurricane Katrina revealed the loss of civility in American life.[61] There was considerable solidarity and civility among the majority of people in New Orleans, as there is elsewhere in the United States. Instead, the disaster revealed the ongoing and unchanged lack of civility of a few at the bottom rungs of society. A brutal social order with few checks on the exploitation of the poorest is capable of generating a criminal backlash among the urban underclass during a natural disaster, a backlash whose lack of pity and predatory nature mirrors the oppression of the communities from which it springs.

A third feature of the Katrina disaster is the decidedly mixed nature of the NOPD's response to it. Unlike the police and fire personnel of

New York City, who were hailed as heroes after September 11, the NOPD suffered considerable criticism of its actions in the days and weeks after Hurricane Katrina. Granted, the conditions in which it operated were unprecedented and horrendous. Communications within the city broke down. The police ran out of gasoline for their vehicles, as well as ammunition, food, and water. Officers had to wade in contaminated water, and many lost their homes and were unable to locate their families. An atmosphere of chaos prevailed in the city for about a week after the hurricane.

Nevertheless, defections from the force were numerous, with one source estimating that as many as 200 officers deserted. Two overwhelmed officers committed suicide,[62] while some others participated in looting. In one incident, police and firefighters participated in the looting of a Wal-Mart on Tchoupitoulas Street. One man interviewed in the store by a reporter said "The police got all the best stuff. They're crookeder than us."[63]

In the face of these actions, Police Superintendent Eddie Compass tried to defend the NOPD. "In the annals of history, no police department in the history of the world was asked to do what we were asked," he is reported as saying. "We won. We did not lose one officer in battle."[64] Despite this strong defense of his force, the perception lingered that the NOPD's performance during Katrina had been disappointing. On September 27, 2005, Compass resigned amidst speculation that Mayor Nagin had forced him out.[65] Compass was later replaced by an NOPD insider, Warren Riley.

The flood of 2005 exposed to the world the steep inequality of rights, the prevalence of violent crime, and the legacy of distrust between the police and many residents in New Orleans. It is too early to tell to what extent these problems will be alleviated or exacerbated by the reconstruction of the city. While planners speak encouragingly of a New Deal, and of homestead provisions that will provide new opportunities for home ownership to poor people who return, the rapid distribution of reconstruction contracts to powerful business interests might ultimately reexclude the very people who have been marginalized by the city's politics all along. The nature of New Orleans' resurrection is thus difficult to foresee.

Conclusion

The police in New Orleans face many challenges. Social deprivation and violent crime are both relatively high. The city is also unusually vulnerable to natural disasters, especially hurricanes and flooding. Both human and natural predators tax the NOPD's capacities. Poverty and repression combine to produce a uniquely variable distribution of rights to human security in the city.

While relatively effective in controlling crowds and making street arrests, the New Orleans police force has a low investigatory capacity, which it applies selectively. The tourist industry and property in general are prioritized. Drug crimes are heavily repressed, while the rate of successful prosecution of murder is low. The use of force in poor neighborhoods is often exaggerated and indiscriminate. The department's crime reporting system, COMPSTAT, has been subject to manipulation by district commanders trying to please supervisors and reassure the public that crime was declining. Mistrust between the city's residents and the police is widespread.

Internally, the NOPD suffers from low morale. Many officers seem to regard their leadership as ineffective and unfair. Turnover is high and the police are understaffed and underfunded. This creates poor working conditions, which exacerbate the problem of morale. This vicious circle erodes the possibilities for high-quality policing and a strong degree of confidence and trust in the police by residents.

The NOPD is part of a criminal justice system with a high capacity to control, arrest, convict, and incarcerate a large segment of the population. However, the police force's autonomy is limited, and it has a relatively high degree of accountability to the court system, through the DA's Office. Unfortunately, this prosecutorial oversight over the NOPD does not necessarily ensure that police power operates in strict conformity to constitutional provisions. Courts in New Orleans are marred by corruption and the kind of politicization that comes with judicial elections and a clientelistic political culture. Furthermore, private assistance to both the NOPD and the DA's office poses the danger that public institutions will favor the interests that provide such assistance. The weak provision of social rights, with poor public education and health systems, and an economy dominated by low-salary service sector jobs, combines with the state's repressive apparatus to produce a starkly inegalitarian social order. To give one final statistic, in 2004, more than 40 percent of children in New Orleans lived in poverty.[66] Barriers to the realization of equality before the law for all residents seem higher in New Orleans than in other U.S. cities.

The September 11 terrorist attack and subsequent reorientation of the national security regime in the United States have had little impact on New Orleans policing so far. Residents' rights have still largely been shaped by local forces. This could be seen in a disaster that had far more impact on New Orleans than September 11: the 2005 Hurricane Katrina. The subsequent flood exposed the inequality of New Orleans' social order to the world. Most residents evacuated, while a minority was left to save itself in the days after the emergency, eventually being relocated by Federal authorities. The performance of the NOPD in the flood was mixed. The dedication to duty of many was marred by the desertion and looting of a minority, while criminal gangs took advantage of the situation to acquire arms and to loot nonessential items.

As New Orleans is rebuilt, a vital question will be whether a more egalitarian and fair regime of human security can be constructed in the city along with the new infrastructure and buildings. The disturbing images of the 2005 flood underlined the importance of the social dimension of public security issues in the United States. The criminal justice system can have, as it did in New Orleans, a high capacity for arresting, convicting, and imprisoning a large portion of the population. However, when it operates in a context of grave inequalities and social deprivation, it may still lack elements of predictability, equality, and fairness. The challenge of New Orleans is an important part of the effort to improve policing and access to human security in the United States and the rest of the world.

Acknowledgments

I would like to thank Sarah Miller for assistance with research for this chapter, and Andrea McArdle and Stacy McGoldrick for helpful comments on an earlier draft. This chapter is dedicated to the future of the International School of Louisiana, whose facilities were destroyed in the great flood that occurred in New Orleans in the wake of Hurricane Katrina on August 30–31, 2005, but which was re-opened later that year.

Notes

1. The problem of violent crime in New Orleans can be seen in its homicide rate. In 2004, New York City, with a population of about 8 million, had 572 murders. New Orleans, with a population less than one-sixteenth of New York's, had 264 homicides in the same year. From Bob Herbert, "No Stranger to the Blues," *The New York Times* (September 8, 2005) at http://www.nytimes.com accessed on September 8, 2005. More evidence of the comparatively high violent crime rate in New Orleans can be found at the web page of the U.S. Department of Justice's Bureau of Justice Statistics at http://www.ojp.usdoj.gov. The data from 2002, for example, show that New Orleans had 258 murders, more per capita than most other cities. Phoenix, Arizona, with almost three times the population of New Orleans, had 177 homicides in the same year, while Oakland, California, with about 80% of New Orleans' population, had 108 homicides.
2. From "A Necessary Safeguard," *The Gambit* (April 6, 2004), p. 7. Such complaints are not new. In 1998, an expert on police abuse, Professor James

Fyfe, said that while departments in various cities were known for brutality, corruption, or inefficiency, New Orleans was prominent nationally for all three. From Stacy McGoldrick, *Not at Liberty to See: Police, Party Politics and Violence in New Orleans, 1852–1880*, Ph.D. Dissertation, Graduate Faculty of Political and Social Science, New School University, New York City, 2003, p. 24, footnote 2.

3. From Paul Constance, "The Police That We Deserve," *BID America* (July–August, 2000), pp. 1–4.

4. Quoted in Michael Peristein, "Feds End 8-Year NOPD Probe," *The Times-Picayune*, (March 30, 2004), pp. B1–B2.

5. For recent criticisms of the NOPD's use of lethal violence, see Michelle Hunter, "Deadly Force," *The Times-Picayune* (June 5, 2005), pp. A-1, A-14, A-15.

6. From Trymaine Lee, "NOPD Aims to become Friendlier Force," *The Times-Picayune* (June 10, 2005), pp. A-1, A-12.

7. The 2001 population of Orleans parish was 476,492. From *The World Almanac and Book of Facts, 2003* (New York: World Almanac Books), p. 450.

8. From author's notes of comments by Second District Commander Edwin Hosli, district police-citizen (NONPACC) meeting, Touro Hospital, New Orleans, June 21, 2005.

9. Walt Philbin, "Homicide Detectives Return to Districts," *The Times-Picayune* (exact date missing, 2002).

10. The same study offers a sobering assessment of the effectiveness of police investigations. The 1967 President's Commission on Law Enforcement and Administration of Justice revealed that only 25% of major crimes resulted in arrest, and the rate of conviction after arrests was 35%. From Michael J. Palmiotto, *Criminal Investigations*, 2nd ed. (Bethesda, MD: Austin and Winfield, 1998), p.16.

11. This includes multiple arrests of the same person, and arrests for relatively trivial crimes. For example, nearly 1,000 people are arrested annually in the French Quarter for urinating in public, with about 200 of those arrests taking place during Carnival. From "The Costs of Plumbing, Patron Vandalism Add Up," *The Times-Picayune* (February 16, 2004), p. A-8. While the population of Orleans Parish, the city limits, is less than 500,000, the greater metropolitan area of New Orleans has a population in the vicinity of 1.2 million.

12. Gwen Filosa, "Delays Cut Convictions in N.O., Study Finds," *The Times-Picayune* (August 16, 2002), pp. A-1, A-6.

13. A study of 54,590 felony cases filed in state courts of the nation's seventy-five largest counties in May 2000, conducted by the U.S. Department of Justice, found a conviction rate of 78%. From Criminal Case Processing Statistics, Summary Findings, U.S. Department of Justice, Office of Justice Programs, Bureau of Justice Statistics at http://www.ojp.usdoj.gov, accessed on September 22, 2005. In another study of a sample of felony cases in forty of the seventy-five largest counties in the United States in May 1998, the conviction rate was 77%. From Brian Reaves, *Felony Defendants in Large Urban Counties 1998*, U.S. Department of Justice, Office of Justice Programs, Bureau of Justice Statistics, November 2001 (NCJ 187232), p. iv, at http://www.ojp.usdoj.gov/bjs/accessed on September 22, 2005.

14. Gwen Filosa, "Delays Cut Convictions in N.O., Study Finds," *The Times-Picayune* (August 16, 2002), pp. A-1, A-6. A national study published in the United States in 1967 revealed that only 25% of major crimes led to arrests, and the rate of conviction after arrest was 35%. From Palmiotto, *Criminal Investigations*, p.16.

15. Quoted in Gwen Filosa, "Scared Silent," *The Times-Picayune* (February 13, 2004), pp. A-1, A-9–12; the quote appears on p. A-12. This is part six of a seven-part investigation of murder in New Orleans.

16. From Michael Peristein, "Evidence Lost in Cleaning of NOPD's Storage Room," *The Times-Picayune* (February 4, 2004), pp. A-1, A-4. See also Michael Peristein, "Evidence Purge Likely to Haunt NOPD," *The Times-Picayune* (January 11, 2003), pp. A-1, A-8; Gwen Filosa, "Evidence Lost, Police Chief Concedes," *The Times-Picayune* (February 6, 2003), pp. A-1, A-9; Michael Peristein, "DA is Reviewing Evidence Purge," *The Times-Picayune* (May 9, 2004), pp. A-1, A-14; Michael Peristein, "NOPD Punishes Pair for Evidence Loss," *The Times-Picayune* (November 21, 2003), pp. B-1, B-2. Another complaint about NOPD's limited investigatory capacity is that the fingerprint division consists of only three people who must serve all eight districts, delaying the investigation of cases involving fingerprints. From Gwen Filosa, "Delays Cut Convictions in N.O., Study Finds," *The Times-Picayune* (August 16, 2002), pp. A-1, A-6; the reference is to p. A-6.

17. Gwen Filosa, "Scared Silent," *The Times-Picayune* (February 13, 2004), pp. A-1, A-9–A-12.

18. The Justice Department study of 54,590 felony cases filed in state courts of the nation's 75 largest counties in May 2000, cited in note 13, found a conviction rate of murder of 64%. From Criminal Case Processing Statistics, Summary Findings, U.S. Department of Justice, Office of Justice Programs, Bureau of Justice Statistics at http://www.ojp.usdoj.gov, accessed on September 22, 2005. Admittedly, the Justice Department data tracked the cases over the course of an entire year, while many of the cases in the New Orleans data were less than a year old. But the New Orleans conviction rate in early 2004 was only 11%; even if many more cases ended in conviction during the course of the year, it is unlikely that the rate approximated 64%.

19. Quoted in Gwen Filosa, "Scared Silent," *The Times-Picayune* (February 13, 2004), p. A-12.

20. Steve Ritea, "Crime, Coercion, and Coverup," *The Times-Picayune* (October 25, 2003), pp. A-1, A-8–A-9; Gordon Russell, "Cooked Books Hardly Unique to 1st District," *The Times-Picayune* (November 4, 2003), pp. A-1, A-4.

21. A public good is one that is nonrivalrous (its benefits can be enjoyed by anyone without reducing another person's consumption of the good) and nonexcludable (people cannot be prevented from consuming the good). In contrast, private goods are both rivalrous and excludable, easily divided into parts, sold on the market, and withheld from others. (From Wikipedia at *http://enwikipedia.org/wiki/Public_good*, accessed on September 20, 2005.) Law enforcement has often been thought of as a public good. However, given modern security technology and practices, security is increasingly taking on

characteristics of a private good or at least a collective good (a good provided only to a subset of society).

22. John Treadway, "400 Cops Get Promotions, Pay Raises," *The Times-Picayune* (March 6, 2004), pp. B-1, B-3.

23. Elizabeth Mullener, "Strength and Honor," *The Times-Picayune* (April 27, 2003), pp. A-1, A-8–11.

24. John Treadway, "400 Cops Get Promotions, Pay Raises," *The Times-Picayune* (March 6, 2004), p. B-3.

25. According to the 2000 U.S. Census, the median household income was $36,824. From Sasha Abramsky, "Supporting the Troops, Doubting the War," *The Nation* (October 4, 2004), pp. 11–15; the reference is to p. 11. In New Orleans, the median household income in 2004 was $27,133. From "Area Overview—New Orleans," at KnowledgePlex at *http://www.dataplace.org/* accessed on September 21, 2005.

26. Mark Schleifstein, "Study Finds Low Morale in NOPD," *The Times-Picayune* (January 9, 2004), pp. A-1, A-10.

27. Ibid. The figures from the survey can be found on the latter page.

28. From Steve Ritea and Tara Young, "Cycle of Death," *The Times-Picayune* (February 8, 2004), pp. A-1, A-5–A-9; the murder rate data is published on p. A-9.

29. See Associate Press, "New Orleans Murder Rate on the Rise Again," August 19, 2005, at MSNBC.com at *http://www.msnbc.msn.com* accessed on September 23, 2005.

30. Tara Young, "Hot Zone," *The Times-Picayune* (February 9, 2004), pp. A-1, A-6–A-8.

31. Ashley Nelson, *The Combination* (New Orleans: Neighborhood Story Project, 2005), p. 66. The Neighborhood Story Project is a series of books produced by New Orleans area high school students. For a year, students kept notes and interviewed and photographed people in their neighborhoods, creating detailed narratives of their communities. Some of these projects were then published. For more on the project, see www.neighborhoodstoryproject.org.

32. From Gwen Filosa, "Legal experts praise Connick," *The Times-Picayune* (January 7, 2003), pp. A-1, A-7. Upon retirement, Connick registered with the Republican Party. While he might have always been philosophically close to the Republicans, his affiliation to the Democrats while in office reflects the continued dominance of the Democratic Party in New Orleans city politics. Sixty-seven percent of the city of New Orleans is black. From "Area Overview—New Orleans," at KnowledgePlex at *http://www.dataplace.org/* accessed on September 21, 2005.

33. From information provided to research assistant Sarah Miller by Mark Gonzalez, an attorney at NOLA-LAW.com, June 2004.

34. Quoted in Gwen Filosa, "Delays Cut Convictions in N.O., Study Finds," *The Times-Picayune* (August 16, 2002), p. A-1.

35. From "Tackling the Backlog," an editorial in *The Times-Picayune* (February 26, 2003), p. B-6.

36. From Rebecca Mowbray, "Crime May Jeopardize New Orleans' Image," *The Times-Picayune* (February 8, 2004), pp. F-1, F-2–F-3.

37. From Gwen Filosa, "Jordan Targets Backlog of Cases," *The Times-Picayune* (February 25, 2003), p. A-1. The story continues on p. A-8.

38. Information provided to researcher Sarah Miller by the Metropolitan Crime Commission, June 2004.

39. From Michelle Krupa and Manuel Torres, "Judge Indicted: Green Charged in Jeff Bonds Scandal," *The Times-Picayune* (September 30, 2004), p. A1. The story continues on pp. A-6–A-7.

40. Personal communication from Suffolk University law professor Miguel Schor, September 21, 2005.

41. From Gwen Filosa, "Legal Experts Praise Connick," *The Times-Picayune* (January 7, 2004), pp. A-1, A-7.

42. Quoted in Gwen Filosa, "Legal Experts Praise Connick," *The Times-Picayune* (January 7, 2004), p. A-7. Wright coauthored the article in the *Stanford Law Review* where the data in the above paragraph were first published. Then-DA Harry Connick paid for Wright and his coauthor to present their findings in New Orleans in January of 2003.

43. Gwen Filosa, "Legal Experts Praise Connick," *The Times-Picayune* (January 7, 2004), p. A-7.

44. This astounding rate of conviction for burglary seems to indicate the seriousness with which violations of the property rights of homeowners are treated in the New Orleans courts.

45. This is the method favored by anticrime watchdog groups in New Orleans such as the Metropolitan Crime Commission. However, it can be misleading because it seems to assume that everyone arrested should be convicted. Given the inevitability of false arrests, it seems better to also look at the conviction rate of those who are actually charged with crimes. As the statistics show, the majority of those charged with crimes in New Orleans are convicted, even in murder cases.

46. The figures in this paragraph come from Gwen Filosa, "Delays Cut Convictions in N.O., Study Finds," *The Times-Picayune* (August 16, 2002), pp. A-1, A-6.

47. From Criminal Case Processing Statistics, Summary Findings, U.S. Department of Justice, Office of Justice Programs, Bureau of Justice Statistics at http://www.ojp.usdoj.gov, accessed on September 22, 2005. This study, previously cited, is of 54,590 felony cases filed in state courts of the nation's seventy-five largest counties in May 2000.

48. The seven-part investigation of murder in New Orleans that ran in *The Times-Picayune* in February 2004 emphasized the criminal background of many murder victims. See, for example, Steve Ritea and Tara Young, "Cycle of Death" in the *Times-Picayune* (February 8, 2004), pp. A-1, A5–9. Several readers of the newspaper wrote letters to the editor complaining that the authors of the series appeared to be excusing the poor record of investigating these crimes on this basis.

49. From Roy Walmsley, "World Prison List, fourth edition," *Home Office Findings* No. 188 (2003), pp. 1–6. The figure for southern Europe is the median rate. The U.S. incarceration rate is listed as 686 per 100,000 in this document, with Russia at 638. Ibid., p. 1.

50. The overall U.S. rate comes from Walmsley, "World Prison List," cited above. The Louisiana rate comes from "Prison Numbers" in *The Angolite*, 28(2) (March/April 2003), p. 13. The same column lists the 2002 prison population in the United States as 2,019,234, with black males making up 41% of that total. *The Angolite* is an award-winning magazine produced by prisoners in Louisiana's Angola state penitentiary, one of the largest state prisons in the country.

51. In the early 1970s, Angola was known as the "bloodiest prison in America." From Anita Roddick, "Innocence Bound: Inside Angola Prison," *Counterpunch* (September 10, 2002) at *http://www.counterpunch.org* accessed on September 21, 2005. Author Daniel Berger claims that Angola warden Burle Cain tried to extort money from him in exchange for access to prisoners; see Daniel Berger, *God of the Rodeo: The Quest for Redemption in Louisiana's Angola Prison* (New York: The Ballantine Publishing Group, 1998). See also the documentary film *The Farm: Life Inside Angola Prison*, an A & E Home Video, released March 30, 1999.

52. From "Angola Facts" at *http://www.georgetown.edu* accessed on September 21, 2005.

53. Data from this paragraph comes from Martha Carr, "Aging Inmates," *The Times-Picayune* (May 21, 2001), pp. A-1, A-6.

54. The NOPD budget in 2003 was $126 million. From Gordon Russell, "City Loosening Purse Strings for Police," *The Times-Picayune* (November 12, 2003), p. A-1. The Sheriff's Office budget and personnel numbers are from a political advertisement for Marlin Gusman, candidate for the office of Orleans Parish Criminal Sheriff, dated September 12, 2004.

55. In 2004, New Orleans' home ownership rate was 46.5%, while the national rate was 69%. From "Area Overview—New Orleans" at KnowledgePlex at *http://www.dataplace.org/* accessed on September 21, 2005.

56. William Finnegan, "Homeland Insecurity," *The New Yorker* (February 7, 2005), p. 29.

57. In New York City in 2002, Police Commissioner Ray Kelly founded a counter-terrorism bureau with 125 officers, a global intelligence room, and language specialists competent in Arabic, Pashto, Urdu, and other languages. From Craig Horowitz, "The NYPD's war on terror," *New York* (February 2003), at *http://www.newyorkmetro.com/nymetro/news/features*, accessed on September 21, 2005. Commissioner Kelly writes that "In March [2004], we had someone in Madrid the day of the bombing on that city's subway [sic]. Our world has gotten smaller, and we need information of any sort that's going to help us protect this city." From Raymond Kelly, "May the Force Be with You," *Gotham Gazette* (May 5, 2004) at *http://www.gothamgazette.com* accessed on September 21, 2005.

58. For example, at a Second District NOPD-citizen meeting held on June 21, 2005, and attended by the author, Second District Commander Edwin Hosli made no mention of the change in orientation in his presentation on policing in the district to the residents. The NOPD holds monthly meetings between the district commanders and members of the public in all eight of the city's

districts. According to the author's notes, twenty-eight residents attended the meeting mentioned above, with twelve white males, twelve white women, and four black women in attendance. While black males make up a disproportionate number of criminal suspects in New Orleans, none were in attendance at this particular meeting.

59. From Jamie Wilson, "Mercenaries Guard Homes of the Rich in New Orleans," *The Guardian* (September 12, 2005), at *http://www.informationclearinghouse. info* accessed on September 18, 2005.

60. See, for example, John Broder, "Storm and Crisis: Racial Tension; Amid Criticism of Federal Efforts, Charges of Racism are Lodged," *The New York Times*, at *http://nytimes.com* accessed on September 23, 2005.

61. See Kenneth Serbin, "A Civilidade Americana no Olho do Furacão," *O Estado de São Paulo* (September 4, 2005), accessed online on September 5, 2005.

62. Joseph Treaster, "Law Officers, Overwhelmed, Are Quitting the Force," *The New York Times* (September 4, 2005), at *http://nytimes.com* accessed and sent to me by Andrea McArdle on September 12, 2005. On September 5, Deputy Police Superintendent Warren Riley said that between 400 and 500 NOPD officers were unaccounted for. From Melinda Deslatte, "New Orleans Police Chief Defends his Force" from WWL-TV at *http://www.wwltv.com/*, accessed on September 8, 2005.

63. Quoted in Michael Peristein and Brian Thevenot, "Even a Cop Joins the Looting," *The Times-Picayune* (August 30, 2005), at *http://www.nola.com/ newslogs/breakingtp* accessed on August 30, 2005.

64. Quoted in Gwen Filosa, "N.O. Police Chief Defends Force," *The Times-Picayune* (September 5, 2005), at *http://www.nola.com/newslogs/breakingtp* accessed on September 5, 2005. See also Melinda Deslatte, "New Orleans Police Chief Defends his Force," Associate Press, September 5, 2005.

65. From James Varney and Michael Peristein, "Compass Resigns" in *The Times-Picayune* (September 28, 2005), at *http://www.nola.com/newslogs/breakingtp* accessed on September 28, 2005.

66. From Joan Treadway, "27% of LA.'s Children are Poor, Study Finds," *The Times-Picayune* (October 13, 2004), p. A-4. Poverty is defined by the Federal government's threshold of $18,400 for a family of four, from Leslie Williams, "N.O. Child Poverty is above 40 Percent," *The Times-Picayune* (January 13, 2004), p. B-1. The New Orleans rate is almost twice that of the United States as a whole which, at 22%, is one of the highest among the advanced capitalist countries. From "US high in UN child poverty table," at BBC News World Edition, March 1, 2005 at *http://www.news.bbc.co.uk* accessed on September 23, 2005.

Bibliography

Berger, Daniel (1998) God of the Rodeo: The Quest for Redemption in Louisiana's Angola Prison. New York: The Ballantine Publishing Group.
Carothers, Thomas (1998) "The Rule of Law Revival" in *Foreign Affairs*, Volume 77, Number 2, March/April, pp. 95–106.

Davis, Diane and Pereira, Anthony (2003) *Irregular Armed Forces and Their Role in Politics and State Formation*. New York: Cambridge University Press.

Howard, L. Vaughan and Robert S. Friedman (1959) *Government in Metropolitan New Orleans*. New Orleans: Tulane Studies in Political Science Volume VI, Tulane University.

Kant de Lima, Roberto (1995) "Bureaucratic Rationality in Brazil and the United States: Criminal Justice Systems in Comparative Perspective" in David J. Hess and Roberto Da Matta, eds. *The Brazilian Puzzle: Culture on the Borderlands of the Western World*. New York: Columbia University Press, pp. 241–269.

King, Gary and Christopher Murray (2001/2002) "Rethinking Human Security" in *Political Science Quarterly*, Volume 116, Number 4, Winter, pp. 585–611.

Mann, Michael (2002) "Globalization After September 11" in *New Left Review*, Volume 15, November/December, pp. 75–92.

McGoldrick, Stacy (2003) *Not at Liberty to See: Police, Party Politics and Violence in New Orleans, 1852–1880*. New York City: Ph.D. dissertation, Graduate Faculty of Political and Social Science, New School University.

Mendez, Juan, Guillermo O'Donnell, and Paulo Sergio Pinheiro, eds. (1999) *The (Un)Rule of Law and the Underprivileged in Latin America*. Notre Dame, IN: Notre Dame University Press.

Nelles, Wayne, ed. (2003) *Comparative Education, Terrorism and Human Security: From Critical Pedagogy to Peace Building?* New York: Palgrave MacMillan.

O'Donnell, Guillermo (2000) "The Judiciary and the Rule of Law" in *The Journal of Democracy*, Volume 11, Number 1, pp. 25–31.

Ogata, Sadako and Johan Cels (2003) "Human Security: Protecting and Empowering the People" in *Global Governance*, Volume 9, Number 3, July–September, pp. 273–283.

Palmiotto, Michael J. (1998) *Criminal Investigations*. Bethesda MD: Austin and Winfield, second edition.

Pereira, Anthony and Mark Ungar (2004) "The Persistence of the 'Mano Duro': Authoritarian Legacies and Policing in Brazil and the Southern Cone" in Paola Cesarini and Katherine Hite, eds. *Authoritarian Legacies in Southern Europe and Latin America* (South Bend, IN: University of Notre Dame Press, 2004), pp. 263–304.

Ungar, Mark (2002) *Elusive Reform: Democracy and the Rule of Law in Latin America*. Boulder: Lynne Rienner.

Zaverucha, Jorge (2003) *Polícia Civil de Pernambuco: O Desafio da Reforma*. Recife: Editora Universitária.

7

Willie Horton to Osama bin Laden: The New Framing of Police and Crime in the 2004 Presidential Campaign

Stacy K. McGoldrick

While teaching a criminology course in the fall of 2004, I asked my students to write a paper comparing the Democratic and Republican positions on crime and policing in that year's presidential campaign. My goal was not only to engage students with the campaign, but to suggest how presidential campaign language about crime almost always focuses upon street crime, is heavy on a "get tough" message, and seeks to unite party supporters around the perception of shared values in juxtaposition to the "criminals" opposing us. To my, perhaps misguided, surprise many students informed me that they were unable to find positions on crime at either the party or candidates' web sites. What they did find was a lot of information about "first responders" (police, fire, and emergency medical technicians) and Homeland Security.

In class we had discussed how the national conversation about crime was shifting from the street and white-collar crime they read about in their 2004 edition textbook to international political crime and terrorism. But their findings suggested that what I had seen as an event-driven topic shift might better be grasped as a profound change in how political campaigns operate, garner support, define the enemy, and construct fear of crime as a concern for the electorate. The specter of street crime, which long shared campaign stages with and even outlasted the Soviet threat, had been entirely displaced in 2004 election rhetoric by a new, far less concrete geopolitical nemesis. My students' inability to find the once reliable "street crime" trope that I had confidently sent them looking for led me to rethink the relationships between crime fears, visions of government, political campaigns, and the accountability structure of police power in the United States. I began with the hypothesis that the fears generated by September 11 had not only spawned institutions like the Office of Homeland Security but had created a starkly new discourse about what it is that police are supposed to do. This new discourse, I believed, set into motion a nation-protecting vision of policing that stood at a sharp tension with the traditions of local governance and oversight of municipal forces.

To explore my hypotheses, I pursued a multiple-methodology research project that merged historical accounts of policing, social theory, and an empirical study of "crime talk" in the 2000 and 2004 presidential campaigns. My first step was to revisit two tracks of U.S. history—the histories of late-twentieth-century campaigns and of policing as an American institution and aspect of political culture—and explore when and how they intersect. In the second step I consulted literature on issue "framing" to consider the extent to which the new discourse of policing represents a change in political culture. I then joined that literature's insights with a qualitative and statistical analysis of party platforms, nominee speeches, and media coverage in the 2000 and 2004 presidential campaigns. The data for my media research were a random sample of articles found in a Lexis-Nexis (a search engine for major English-language newspapers) search of all American newspapers' 2000 and 2004 political campaign coverage. I used a random number table to select ten articles on the campaign for each month from November 1999 to November 2000 and again from November 2003 to November 2004. I then replicated this search, but cross-listed the term "presidential campaign" with "police," "crime," "law enforcement," and "terrorism." Finally, I explored the relation of these changes in campaign discourse to changes in the discipline of criminology.

What I found was that the discourse of crime and policing changed remarkably between the presidential campaigns of 2000 and 2004. This is significant because how we imagine crime (by processing media images of it), and police forces, has always been linked to a vision of government.[1] Up to now this link was checked by a structural barrier. Though presidential contenders have long run on police and crime issues, police organization and management have always remained local. The distance between the federal executive and local police has paid dividends to citizens in police responsibility and responsive oversight. The 2004 campaign provides those same citizens with reasons to worry. While the United States has been markedly moving away from a local policing model due to the newly developing Homeland

Security policies, this seismic shift in authority was taken as a given rather than debated over as a problematic issue in the campaign of 2004.

The fact that terrorism was an all-consuming factor in the 2004 campaign and has far-reaching media consequences will surprise no one, but the reality that almost all conversation about crime and police were subsumed under the rubric of international politics and terrorism is a phenomenon that deserves analysis. Since at least the presidential campaign of Barry Goldwater in 1964, "tough on crime" (meaning street crime) rhetoric has been a mainstay of political campaigns. For this reliable talking point to become a near nonissue marks a real change in public discourse. More significantly, by representing police forces as protectors of the nation-state, political candidates foster an understanding of policing that is nationalized in both its vision and orientation. This change in representation and expectation about the scope of police responsibility can, in turn, contribute to a different distribution of power in American policing, one that displaces the tradition of local autonomy and responsibility to local communities and reconfigures legitimate state violence as tied to national institutions and norms. This new conversation, combined with the realities of Homeland Security, could portend a new and dangerous political culture, one in which ideas about public vigilance over police action remain unformed or unstated. Thus, if the public loses a sense of responsibility over local police forces, widespread abuses may come to be an increasing outcome of Homeland Security.

Furthermore, this new policing narrative should be understood both for its impact on civil society and practical application to police operations and bureaucratic structure. First, funding for the organization and management of municipal forces may continue to shift in theme and priority. Currently, police forces are feeling the crunch of a shift in expectations and personnel hours, without a guaranteed increase in funding and officers.[2] Police managers have had to find new sources of funding beyond their municipal tax base and they do this by asking for Homeland Security grants. This dependence on grants has been true since 1968, when federal matching grants were instituted to encourage increases in police forces (Chambliss 2001: 18). Second, the narrative of "first responders" protecting the nation implies a more hands-off approach by the public to discretionary police action and less attention to police critics. Similarly, the national and geopolitical framing of visions about crime and policing may lead to a new situating of responsibility and place more local police actions within the purview of federal government.

In order to best understand the characteristic of this shift and its possible implications, first I will outline the importance of policing and crime in American national politics and how that political theme relates to the history of policing. I will then turn to scholarly opinion on media's role in shaping political sentiment and apply that to the most recent elections.

Law and Order Campaign—"Crime Talk" as Race-Baiting in the Late-Twentieth-Century United States and the Persistence of Local Police Control

"Law and order" policies became strategically important because they allowed politicians to court racially anxious white voters after the tumult and triumphs of the civil rights movement. Though the Dixiecrat bolt from the Democratic Party and George Wallace's segregationist and counter-culture-baiting presidential campaign in 1964 revealed fissures in the New Deal Order's southern electoral Democratic Party majority, the explicitly racist appeal of those political efforts kept their agents from moving into a mainstream coalition.[3] But, in his 1968 and 1972 presidential campaigns, Richard Nixon's strong "law and order" rhetoric offered racially anxious constituencies a legitimizing code name and a "southern strategy" to political victory. The "law and order" platform became a key component of American political campaigns for the remainder of the century at the presidential level, and indeed in many state legislative, sheriff, judicial, and gubernatorial campaigns. (This strategy had been a potent weapon for insurgent Republicans, but Bill Clinton signaled that this rhetoric had permeated both parties in his 1992 presidential campaign. In a move many believed was calculated to solidify his image as a tough-on-crime Democrat, the then Arkansas governor refused to commute the death sentence of a mentally disabled man (Chambliss 2001: 25).)

Despite the ubiquity of police and crime as a presidential campaign topic in the last half of the twentieth century, historians of U.S. policing have long highlighted the inherent localism of police forces. Since their inception, police forces in the United States have been subject to local control and politics. In other words, control of municipal police forces has been a local issue and responsibility for police actions and relations with the public has rested on local government (unlike controversies over the actions of the FBI, for example). Police forces, then, despite long-standing dependency on federal grant dollars and vulnerability to federal law suits (see Marilynn Johnson's chapter 4 in this volume) maintained significant local autonomy.

Crime levels and police responses have been important barometers of white flight, racism, and the rhetoric of public order in presidential campaigns. Openly segregationist and racist campaign language has been replaced by talk of safe streets and social order (Beckett and Sasson

2004: 48–50). Many scholars have documented, for example, the singular significance of the Willie Horton "Weekend Pass" ad to the presidential campaign of then Massachusetts Governor Dukakis when Republicans aired a national commercial stating that Willie Horton, an African-American man imprisoned for murder, raped a young white woman while he was out on furlough from a Massachusetts prison. Although the ad was widely criticized for race baiting, nevertheless Dukakis was effectively characterized as soft on crime and by extension as a dangerous and irresponsible leader (Chambliss 2001: 24).

If this has been a national conversation coded with racial animosities, the threat of random violent crime has always been framed locally in terms of both the protectors (police) and the enemy (street thugs). The threat has been from within and has not, until recently, had a geopolitical perspective. It is local criminals who would terrorize and therefore local police who could protect the middle class. This perception of danger is connected to media coverage of local crime. When local media heavily cover local crime, community members' perception of threat increases. An accompanying fear of street crime has increased even when rates of violent crime have lowered and despite the fact that random and stranger, more violent crime has always been relatively rare (Johnson-Cartee 2005: 301–305).

The History of Localist Police Authority in the United States

The most famous federal investigative force, the Federal Bureau of Investigation, started out as The Bureau of Investigation and was conceived in 1908 and expanded to become the Federal Bureau of Investigation in 1933. The FBI was charged with investigation of federal and interstate offenses (not without significant turf wars between local and federal forces) and did not officially interfere with the patrolling, traffic enforcement, and service calls that characterize municipal police. Local police forces remained by far the most visible in terms of interaction with the public, with state troopers having the widest regional breadth. This local conception and organization of the police sharply distinguish the history of American police forces from their contemporaries in Western Europe.

Unlike the French or British police, police units in the United States emerged at the municipal level, at the instigation of county or city governments, and to this day local police chiefs (as distinguished from mayors or other chief executive officers of city government) exercise some autonomous power over the character of municipal police (Miller 1999: 12–15), though the ultimate check on their power is that they can be let go at the pleasure of the mayor—like William Bratton in New York. Moreover, these police forces were created to serve very different needs in different regions. Thus, the history of the police is closely associated with American republicanism; the dual drives for locally controlled law enforcement and locally autonomous politics are central to the cultures that developed around security forces and the level of acceptance they received. For example, early southern police forces developed out of slave patrols, loosely organized bands of white men that would patrol the land around plantations looking for slaves out without a pass, in the first half of the nineteenth century, while police forces in northeastern cities were created to protect property and quash social disorder.[4] Moreover, the popular acceptance of police could never be taken for granted before the last third of the nineteenth century, and their presence was always controversial to local populations made nervous by a standing, organized, and often (but not always) armed police force with power to arrest (Ryan 1997). Tightly allying the police forces to local governments through organized political parties helped to alleviate some of the anxiety around their creation.[5]

Throughout the nineteenth and twentieth centuries, police forces in the United States continued to respond to local social and political conditions. Whether they were enforcing state segregation laws (sometimes battling Federal Marshals as in the case of Mississippi) or breaking up striking workers (Fogelson 1977), police forces have often operated in both legal and extralegal ways to accommodate their own interests as well as the interests of local elites. For example, in the nineteenth century, economic interests led many police to not "see" local brothels either because the procurers would bribe them or because local elites owned the brothels (as in the case of nineteenth-century New Orleans).

However, it would be a mistake to characterize local autonomy as unjust by definition. Local police discretion can often allow for richer community-police interactions and facilitate changes of priorities by the local government or even community members. For instance, many municipalities were able to adopt models of community policing after local activists highlighted the benefits of a police force more intimately familiar with or even native to a community (Wyckoff 1988: 103–120). Some of the best community-police relationships are built upon a municipal police force's ability to adapt to the particular problems at hand. For example, a district captain might assign more patrol in a particular area after learning more about local community members' concerns. Furthermore, with local autonomy, community access to those responsible for policing can, in key moments, shape the nature of policing. When, for example, New York City residents demanded citizen complaint review boards or programs bringing police into classrooms, legislative and mayoral candidates knew that they would have to speak to these demands when campaigning and act on them if elected. Localization, then, can make communication and accommodation between communities and police more viable. If, however, police forces become increasingly beholden to national concerns as they now are under the organization of Homeland Security, then they will also more likely be unable or unwilling to adjust their behavior toward matters of immediate community interest.

Up until quite recently only two sources of federal oversight—federal grant programs and federal prosecution of police abuses—have mitigated this historically local dynamic. Federal grant programs have created a few new mandates for police forces, but even as these grants increased in the late decades of the twentieth century, local autonomy and discretion remained the most salient characteristic of American policing. This enduring local dominance is the result of the continued organization of sheriffs by counties, police by cities, and the lack of any cohesive coordination among those forces, the FBI, and other federal law enforcement agencies. And although jurisdictions have long overlapped and been somewhat competitive with one another, presidential campaigns have not historically turned on a perceived need for the federal government to streamline and coordinate jurisdictional boundaries. So, although it is true that presidential candidates have both relied heavily on policing issues in their campaigns and used policing debates to convey messages of coded racial antagonism or support for law and order, the relative lack of federal executive control over police has made their discourse on the matter largely symbolic and commitment-free. It has been easy to tap into community fears and concerns, race bait, and create a wedge between the "pathology sponsoring" welfare policies and those who advocate "personal responsibility." This has led presidential candidates to adopt law-and-order issues as a campaign mainstay, although they have not had to show actual follow-up action in respect to policing when it came to police actions, as distinguished from numbers of officers on the street (Beckett and Sasson, 2004: 52–55).

Framing Past and Present: From the Politics of Race Fear to the Politics of National Mobilization

Both Democratic and Republican candidates have used the issue of crime and police in order to garner votes. This, in turn, has made policing a common theme in presidential rhetoric. Policing street crime, then, has been "framed" as a presidential issue. If framing contributes both to the creation of social meaning and the creation of consensus around certain policy, then the reframing of presidential political rhetoric about crime and policing is indeed important to understanding the viability of public debates on these subjects. Understanding public perceptions of political and social problems helps us to consider the issues of power and how institutions operate in discourse. "Framing is the process by which a communication source, such as a news organization (or a political leader, public relations officer, political advertising consultant, or news consumer), defines and constructs a political issue or public controversy," (Nelson et al. 1997: 567). For example, fear of crime is, according to many scholars, not correlated with the actual crime rate. Moreover, fear of crime will go up when news coverage of crime goes up, even if the crime rate itself is going down (Beckett and Sasson 2004: 74–75). This, in turn, impacts where politicians feel they need to stand on the "crime issue" and a vicious cycle is born. The national venue of presidential campaigns creates a unique opportunity to gauge the political temperature and, in the case of crime and police, sometimes to manipulate the public. As Gamson et al. have argued, the role of media in politics and the construction of political meaning are crucial:

> We walk around with media-generated images of the world, using them to construct meaning about political and social issues. The lens through which we received these images is not neutral but evinces the power and point of view of the political and economic elites who operate and focus it. And the special genius of this system is to make the whole process seem so normal and natural that the very art of social construction is invisible. (Gamson et al. 1992: 373)

The usefulness of studying media images of campaigns in order to discern their relationship to policy and power has also received scholarly attention. As Johnson-Cartee states, "Meaning has been socially constructed through a process often dominated by the mass media. Because of this, research analysis of the images found in mass-mediated messages reveal important social indicators." (Johnson-Cartee 2004: 4). By understanding how the subjects of presidential campaigns have represented themselves through their own production (speeches, debates, party platforms), and how they have been represented (articles in large media outlets), we can better assess how the terms of discussion have changed in the last five years. My research indicates that there has indeed been a shift in focus from street crime to geopolitical crime or terrorism, and from local policing to Homeland Security.

Changing Media Frames in the 2000 and 2004 Presidential Campaigns

Keeping this potential shift of frame in mind, changes in media coverage and campaign materials can illuminate the dynamics of this shift manifested in

Table 7.1   Analysis of newspaper coverage and
article content in 2000 and 2004

Articles	2000	2004
Presidential campaign	114	114
Presidential campaign/law enforcement	8	38
Presidential campaign/police	33	37
Presidential campaign/crime	66	78
Presidential campaign/terrorism	11	102
Total	232	396

new characterizations of crime, threat, and policing. In other words, if this
frame-shifting is true, then we can expect more characterization of police as
national defenders and less of a rhetorical concern with street crime. When
I analyzed the articles in 2000 and 2004 (table 7.1), I found this hypothesis to
be confirmed. After eliminating irrelevant and repeated articles (and allowing for the fact that not all topics generated ten articles for each month and
simply taking all the articles listed), I analyzed 232 articles for 2000 and 396
in 2004. I analyzed the articles for the language they used to describe the
campaigns and their content. I also looked at the content of the presidential debates to see how often crime and police were referred to, and in what
context. Through this analysis of newspaper coverage and campaign content, I discerned noticeable shifts in discourse between 2000 and 2004; the
great difference between the campaign years reflected a sharp shift in the
content of terms associated with crime and policing after the September 11
attacks.

Through this analysis of media coverage and campaign output I found
that not only was there a significant shift in the framing of police (local to
national) and crime (local to international) but that the shift itself was not
justified or problematized within the discourse. In fact, besides limited
debate about the proper scope of the PATRIOT Act, little attention was
devoted to the significant changes in the organization of the FBI, training
of local police forces, and organization of Homeland Security. The cause
for this shift in frame, which the major 2004 presidential contenders
accomplished without any demonstrable need to explain, is uncertain.
The ease of this transition could be explained as the result of the collapse
of rigorous criticism in mainstream American media. This loss of a critical perspective, in turn, may have been informed by—or it may have

contributed to—the quickly hallowed framing of police as "first responders" after many New York City police died in the World Trade Center towers collapse, which made it unpatriotic and therefore politically impossible for a mainstream political candidate to criticize this new vision. But whatever the reason, the 2004 presidential campaign introduced a dramatically new and starkly different discourse of police as guardians of the national interest that was, nevertheless, treated as a political given.

The Shifting of Party Platform Frames in 2000 and 2004

I found that the discourse on both policing and crime during the 2004 campaign was broadly pitched and conflated with two distinct conceptions of policing. Policing could mean either the traditional "street" concerns of attending to the local order and fighting random violent crime or enacting the new, geopolitical vision of impeding, or responding to, terrorists. Consider the following quote from the Democratic Party platform in 2000:

> Today, America finds itself in the midst of prosperity, progress, and peace. We have arrived at this moment because of the hard work of the American people. This election will be about the big choices we have to make to secure prosperity that is broadly shared and progress that reaches all families in the new American century.

The varying issues that the Democratic Party took on in the 2000 platform complement this broad vision. In 2004, by contrast, the platform stays close to issues of security and war. The laundry-list nature of the Democratic platform in 2000 compared to the focused, serious platform in 2004 demonstrates this shift of frame. Moreover, in 2000 the Democratic Party controlled the executive branch and touted a future vision; in 2004, as the party of opposition, it needed to justify its positions (table 7.2).

When comparing the topics tackled in the respective platforms, one can see that the Democratic Party's focus on terrorism has permeated all other topics. The Republican Party platform went through a similar transition between 2000 and 2004 (table 7.3). The 2004 platform, after celebrating Ronald Reagan, invoking Abraham Lincoln, and offering a reflection on September 11, went on to introduce its major planks. In 2000, their "Renewing America's Purpose" platform had emphasized the need for no-frills prisons, placed attention-grabbing subheadings on the topics "justice and safety" and "children at risk," and introduced themes of moral responsibility, health care, and judicial reform.

Table 7.2 Differences in substantive issues covered in the 2000 and 2004 Democratic Party platform, listed in order of appearance

2000	2004
Prosperity	Defeating terrorism
Fiscal discipline	Keeping weapons of mass Destruction out of the hands of terrorist
Retirement security	Promoting democracy, peace and security
Investing in America	Strengthen our military
Education	Achieving energy independence
Investing in innovation	Strengthening Homeland Security
Protecting consumers	Creating good jobs
Investing in communities (Street crime, new urbanism)	Standing up for the great American middle class
Valuing work: safe working conditions and "ergonomic standards"	Reforming health care
Progress: crime rate down, adoptions up, teen births down, people moved off welfare	Improving education
Fighting crime	Protecting our environment
Peace: weak states, pollution, global epidemics	A strong American community

Table 7.3 Republican Party platforms, 2000 and 2004

2000	2004
The American dream: prosperity with a purpose	Winning the war on terror
Education and opportunity: Leave no American behind	Ushering in an ownership era
Parents	Building an innovative, globally competitive economy
Renewing family and community	Strengthening our communities
Retirement security and quality health care: our pledge to America	Protecting our families
American partners in conservation and preservation: Stewardship of our natural resources	Summary and call to action
Government for the people	
Principled American leadership (where terrorism and foreign police were discussed)	

Domestic issues were central to both the Democratic and Republican platforms in 2000. In particular, the Democratic Party emphasized the falling street crime rate. In 2004, street crime went almost unmentioned in both party platforms.

Presidential campaign discussions of crime in the 2000 race looked similar to those of the previous twenty-five years. Law-and-order issues revolved around the fear of street crime, and white-collar crime received little, if any, attention. Issues like the death penalty, gun control, and drugs were typical of the campaign messages about crime. Also, while the campaign rhetoric in 2000 acknowledged the drop in street crime in the late 1990s, the context of the conversation still fanned fears of random violent crime and favored reactionary fear-mongering. Note, for example, this language from the 2000 Republican platform:

> Crimes against women and children demand an empathetic response. That is why the Republican Congress enacted Megan's Law, requiring local notification when sex offenders are released, and why we advocate special penalties against thugs who, in assaults against pregnant women, harm them or their unborn children. Federal obscenity and child pornography laws, especially crimes involving the Internet, must be vigorously enforced—in contrast to the current administration's failure in this area. We urge States to follow the lead of congressional Republicans by making admissible in court the prior similar criminal acts of defendants in sexual assault cases. (CNN.com.>allpolitics.com)

Media coverage of the campaigns did not stray far from the agenda laid out by party platforms and speeches. As with the campaigns, there are important differences in discussions of crime and crime control between 2000 and 2004. First, there were twelve more articles about crime in the sample from 2004 than in the sample from 2000 (despite a continued drop in street crime rates). Second, and most obviously, there were a substantially higher number of articles about terrorism in the 2004 sample, and this made for most of the increase in the articles about crime. Third, in the discussions of crime, there were significantly more articles about crimes in other countries. Although in 2000 all but three of the sampled articles about crime addressed crime in the United States, in 2004 thirty-three articles focused on crimes in other countries. Furthermore, this trend toward expanded crime coverage was not just about terrorism, but included Serbian war crimes, Russian mobsters, Colombian drug lords, and, of course, Vietnam and allegations that Democratic presidential candidate John Kerry accused American soldiers of war crimes. Fourth and related, "crime" as a concept covered more territory. There were twenty-five different kinds of articles within the rubric of crime in 2000 and they concentrated on street crime, drug policy, and other domestic issues, versus forty-three different kinds of articles in 2004, which included white-collar crime, street crime, terrorism, and crimes by people in other places (including war crime and identity theft). Thus framing of "crime" was broader in 2004 even when accounting for terrorism, suggesting an overall expansion in the concept within the political media.

The dramatic difference of geographic focus was most evident in the many more articles about crimes in countries other than the United States. This difference in focus puts into relief the real reconceptualization in American media thinking about crime. In 2004, there were twenty-nine more articles in the sample with a geopolitical theme, and, as noted, these were not only about terrorism, but also about Serbs, war crimes, Cambodian crime, and other foreign law-enforcement concerns. Perhaps not surprisingly enough, the hegemony of the Swift Boat controversy is also evident. Numerous articles discussed to what extent John Kerry had earned his service medals or had called American soldiers in Vietnam guilty of war crimes. Others covered the long-running controversy around whether the Swift Boat ads were accurate, who was responsible for them, and who funded them. The evidence suggests that the Bush campaign was extremely successful in exploiting the controversy, because it effectively masked the President's own sketchy Vietnam record.

On the domestic agenda, in the sampled articles street crime played almost no role in the campaign of 2004. Police actions in relation to crime and patrolling were not discussed in the sampled articles. There were only two articles about the death penalty in 2004 (compared to eight in 2000) and four on gun control. In the 2004 sample there were four articles about drugs, but two of them involved new accusations about George Bush's alleged past drug use. Eight out of the seventeen articles discussed domestic issues in 2004 and five of those were about convention or campaign security, harkening back to the issue of terrorism. The issue of campaign security came up in all the categories of search. The cost to local communities, the new priorities of law enforcement, and new tactics toward protesters emerged as more salient issues in 2004 than in 2000.

The change in vantage point becomes even clearer when articles that deal with law enforcement are considered. In the 2004 sample there were thirty more articles than in 2000 that addressed law enforcement. Furthermore, in the 2000 campaign sample no articles concerned law enforcement in other countries or the context of American police responding to geopolitical issues. In 2004, eighteen out of thirty-five articles were global in context, considering issues such as international drug trade, weak states, immigration, or George Bush's military service. Eight out of those eighteen articles dealt directly with terrorism and law enforcement in other countries, for example, Saudi Arabia. Finally, in 2004 seven out of seventeen articles about law enforcement in the United States were concerned with the costs, logistics, or politics of guarding campaign stops of the party conventions. As in the articles about crime, the security of campaigns was of major interest, and could be easily connected to the broader topic of increased costs for security generally in the age of terrorist threat.

If the 2004 vision of crime and law enforcement was expanding beyond the scope of the 2000 campaign, articles that dealt with policing in 2004 were narrower in focus. Municipal-policing-of-street-crime issues were almost absent, and the articles placed heavy emphasis on police as "first responders" in protecting the country from terrorists. Thus, the police forces in this country were recast as (or at least had added to their symbolic repertoire the role of) a national, military-like operation (quite unlike the militarization of local police described by William Allison in chapter 1 of this volume). Although the samples from both campaigns saw a relatively similar number of articles about the police (thirty-three in 2000; thirty-seven in 2004), the tenor of the articles was dramatically different. In both instances the largest number of articles about the police covered cost and organization of campaign security, but the change brought by the mandate to police terrorism, and a lack of significant criticism of policing, are evident in the articles from 2004.

Racial profiling (four articles) and police brutality (five articles) received some coverage in 2000. Coming quickly after the widely covered cases of Amadou Diallo and Abner Louima in New York City, the articles critical of policing did make an impact in 2000.[6] When combined, articles about profiling and brutality made up the largest category in stories about the police, with campaign security coming in second. When these categories are looked at separately, the largest category of articles about the police was that about campaign security, followed by police brutality and racial profiling.

In marked contrast, the sample for the 2004 campaign had no articles about police brutality, racial profiling, or corruption, despite the fact that the campaign took place after years of the Los Angeles Rampart Scandal, in which hundreds of convictions were called into question as a result of accusations of false testimony and evidence tampering by the Los Angeles Police Department. One article detailed how crime and police were not getting much attention, three articles addressed funding for police forces (and whether President Bush had adequately done so), and three other articles discussed a potential police strike in Boston during the Democratic convention. After that, the vast majority of articles dealt with campaign security (fifteen out of thirty-seven articles), and all together twenty-six out of thirty-seven articles involving the police had some connection to terrorism. There was only one article that dealt with local police power and the PATRIOT Act. There were no articles manifestly critical of police actions.

During the 2000 campaign, the media representations of crime revolved around domestic policy and street crime.[7] Discussions of police forces typically consisted of controversies over racial profiling and community policing. Although both Vice-President Al Gore and Governor George Bush were expected to have a position on racial profiling and capital punishment, it was also understood that these were largely symbolic "bully pulpit" positions over which, as candidates for federal office, they would have little jurisdiction. Nevertheless candidates' positions on crime and policing continued to be a salient campaign topic. Not surprisingly, in 2004 the discussions of crime concentrated on terrorism, and highlighted the work of the police as the "first responders" and the home-line defense in protection of the nation from geopolitical events. Stories about border protection (often thought of as racially coded policing itself), for example, were more common than stories about racial profiling.

In contrast, I found that the domestic agenda loomed large in 2000, with media coverage and party platforms about how to spend the surplus and harness the economic boom of the late 1990s revolving around a smorgasbord of social issues including Medicare, childcare, environmental protection, and ergonomic standards for workers. Furthermore, community policing continued to be widely discussed after President Clinton's 1996 promise to fund 100,000 more cops dedicated to community policing work.[8] Many debates also raged over whether "zero-tolerance policing," commonly held to be arrest-driven policing with problematic civil liberties consequences, was responsible for the drop in crime rate. In 2000, the then staple criminological issues of street crime, babies born addicted to drugs, and effective policing played a prominent role in presidential campaign dialogue. Both campaigns discussed these issues in their platforms and they appeared in media coverage of the campaigns.

By contrast, classic policing and criminal justice issues—the death penalty, drug policy, and racial profiling—were all but absent in the media coverage studied from 2004. Only a cursory discussion of gun control emerged when the 1994 assault weapons ban came up for renewal near election day and even that issue was subsumed under the rubric of terrorism when Democratic nominee John Kerry couched it as an issue about "keeping guns out of the hands of terrorists." This rhetoric stood in marked contrast to Al Gore and other Democrats' concentration on police safety and street crime in 2000. Not only were traditional issues of crime eclipsed in the 2004 campaign, but also policing was reconceptualized as the first line of defense against terrorists, rather than as an essential defense of local order.

The Reframing of Crime in Academia

Furthermore, there is some evidence to suggest that the war on terror is not just changing the discussion of crime and policing, but changing the very field of criminology. In a 2003 edition of *Law Enforcement News* (Rosen 2003: 1), Marie Simonett Rosen called terrorism "the monster that ate criminology." Criminologists have historically centered their work upon street crime while some critical scholars in the field often concentrated on the consequences of white-collar crime. But now criminology textbooks about terrorism are flooding the market, as are classes on terrorism and geopolitical conflict within criminology departments. Police studies curricula are going through a similar transformation, with classes on intelligence gathering and crisis management emerging throughout the country.[9] And the momentum of this direction in criminology is unlikely to change, especially as noted criminologists are getting millions of dollars in grants from the federal government to study terrorism.[10] Thus the fast moving changes in media coverage of crime and policing are mirrored in college curricula.

Conclusions and Questions

What I found is a significant shift in the media and campaign rhetoric both about what crime is and what kinds of crime people ought to fear. Moreover, I discovered a shift had taken place in the cultural representation of who police are, what their roles are, and what they should be, despite the relatively scant debate over whether this new "nation-state" perspective on policing is a good idea. Very little about this new frame of policing and fear of crime had been problematized by the public, press, or candidates. Furthermore, in the random sample there were more articles about the presidential campaign itself and its consequences and strategies than about the substantive issues at hand. This was true in both the 2000 and 2004 races. Although the shift in frame was evidenced everywhere, there was much less reflection by either media outlets or candidates on what this shift might mean for local police forces.

Analysis of the dramaturgical presentation and framing of political narratives, through media and other outlets, can help us understand the importance of the shift in discussion between 2000 and 2004. The combination of lower street crime rates with the emergence of a new and nebulous enemy has pushed the once domestically focused national political discussion of crime into a geopolitical frame. This chapter demonstrates the consequences that may flow from this change in frame—beginning with the directions we can glean from the most recent campaign, in which nearly all discussion of police and crime fell under this rubric of terrorism and Homeland Security.

Thus, it is clear through an analysis of how frames change, the historical situating of the police, and the changes in the characteristics of that situating, that the role of policing, crime, and fear of crime has shifted between the presidential campaigns of 2000 and 2004. The fact that the war on terror has impacted the presidential campaign is no surprise, but the idea that fear of street crime, a constant refrain in presidential campaigns since at least the mid-1960s and Nixon's southern strategy, has been exchanged for thinking of the police as "first responders" in the war on terror is an important shift in political imagination that needs to be further investigated.

There are several consequences that may arise out of this new vision. First, if police actually are responding to the orders of the Department of Homeland Security in the everyday execution of their jobs, then the historic localism of American police forces may be exchanged for a more nationalistic vision. This may, in turn, create police forces that have less capacity to respond to community concerns and less responsibility for their actions. Second, this discourse of police as defenders against terrorism not only alleviates responsibility of the police toward the community, but also creates a problem within communities; citizens will have no clear source of authority to whom they should go, and who would be expected to respond to their concerns, particularly when it comes to abuse and brutality. Finally, if local communities have police forces that are not distinguished from a force protecting the nation state, then, in the current political climate, a critical stance toward policing, and local accountability for abuses of police power, become far more difficult to maintain.

Notes

1. See David Garland, *Mass Imprisonment in the United States: Social Causes and Consequences* (London: Sage Publications, 2001) for an examination of how the public gains its impressions of crime threat and rate through media coverage of crime, not through personal experience, and how this can lead to an exaggerated sense of threat.

2. The economic pressures on local police forces to react to "yellow alerts" and terrorist threats combined with the fiscal crunch of the recent recession have led to a new set of financial concerns for local police departments, particularly in smaller towns that don't have reliable or prosperous tax bases. According to

Fleury-Steiner and Wiles there is the small but growing trend of corporate-sponsored police cars. The program offers police departments well-equipped cars for $1, decorated with the logo of the corporate sponsor. Police departments turn to the savings of such offers in the sight of budget crunches, but this kind of privatization of policing may lead, according to Fleury-Steiner and Wiles, to increased bias (what if they are asked to break up a demonstration outside of McDonalds in a McDonalds car?), erosion of public authority, and loss of legitimacy. Fleury-Stiener, Benjamin and Kristian Wiles, "The Use of Commercial Advertisements on Public Police Cars in the United States, Post 9/11," *Policing and Society*, 13(4) (2003), 441–450.

3. George Wallace famously couched his "states rights" rhetoric in racially motivated pro-segregationist positions. Besides attempting to block the integration of Alabama schools, Wallace ran on a pro-segregationist position throughout his political career, famously declaring, in his inauguration speech "segregation today, segregation tomorrow, segregation forever." See Dan T. Carter, *The Politics of Rage: George Wallace, The Origins of New Conservatism and the Transformation of American Politics* (Baton Rouge, LA: Louisiana State University Press, 2000).

4. See McGoldrick, Stacy K. "Not at Liberty to See: Police, Party Politics and Violence in New Orleans, 1852–1880," *Sociology*, Graduate Faculty, New York: New School University, 2003; McGoldrick, Stacy K. "Confederate Police and a New Racial Order: The New Orleans Riot of 1866," in Rodney D. Coates, ed., *Race and Ethnicity: Across Time, Space, and Discipline* (Boston: Brill Academic Press, 2004); Miller, Wilbur R. *Cops and Bobbies: Police Authority in New York and London, 1830–1870* (Columbus, OH: Ohio State University Press); Rousey, Dennis C. *Policing the Southern City: New Orleans 1805–1889* (Baton Rouge, LA: Louisiana State University Press, 1996); Ryan, Mary P. *Democracy and Public Life in the American City During the Nineteenth Century* (Berkeley, CA: University of California Press).

5. See Miller, *Cops and Bobbies*, p.17 for an analysis of this process in New York. I think his argument holds for most early American police forces.

6. Amadou Diallo was shot in front of his building by New York police officers who claim they saw a gun. Abner Louima was sexually assaulted in a police precinct bathroom. Both cases were widely covered in New York and through the country.

7. Street crime, as commonly seen in criminology and sociology textbooks, includes juvenile delinquency, mugging, robbery, car theft, and so on, most of what we think of as crime when watching cops shows and movies.

8. Clinton wanted the police officers to engage in "community policing" specifically, demonstrating the popularity of the idea in 1996. See: *Times*, New York, 1996. "Excerpts From Platform Adopted at Democratic Convention." *New York Times*, August 28.

9. For example, Thomson Wadsworth, a well-known publisher of criminology textbooks, offers eleven different textbooks about terrorism, all of them first published after 2001. Numerous universities are also currently offering classes on terrorism within their criminology curriculum.

10. The University of Maryland recently was awarded a $12 million grant to open the Center of Excellence for Behavioral and Social Research on Terrorism and Counter-Terrorism headed by Gary Lafree at (www.umd.edu/umnews.new-center.html accessed on June 22, 2005).

Bibliography

Beckett, Katherine and Theodore Sasson, 2004, *The Politics of Injustice: Crime and Punishment in America*. Thousand Oaks, CA: Sage Publications.

Carter, Dan T., 2000, The Politics of Rage: George Wallace, The Origins of New Conservatism and the Transformation of American Politics. Baton Rouge, LA: Louisiana State University Press.

Chambliss, William J., 2001, *Power, Politics and Crime*. Boulder, CO: Westview Press.

Fleury-Stiener, Benjamin and Kristian Wiles, "The Use of Commercial Advertisements on Public Police Cars in the United States, Post 9/11," *Policing and Society*, 13(4) (2003), 441–450.

Fogelson, Robert M., 1977, *Big City Police*. Cambridge, MA: Harvard University Press.

Gamson, W.A., D. Croteau, W. Hoynes, and T. Sasson, 1992, "Media Images and the Social Construction of Reality," *Annual Review of Sociology*, 18: 373–393.

Garland, David, 2001, *Mass Imprisonment in the United States: Social Causes and Consequences*. London: Sage Publications.

Johnson-Cartee, Karen S., 2004, *News Narratives and News Framing: Constructing Political Reality*. New York: Rowman & Littlefield.

McGoldrick, Stacy K., 2003, "Not at Liberty to See: Police, Party Politics and Violence in New Orleans, 1852–1880," *Sociology*, Graduate Faculty, New York: New School University.

McGoldrick, Stacy K., 2004, "Confederate Police and a New Racial Order: The New Orleans Riot of 1866," in Rodney D. Coates, ed., *Race and Ethnicity: Across Time, Space, and Discipline*. Boston: Brill Academic Press.

Miller, Wilbur R., 1999, *Cops and Bobbies: Police Authority in New York and London, 1830–1870*. Columbia, OH: Ohio State University Press.

Nelson, T.E., R.A. Clawson, and Z.M. Wildavsky, 1997, "Media Framing of Civil Liberties Conflicts and its Effect on Tolerance," *American Political Science Review*, 91: 567–583.

Rosen, Marie Simonett, 2003, *Law Enforcement News*. New York: John Jay College of Criminal Justice.

Rousey, Dennis C., 1996, *Policing the Southern City: New Orleans 1805–1889*. Baton Rouge, LA: Louisiana State University Press.

Ryan, Mary P., 1997, *Democracy and Public Life in the American City During the Nineteenth Century*. Berkeley, CA: University of California Press.

Wykoff, Mary Ann, 1988, "The Benefits to Community Policing: Evidence and Conjecture," in Jack R. Greene and Stephen D. Mastrofske, eds., *Community Policing: Rhetoric and Reality*. New York: Praeger.

Newspapers Sampled

The Atlanta Journal Constitution
The Australian
The Baltimore Sun
The Boston Globe
The Boston Herald
Buffalo News
Chicago Sun Times
Christian Science Monitor
Columbus Dispatch
Courier Mail, Queensland Australia
The Daily News, New York
The Denver Post
Denver Rocky Mountain News
Financial Times, London
The Gazette, Montreal
The Guardian, London
The Hartford Courant
The Houston Chronicle
The Independent, London
The Irish Times, Dublin
Jerusalem Post
Los Angeles Times
The Milwaukee Journal Sentinel
Newsday, New York
The New York Times
Omaha World Herald
The Oregonian
The Ottawa Citizen
Pittsburgh Post-Gazette
The Plain Dealer, Cleveland
Sacramento Bee
San Antonio Express- News
The San Diego Union-Tribune
The San Francisco Chronicle
The Seattle Times
The St. Louis Post-Dispatch
The St. Petersburg Times
The Star Tribune, Minneapolis
The Straits Times, Singapore
Sunday Telegraph, London
Sunday Times, London

Tampa Tribune
Times-Picayune, New Orleans
Toronto Star
USA Today
The Wall Street Journal
The Washington Post
The Weekend Australian

8

Policing after September 11: Federal–Local Collaboration and the Implications for Police–Community Relations

Andrea McArdle

Increasingly since the events of September 11, local police forces have been recruited to participate in federal initiatives to combat international terrorism. Shortly after September 11, the passage of the USA PATRIOT Act (the acronym for Uniting and Strengthening America by Providing Appropriate Tools Required to Intercept and Obstruct Terrorism Act), promoted one form of federal–local cooperation by adopting measures to coordinate inter-agency responses to suspected terrorist initiatives.[1] Since that time, the federal government has advanced a variety of measures to extend and reinforce the role of local police forces in antiterrorist policing. The executive branch of the federal government has advocated a specific role for local law enforcement in apprehending unauthorized immigrants. The contours of such a plan were reportedly outlined in a draft Department of Justice opinion in April 2002 that the department never released[2] but that a federal appeals court, affirming a lower federal court ruling, recently ordered should be disclosed to the public under the Freedom of Information Act.[3]

An amendment to the Department of Homeland Security Authorization Act for Fiscal Year 2006, which passed in the House of Representatives on May 18, 2005, the recently reintroduced Clear Law Enforcement for Criminal Alien Removal Act, and the Homeland Security Enhancement Act, would go even farther in federalizing the role of local police enforcement of immigration laws. These legislative proposals have prompted expressions of concern and even vocal opposition among some local police agencies. The recently adopted REAL ID Act, which, among other things, sets federal standards for states' issuance of drivers' licenses to immigrants,[4] enlists state regulatory mechanisms in the campaign to restrict the activities and income-producing capabilities of persons who are for any reason without status.

New York City has been a focal point for much of this drive to enlist local law-enforcement agencies into a collaboration with federal authorities in the war on terror. Currently, the NYPD works with the FBI in the Joint Terrorist Task Force, deploys detectives in locations outside the United States, and participates in networks of information such as the State Department's database of 50 million overseas requests for U.S. visas.[5] Moreover, under the stewardship of Commissioner Raymond Kelly, a former Commissioner of the U.S. Customs Service and later Under Secretary for Enforcement at the U.S. Treasury Department, the NYPD has imported career federal officers into the force at the deputy commissioner level to serve in key posts in New York City's post–September 11 antiterrorist initiatives. Early in 2002, David Cohen, former Deputy Director of Operations for the CIA and a thirty-five-year veteran of the CIA, was named the NYPD's Deputy Commissioner of Intelligence.[6] In June 2003, Michael Sheehan, formerly a Lieutenant U.S. Army Colonel, a Deputy Assistant Secretary of State, and Department of State Ambassador at Large for Counter Terrorism, joined the NYPD as Deputy Commissioner of Counter Terrorism.[7]

It is in the context of its antiterrorism policing role that the NYPD, certainly at the managerial level, seems to have altered its traditional orientation as an agency responsive to locally based and determined priorities, with its new focus, under the rubric of national security, on surveillance of Islamic institutions and Arab, Muslim, and South Asian immigrants. Most notably, in September 2002 Deputy Commissioner Cohen asserted in a court proceeding that court-imposed guidelines requiring that the NYPD show suspected criminal activity before it could launch a political investigation, and limiting the NYPD's ability to gather, retain, and share information, were "no longer consistent with the public interest" and "counterproductive"[8] to policing the post–September 11 city. Instead, he contended, the NYPD now required considerable leeway in developing intelligence to combat the threat posed by Al Qaeda and "extremist Muslim fundamentalism."[9] In effect, Cohen was describing the way in which the NYPD was reassessing enforcement functions, suggesting a shift from a mainly reactive to an investigative orientation to police work.

At the same time that the City's principal law-enforcement agency has embraced an antiterrorist operations framework, one that is national, even international, in scope, other New York City public institutions have asserted some localist independence, by supporting initiatives that would limit local participation in federal initiatives. In September 2003 New York City Mayor Michael Bloomberg issued an amended executive order that, in a variation of a "don't ask/don't tell" policy, purported to limit inquiries, and ultimately, disclosures, by city agencies concerning confidential information, including individuals' immigration status.[10] In February 2004, the New York City Council, with the support of a broad coalition of grassroots organizations, adopted a Bill of Rights Defense resolution calling for transparency in the federal enforcement of the USA PATRIOT Act and rejecting the use of racial, ethnic, or religious profiling, and secret detentions or other immigrant enforcement actions infringing on civil liberties. In June 2004, the City Council adopted an ordinance barring the NYPD from using racial profiling as a determinative factor in any law enforcement actions.[11]

The exceedingly complex and contradictory legal landscape in New York City with respect to antiterrorist enforcement efforts has been replicated on a national scale in a kind of thrust and parry between a long-entrenched tradition of police localism and the current urgency around national security initiatives. The contradictory impulses to cooperate with federal enforcement policies and to resist federal efforts to preempt local enforcement priorities have crystallized in the continuing national debate around immigration, and its implications both for national security and employment opportunities for U.S. nationals in a job-sluggish economy.[12] Federal agencies want to incorporate phalanxes of state and local police forces into the enforcement of civil, in addition to criminal, immigration laws, to augment the limited number of federal immigration law agents available to enforce these laws,[13] on the theory that these more localized police forces might uncover terrorists living among local immigrant communities.

Many state and local police agencies have not embraced this civil enforcement function, in part because of the increased personnel costs entailed in expanding their scope of operations, and their general unfamiliarity with civil immigration law. Moreover, taking on such a role would have a "chilling effect" on immigrants' reporting crime and cooperating in police investigations, risking a further breakdown of trust between local police forces and immigrant communities.[14] Immigrant advocates point out that in New York City the chilling effect includes the ubiquitous presence of NYPD officers in the Jackson Heights, Queens, subway station—an area heavily populated by immigrants but not known for its incidence of crime—and the "random" traffic stops and ticketing of predominantly immigrant taxi drivers by Port Authority officers at New York City's bridges and tunnels.[15] These advocates discern the chill as well in the operation of an Immigration and Customs Enforcement "office" at Rikers Island, New York City's principal detention facility, where information concerning detainees' immigration status and country of origin is continuously accessible.[16]

This chapter will examine the asserted justifications for an expanded role for local law-enforcement agencies in policing an "antiterrorist" state, a role that is in tension with a localist tradition of policing (which, at its best, is attentive to community needs and priorities and fosters community participation in problem-solving policing).[17] It will also assess the implications for the increasingly threatened networks of police-community communication and cooperation that have long existed, even if tenuously, at the local level. Focusing attention on New York City, the chapter considers the NYPD's articulation of its role in counterterrorist policing as a reflection of contradictions in government discourse concerning the appropriate contours of local law-enforcement authority. It addresses the linkage of local law enforcement, intelligence gathering, and racial profiling after September 11, and points to continuities between post–September 11 urban policing and the racially inflected public-order and anticrime policing of the 1990s. It concludes with a brief consideration of community-level opposition to federal-local governmental assaults on civil liberties and the targeting of immigrants: a localism rooted in engaged civic participation and exchange among multiple constituencies, and made possible by the smaller scale and accessibility of local government institutions.

Drafting Local Police Forces into the National Security Network

If the hallmark of John Ashcroft's tenure as Attorney General was the aggressive implementation of the USA PATRIOT Act, a critical component of the strategy was his promoting the view of the immigration law violator as proxy for international terrorist. Concluding that undocumented immigrants are a major threat to national security, federal law-enforcement agencies, especially the Departments of Justice and Homeland Security, have considered it critical to extend the reach of their enforcement capabilities to these immigration law violators. John Ashcroft's interpretation that local governments have "inherent" authority to enforce civil immigration laws, expressed in a number of public contexts, including an October 2002 address to the International Association of Police Chiefs, was one such effort. This interpretation significantly expands local enforcement authority over immigration law, which resides principally in the Illegal Immigration Reform and Immigrant Responsibility Act of 1996. That statute empowers state and local law-enforcement agencies to enter into agreements with the Attorney General to train and deputize local officers as immigration agents,[18] and authorizes the Attorney General to enlist local forces in an immigration emergency.[19] In addition, a 1996 opinion of the Clinton-era Department of Justice had recognized state and local enforcement authority over violations of the criminal provisions of the immigration laws.[20] By statute, Congress has empowered state and local law-enforcement agents to arrest violators of two specific provisions of the criminal immigration law, section 274 of the Immigration and Nationality Act, banning the smuggling of unauthorized immigrants, and section 276 of the Act, criminalizing the illegal reentry of previously deported persons.[21]

As support for his view that local enforcement authority exists independently of such statutory authority, and extends to *civil* immigration law (typically committed to enforcement by federal immigration agents), as distinguished from the provisions of immigration law that are defined as crimes, Ashcroft apparently relied on an unpublished April 2002 draft opinion from the Justice Department's Office of Legal Counsel. Whether or not, as one conservative commentator had reported, the opinion remained under wraps because the Bush administration was concerned about how it would be perceived by Latino voters,[22] the Department of Justice's continuing refusal to disclose it while invoking it in various public settings prompted immigration advocacy groups to force production of the memorandum through the previously mentioned Freedom of Information suit.[23] (In October 2004, a federal district court ordered the Justice Department to produce a redacted version of the April 2002 draft memorandum.[24] The Department appealed,[25] and on May 31, 2005, the Second Circuit affirmed the district court, ordering disclosure.[26])

As a practical matter, the Departments of Justice and Homeland Security have acted on the Ashcroft view by placing information concerning hundreds of thousands of alleged *civil* immigration law violators in the National Criminal Information Center (NCIC) database, which is widely used by a host of law-enforcement agencies to assist in apprehending suspected *criminal* law violators. Typically, a local police officer consults this database after a traffic stop prompts further inquiry on a possible criminal record. Based on its plain language as well as case law interpretations, the federal statute governing the NCIC database limits the information within its purview to records relating to criminal law violations and to specifically delineated categories of civil records, such as orders of protection against stalkers, and deportation orders against persons convicted of a felony.[27] With the addition of data concerning violation of civil immigration laws (e.g., presence in the United States with a removal order), federal authorities have a "captive" audience of local law-enforcement officers who can hardly "avert their eyes" from seemingly relevant information appearing in an official data source. As a result, local law officers are arresting and reporting thousands of persons on alleged immigration law offenses that would otherwise have gone unnoticed and unenforced because it was seemingly beyond their jurisdiction to enforce the provisions of criminal law.[28] Immigrant advocates including National Council of La Raza, the New York Immigration Coalition, and the American-Arab Anti-Discrimination Committee have challenged this use of the NCIC database in a class action lawsuit filed in December 2003.[29]

Significantly, not only the executive branch seeks to incorporate local police forces into immigration law enforcement. As immigration law scholar Michael Wishnie has documented, increasingly Congress has sought to devolve its immigration policy-making authority, long under-stood to be exclusively federal in nature, to state and local entities.[30] For example, an amendment proposed by Representative Charles Norwood (R.-Ga.), and included in fiscal legislation passed by the House of Representatives on May 18, 2005, would "clarify" that state and local police agencies have the authority to enforce civil immigration law, and would facilitate local enforcement by affording training.[31] This proposal carries forward key provisions of the proposed Clear Law Enforcement for Criminal Alien Removal Act of 2003 (also sponsored by Norwood), which was recently reintroduced into the House of Representatives. In its current form, the CLEAR Act would all but coerce localities into enforcing civil immigration laws by making states and localities that do not have in effect a policy or practice of assisting enforcement of immigration laws, or that prohibit cooperation with federal immigration authorities, ineligible for federal funding related to enforcement. To "sweeten" the package, the CLEAR Act would authorize federal equipment grant assistance for cooperating localities, and provide immunity from liability for law-enforcement personnel and agencies that enforce immigration laws.[32]

Another legislative proposal, a failed amendment to the Homeland Security Appropriations Act of 2005, sponsored by Congressman Tom Tancredo, Republican from Colorado, would have punished localities that had adopted or enforced a "sanctuary policy"—a policy barring local employees and police officers from inquiring into or reporting a person's unlawful immigration status—by denying them Homeland Security fund-ing.[33] A favored tactic of the so-called immigration reform movement—the campaign of those who support strict enforcement of immigration laws—these efforts to punish sanctuary cities point to provisions of two federal statutes adopted in 1996 that bar localities from prohibiting their employees' reporting an immigrant's unlawful status to federal authorities.[34]

These statutes, in turn, were a response to nondisclosure policies adopted in the 1980s to encourage undocumented immigrants who were crime victims or witnesses, or otherwise in need of city services, to come forward to local police for help.[35] New York City's own sanctuary provision, originally adopted as an Executive Order in 1989, specifically prohibited its employees from voluntarily disclosing information to federal immigration authorities. A 1999 ruling of the Second Circuit Court of Appeals rejected the City's arguments that the 1996 federal statutes interfered with its sovereignty under the Tenth Amendment by limiting the City's right to elect not to participate in federal regulatory programs, and by purporting to dictate the use of information acquired by local employees in the course of their official duties. The court held (1) that the challenged federal statutes were valid enactments barring states from requiring "passive resistance" to specific federal programs,[36] and (2) that the Executive Order effectively singled out a specific federal policy and agency, and a specific category of information with respect to which City employees were forbidden to cooperate, while permitting City employees to divulge the information to the "rest of the world." Because the City's no-voluntary-cooperation policy did not protect this confidential information in all circumstances, and did limit the effectiveness of a federal policy, the City's Tenth Amendment defense was unavailing. The Order conflicted with the 1996 law and thus was preempted by it under the terms of the Supremacy Clause (Article VI, Clause 2, of the U.S. Constitution) declaring the priority of federal law in the event of a conflict with state law.[37] (The Court emphasized, however, the narrow scope of its ruling and thus did not consider whether, if New York City were to adopt a more general confidentiality provision that was not limited to communications with federal immigration authorities, such a law would pass muster.[38]) If there was any remaining doubt about the status of the Executive Order, in January 2003 New York City received notification from the "reform" organization Friends of Immigration Law Enforcement (as did Houston and Los Angeles during that same year) that its sanctuary policy, still on the books, was in violation of federal law and subject to legal action.[39]

Touted as the "most comprehensive privacy policy in the history of New York City,"[40] the Executive Order currently in effect, signed into law September 2003, limits disclosures of confidential information (defined broadly to include receipt of public assistance, sexual orientation, status as a victim of domestic violence or sexual assault, status as a witness to a crime, as well as immigration status), to enumerated circumstances. These include where the disclosure is "required by law" or has been authorized in writing by the person to whom it relates, or, in the case of confidential information relating to immigration status, where the information concerns suspected "illegal activity" (defined as unlawful activity, including infractions and minor violations of law, not necessarily activity that would result in a criminal conviction) other than undocumented immigration status, or is needed to further an investigation of "potential terrorist activity."[41] In separate sections, the Order prohibits City personnel other than law enforcement officers from asking about a person's immigrant status unless required by law to do so or to ascertain whether the person qualifies for a City service.[42] The Order bars law enforcement officers from asking about a person's immigration status "unless investigating illegal activity other than mere status as an alien," declares the "policy of the Police Department" not to ask about the immigration status of crime victims, witnesses, or persons who ask for police assistance, and provides that police officers "shall continue to cooperate with federal authorities in investigating and apprehending aliens suspected of criminal activity."[43]

In adopting a confidentiality policy broader than the coverage of the Executive Order invalidated by the Second Circuit in 1999, Executive Order 41 does not by its terms fall within the narrow ban of that court's ruling. But even assuming that the Order would not still be open to a challenge that it conflicted with federal law, the Order is hardly problem-free for the immigrant groups that are purportedly the Order's chief beneficiaries. Although the official discourse around Executive Order 41 highlights how the Order is oriented toward confidentiality, by limiting even the occasion of inquiry, the Order does not ban all disclosure of information to federal authorities. Nor is its limitation on inquiry airtight: police may inquire with respect to any illegal activity, which has a potentially broad scope, and only the "policy" of the police department constrains an officer's decision whether or not to inquire of a crime victim or witness. Recent testimony by an assistant deputy NYPD commissioner before a New York City Council Immigration Committee hearing confirmed that NYPD officers regularly advise federal immigration officials when they arrest a noncitizen, and also transmit information on the arrestee's country of origin.[44] In all these respects, the aggressive tactics of Friends of Immigration Law Enforcement in targeting New York City may well have accomplished their purpose.

An assumption behind a sanctuary provision is that law-enforcement officers, perhaps even more than city personnel who dispense benefits, do not want discovery of an immigrant's unlawful status to interfere with the person's willingness to seek police assistance or to cooperate with police in a crime investigation.[45] In fact, the NYPD has gone on record as opposing local law enforcement of federal immigration laws.[46] Yet in the case of New York City, as noted, the dynamics of post–September 11 policing (and the reported funding and turf battles with federal agencies),[47] place the upper echelons of the NYPD, and apparently the rank-and-file as well, in a more complicated, if wary, relation with federal authorities. Much as the provisions of the new Executive Order are porous, and thus unevenly protective of the City's immigrant communities, the localist orientation in policing has been moderated, and compromised, by the requirements of national security policy and interagency cooperation.

Police and Immigrant Community Relations: The Situation in New York City

From the perspective of localities that want to include their immigrant communities within the protective ambit of civic life and services, these federal executive and legislative initiatives, aided by anti-immigrant advocacy organizations, intend to ferret out anyone who may be without lawful immigration status, for any reason. And as a result they threaten to strain the increasingly frayed relations between immigrant groups and local police forces. In New York City, for example, tensions between police and immigrant communities long predated September 11, where an aggressive style of law enforcement—referred to as "zero tolerance"—spawned a grassroots antibrutality movement that came to shape public discourse around policing in New York.[48]

During the eight years of Rudolph Giuliani's mayoral administration, the city's crime rate declined steadily, fueling claims by the Mayor's Office and the NYPD—claims that were never substantiated—that the city's aggressive enforcement strategy had made possible the downward trajectory in crime.[49] The architects of that strategy drew on James Wilson and George Kelling's frequently invoked "broken windows" paradigm, which asserts a link between disorder—particularly in the aesthetic or physical sense—and crime. But while invoking it, the Giuliani administration detached the broken windows theory from its original emphasis—responding to physical disorder using alternatives to traditional law-enforcement methods—and instead vigorously enforced low-level criminal codes that dislodged immigrant street vendors and homeless people from locations catering to tourists and shoppers.[50] At the same time, the NYPD pursued a high-visibility crime-fighting program in the city's poorer areas, inhabited mainly by persons of color.[51] Throughout the latter 1990s, this aggressive style of policing was also associated with a series of heavily publicized incidents in which young men of color, and frequently immigrants, lost their lives or were brutally assaulted in encounters with NYPD officers. The names of Abner Louima, battered and sodomized with a wooden stick in a precinct house, and Amadou Diallo, struck and killed in a burst of forty-one bullets fired by officers of the Street Crime Unit as he stood near the vestibule of his apartment building, quickly come to mind. New York City's communities of color continually called attention to these incidents, and to the evidence that racial indicators and stereotypes drove the NYPD's aggressive policing, and called for vigorous prosecution of the police officers involved.[52]

By the late 1990s, partly as a result of this public advocacy, the NYPD's practices had become the object of five government investigations and the basis for a federal lawsuit. These inquiries focused attention on the disproportionate effects of the city's law-enforcement campaign on poor people of color, including many immigrants. A report by New York State's Attorney General collecting extensive data on the Street Crime Unit's stop-and-frisk campaign documented that blacks in New York City were stopped at a rate that was six times more often, and Latinos four times more often, than whites were stopped. In June 2000, the U.S. Commission on Civil Rights cited NYPD data that "strongly suggest[ed]" that the NYPD used racial profiling in stop-and-frisks and other street encounters.[53]

By some accounts New York City's "broken windows/zero-tolerance" approach to reducing disorder and the incidence of crime was a spectacular success, ready for export to localities both within and beyond the United States. For the city's more marginalized communities, local policing was defined during the Giuliani years more ominously by the struggles over aggressive public-order and anticrime initiatives and racial profiling. Despite some surface similarities between New York City's policing strategies and community-policing approaches, the NYPD during the Giuliani years did not embrace the core approach of community policing, based on community-police partnerships and deployment of neighborhood beat officers who work within communities; instead, the NYPD vested problem-solving responsibility in the precinct commander and intensified its use of traditional law-enforcement methods.[54]

However, during the closing months of the Giuliani administration, the city's response to the September 11 attack on the World Trade Center towers, which depended so heavily on the efforts of uniformed police and firefighters, led to a moratorium of sorts between the NYPD and the city's communities of color. It fell to newly elected Mayor Michael Bloomberg and his Police Commissioner Raymond Kelly to address the simmering tensions between the NYPD and black and Latino communities, as well as the post–September 11 concerns that persons of Middle Eastern and South Asian origin and members of other Islamic groups would become a new focus of profiling.

In this context, it seems significant that, only two months into the Bloomberg administration, the NYPD issued an operations order prohibiting the use of racial profiling, which it defined as "the use of race, color, ethnicity or national origin as the determinative factor for instituting police action." The order required all enforcement actions, including arrests, stops, and questioning, to conform to Constitutional standards; thus, officers must "articulate the factors" that led them to take an enforcement action.[55] At the same time, any analysis of the import of these strictures and their impact on local communities must take into account the globalized context of policing that, after September 11, has supplanted the traditionally more fractionated efforts of local, national, and international law-enforcement agencies.

And it is in this globalized post–September 11 context that the NYPD has asserted that longstanding limitations on domestic police investigation methods are inadequate. Instead, it has sought to justify using the more diffuse and invasive practices customarily employed in intelligence work, including an undisguised form of racial profiling in immigrant communities. Evaluating the argument that the events of September 11 have precipitated a radical disjunction between past and current conditions of policing requires a close examination of New York City's pre–September 11 policing landscape.

The NYPD and Civil Liberties, Pre–September 11:
The *Handschu* Case

In New York City, efforts to maintain a "wall of separation" between criminal law enforcement and intelligence gathering had produced an important legal and political precedent limiting the reach of state power over individual civil liberties. In an earlier dispensation, before the "broken windows" theory had entered the criminal justice canon or "zero tolerance" had become the catchphrase for aggressive law enforcement, embattled but energized communities in New York City—including members of the Black Panther party, antiwar protestors, and gay rights activists—were embroiled with the NYPD in a contentious struggle over policing tactics. This earlier NYPD campaign was aimed not at curbing street crime or maintaining public order but at monitoring political dissent.[56] Yet the violations of civil liberties brought to light in that controversy resonate with more recent clashes between the NYPD and local immigrant communities, pre- and post–September 11, over the reach of police authority.

In the 1960s and earlier, the Public Security Section of the department's Intelligence Division, referred to locally as the Red Squad, used infiltration, interrogation, photographic surveillance, wiretapping, and other investigative tactics to monitor expressive activity.[57] Against a backdrop of urban unrest and antiwar protests nationally, the 1968 Report of the National Advisory Commission on Civil Disorders (the Kerner Report) had approved the use of undercover agents and informers to gather intelligence on "potential as well as actual" civil disorders.[58] During the 1970s and early 1980s in New York, such counterintelligence tactics became the subject of a protracted legal battle, a class action lawsuit, to ensure the department's observance of dissidents' First Amendment rights. Filed in federal court in 1971, the lawsuit asserted the rights of several individual plaintiffs and a class defined broadly to encompass all residents and other persons or organizations physically present in New York City, engaged currently or in the past in "lawful political, religious, educational or social activities" and consequently having faced or being subjected to "infiltration, physical and verbal coercion, photographic, electronic, and physical surveillance, provocation of violence, recruitment to act as police informers and dossier collection and dissemination by defendants and their agents."[59]

Precipitating the lawsuit were revelations surfacing during the conspiracy trial of the "Panther 21" that NYPD officers had infiltrated the Black Panther party and tried to induce party members to commit crimes. (All defendants were acquitted of the charges that they had planned to bomb department stores and police precinct houses in the city.)[60] Roughly contemporaneously with this suit (known as the *Handschu* case in reference to the first-named plaintiff, a lawyer from Buffalo, New York), class actions challenging police intelligence activities were brought against the cities of Chicago and Los Angeles.[61]

The parties in the *Handschu* case ultimately negotiated a settlement approved by the court that incorporated a set of guidelines to govern the launching of a political investigation. Although there was no formal adjudication of wrongdoing in the case, a police commissioner's affidavit made part of the record acknowledged that the challenged police conduct was not limited to investigations of crime but covered any activity that was likely to lead to a "serious police problem."[62] Under the guidelines, the crucial predicate for any investigation of individuals or groups engaged in political activity was "specific information" of criminality. In that event, the Public Security Section (PSS) was required to submit an investigation statement to a newly constituted Authority consisting of two NYPD deputy commissioners and one civilian appointed by the mayor after consultation with the police commissioner. Within thirty days of beginning an investigation, the PSS had to secure approval to continue it by a written request demonstrating good cause for the investigation and the necessity for extending it.[63]

The guidelines required the Authority's prior approval to deploy undercover personnel, as well as to maintain information that a person's name appeared on a political petition or on a mailing list, or that a person provided monetary support for a political or religious group, or published any writing espousing a religious or political position. The guidelines also established a process for individuals and groups to inquire whether they were the subjects of PSS records, and regulated use of investigators, electronic and mechanical surveillance, and the dissemination of information that the PSS had gathered. The Intelligence Division was required to file an annual statement of compliance, while the Authority itself was directed to publish statistics concerning the number of investigations initiated and violations of procedures.[64] Thus, the guidelines contemplated the creation of a paper trail documenting the conduct of criminal investigations connected to political activity.[65] The parties agreed to incorporate the provisions of the guidelines into the court order concluding the lawsuit— thus ensuring that any violations of the guidelines could be punished as a contempt of court. As the 1985 judicial decision approving the terms of the settlement emphasized, the threat of a contempt order was a significant sanction that lawyers representing the *Handschu* class could invoke to protect their clients' legal interests against future encroachment.[66]

On one occasion in the late 1980s class counsel did seek to punish the NYPD for failure to comply with the guidelines after it was revealed that police were taping and transcribing local radio programs featuring black activists and political leaders. In that case, the court did not cite the NYPD for contempt, although it determined that police monitoring of the radio broadcasts violated the guidelines.[67] But the procedural mechanisms put in place by the *Handschu* consent decree, and the resulting press coverage when alleged violations occurred, seemed to have the intended effect of keeping NYPD political surveillance in check. Local activists—those most directly affected by the decree—were quick to invoke the order in response to the NYPD's missteps, and the prospect of having to explain its failures in an official proceeding had some deterrent effect.[68]

Profiling and Political Surveillance in the Post–September 11 City

After functioning under the Handschu Authority procedures for seventeen years, the NYPD in September 2002 applied to the court to modify the guidelines—in effect, to dismantle them. A series of supporting affidavits submitted by Deputy Commissioner Cohen set out the department's rationale: policing the post–September 11 city required far greater leeway in developing intelligence to combat the threat posed by Al Qaeda and "extremist Muslim fundamentalism" generally.[69] Cohen asserted that the Handschu Guidelines' requirement of a criminal predicate before launching an investigation, the restrictions on collecting and retaining information gleaned from publicly available media, and limits on the NYPD's ability to share information gained in an investigation with other agencies obstructed antiterrorist police work. The guidelines developed in an earlier day were "no longer consistent with the public interest" and had become "counter-productive."[70] These strictures on investigation of political and religious expression, Cohen indicated, made it possible for terrorists to plan criminal activities in mosques and other Islamic institutions without risk of detection.[71] What the NYPD proposed instead was to eliminate the required link between political activity and criminality, and remove the Authority's oversight role in NYPD political investigations.[72]

Counsel for the *Handschu* class objected that the NYPD was, by its motion, seeking permission to operate without the Constitutional restrictions that bind criminal law-enforcement agencies and to act as a counter-intelligence agency such as the CIA, with an emphasis on secrecy and breadth of information gathering.[73] Civil liberties scholar and co-counsel for the *Handschu* class Paul Chevigny argued that if the NYPD were allowed to investigate a religious organization because it is Islamic, "only a very slight prejudice, a very slight distortion, will seem to make that religious organization a threat." It was for that very reason, he continued, that some "specific information" indicating criminality should be required to justify a police investigation.[74] Upon prompting from the court, the NYPD eventually conceded that the post–September 11 Department of Justice guidelines for the FBI's conduct of investigations would be adequate to support the NYPD's antiterrorist investigations.[75] Among other things, these guidelines contemplated escalating levels of investigative activity and corresponding thresholds of criminality to justify initiating an investigation at each level.[76] Accepting the NYPD's rationale, U.S. District Court Judge Charles Haight entered an order that limited the Handschu Authority's oversight role along the lines of the NYPD's proposal and revised the guidelines to conform to the FBI standards.[77] The revised guidelines purport to abide by Constitutional mandates, though a closing reservation stated that their purpose is for "internal NYPD guidance" and that they do not create any rights enforceable in a court.[78]

Even as these changes were being debated and ultimately resolved by the court, members of the NYPD were engaging in investigative activity that, under the Constitution and either version of the guidelines, violated the rights of protected class members. On three occasions in February and March, 2003, individuals and organizations protesting the impending U.S. invasion of Iraq gathered in New York City for rallies and marches; on each occasion, the NYPD arrested some protestors on charges of disorderly conduct, obstructing governmental administration, or assault. While the arrestees were in custody, NYPD officers posed questions from a

"Demonstration Debriefing Form" that apparently had been authorized by a high-level Inspector in the Intelligence Division. Among the categories of information that the department sought to elicit were answers concerning individuals' school and organizational affiliations, and prior demonstration history. Arrested persons also reported that officers questioned them more broadly—about their political memberships, their views on President Bush and the war in Iraq, their traveling arrangements and traveling companions on the day of the antiwar rally, their knowledge about future demonstrations, and any past travel to the Middle East or Africa. The information gleaned from this questioning was then entered into an Intelligence Division database.[79]

Although both Police Commissioner Kelly and Deputy Commissioner Cohen denied having knowledge of the debriefing form, the commissioner did not acknowledge that the practice was illegal.[80] When the allegations came to light, counsel for the *Handschu* class applied to the court to incorporate the revised guidelines into the court order itself—to ensure that such unauthorized police conduct as questioning about political belief and activity would be subject to a contempt-of-court sanction.[81] In August 2003 Judge Haight agreed that the *Handschu* class was entitled to the protection of the contempt sanction, which this same judge had considered so significant a safeguard when the original guidelines were approved. Noting that the NYPD had shown itself by these events to be in "some need of discipline," he took issue with the NYPD's characterization that the officers had engaged in debriefing. The procedure, the Judge concluded, was custodial interrogation—and thus raised a serious question about the voluntariness of the responses.[82]

Policing, Panic, and the Rhetoric of Terrorism

While the NYPD sought to justify its antiterrorist measures in court, the Department of Justice was launching a campaign to bolster national support for the enhanced law-enforcement powers authorized under the PATRIOT Act. A Justice Department web site, www.lifeandliberty.gov, asserts, among other things, that the provisions of the Act, including the grant of additional wiretapping authority and the ability to execute secret search warrants, supply necessary tools to combat terrorism. Arguing that the Act simply enables government to use law-enforcement tools that have long been available against organized crime and drug trafficking, the web site in an earlier posting quoted a comment from Democratic Senator Joseph Biden during the floor debate on the Act to the effect that if the FBI can wiretap the "mafia," it should have access to similar law-enforcement tools in the war on terrorism.[83] Echoing these explanations, in 2003 the then-Attorney General John Ashcroft embarked on a series of interviews and speaking engagements before law-enforcement groups and conservative organizations around the country to muster support for the Act's extension of law-enforcement authority.[84]

These Justice Department efforts are, to say the least, disingenuous in suggesting that the FBI lacked *any* authority to wiretap or execute "sneak and peek" warrants against suspected terrorists. Although the PATRIOT Act provisions are more expansive, authority to conduct surveillance already existed under the provisions of the Foreign Intelligence Surveillance Act.[85] At the same time, the department's arguments are contradictory, asserting, on the one hand, a need for heightened law-enforcement authority to combat an unprecedented situation and, on the other, that the investigative authority conferred by the PATRIOT Act is nothing new. The Justice Department's linking of law-enforcement initiatives against terrorism and drug trafficking also reveals, perhaps unwittingly, how the rhetoric of terrorism has long accompanied, and enabled, aggressive law enforcement, particularly policing that occurs in racially targeted, local contexts. The sweeps and arrests of youthful gang members and their families in Southcentral Los Angeles in the late 1980s illustrate the way in which the discourse of policing has embedded the idea and language of terrorism. In *City of Quartz*, the trenchant deconstruction of cultural forces, class dynamics, economics, and politics in Los Angeles, Mike Davis has shown how the LAPD deployed the Street Terrorism Enforcement and Prevention Act to combat gang activities linked to the drug trade, while local politicians embraced the language of terrorism to hammer home antigang, law-and-order platforms.[86]

No less than the current initiatives against immigration law violators, the government responses to "potential as well as actual" civil disorders in the late 1960s,[87] the antigang campaigns in Los Angeles in the 1980s, and zero-tolerance policing in New York City in the 1990s, all depended for their acceptance on a climate of public panic and feared subversion of the moral and social fabric. Under such a climate, the risk of police overreaching in the form of monitoring of political activity and racial and ethnic profiling of South Asian, Arab, and Muslim immigrant communities is particularly pronounced. The NYPD's efforts to dismantle the Handschu guidelines, the Department's custodial "debriefing" of antiwar dissenters, and Deputy Commissioner Cohen's stated determination to target Islamic institutions demonstrate the actual impact of antiterrorist policing on local civil liberties. The department's aggressive monitoring and curtailing of political dissent during the Republican National Convention,[88] and the initiation on July 22, 2005, of random stops and searches of subway commuters, with their implications for racial profiling and the Fourth Amendment requirement of probable cause for searches,[89] highlight the risk of further chilling effects on New York City's besieged immigrant communities.

Grassroots Responses: A New Localism

As advocacy groups have argued for greater safeguards against overzealous policing following the antiwar protests of 2003 and the protests staged at the Republican National Convention in 2004, the federal government promotes local enforcement of immigration law in what one commentator has approvingly called a "broken windows" strategy; in effect, it targets low-level immigration offenses to combat/prevent more serious violations.[90] It is this shared reliance on preventive practice that highlights the continuities between pre–September 11 police strategies to preempt the occurrence of more serious crime and the use of preventive detention after September 11 targeting immigrants from Muslim, Arab, and South Asian communities.[91] In response, affected community members have intensified grassroots organizing and consciousness-raising. Community-based organizations such as Families for Freedom, raising awareness about Federal immigration laws and policies promoting detention and deportation of immigrants, and the impact on immigrant families,[92] and DRUM (Desus Rising Up and Moving),[93] advocating for the rights of low-income South Asian immigrants, particularly with respect to detention and deportation issues, are among the more active New York City-based grassroots groups seeking repeal of federal "immigration reform" laws. Responding to the increasing crisis in Asian communities post–September 11, the New York-headquartered Asian-American Legal Defense and Education Fund has engaged in "frontline lawyering"—combining litigation, policy work, community organizing, and community education—to assist immigrant communities facing secret detention or special registration.[94]

And a broad coalition of grassroots organizations in New York City responded to a sense of federal overreaching through the formation of a Bill of Rights Defense Committee (BORDC) and support of a Bill of Rights Defense resolution, which the New York City Council adopted in February 2004. Among other things, the Bill of Rights Resolution expressed opposition to secret detentions or other secret immigration enforcement actions, surveillance of lawful political activity, and racial, ethnic, or religious profiling.[95] Turning specifically to the context of immigrants working and living in the City, the Resolution refers to aggressive enforcement efforts that "may undermine trust between immigrant communities and the government, and in particular, pose a threat to the civil rights and liberties of the residents of our city who are or who appear to be Arab, Muslim or of South Asian descent." The Resolution also opposed enforcement of federal immigration laws, "except as directed by New York City Executive Order 41," discussed earlier. The BORDC also spearheaded a grassroots initiative to reform the PATRIOT Act, responding to legislation that has been proposed to continue and extend its reach.[96] Thus, the advocacy platform of the BORDC has crystallized and brought together the immigrant/racial targeting issues and general civil liberties concerns that the NYPD and the City's activist and racial minority communities have struggled over in the decades before September 11, and in its aftermath.

To date, the City's Bill of Rights Defense campaign has been replicated in almost 400 U.S. cities and seven states.[97] In declaring themselves "civil liberties safe zones,"[98] these localities recall grassroots campaigns of the late 1970s and the 1980s to secure adoption of local antiapartheid and nuclear weapon-free zone ordinances. Organizers of a national conference, Grassroots America Defends the Bill of Rights, in October, 2003, in Maryland, pointed to these local efforts as evidence of a burgeoning movement of "bottom-up grassroots democracy" in which community-level activism not only responds to local threats to civil liberties but also serves as a platform for influencing national policy.[99]

In New York City, the Bill of Rights Defense group is a broad-based coalition of neighborhood groups (from Astorians for Peace and Justice to the Brooklyn Greens), churches, civil rights advocacy organizations, political parties, and issue-based groups (pro-choice, global health, and antiwar, among many others). The resort to grassroots organizing against federal overreaching, and the well-documented history of antibrutality activism in New York City, suggest a strategy through which presently targeted immigrant and ethnic communities may enact a sense of vibrant localism, through an engaged participation in public life. Occurring at a local scale, discussion and collective action in interaction with, or response to, local government institutions create opportunities for influencing the terms of public debate,[100] whether or not the participation results in formal governmental action. Some commentators have noted the limits of local participation, given patterns of mobility, and the fact that individuals typically identify with more than one locality.[101] Others cite the concerns of parochialism, exclusionary impulses, or inattentiveness to extralocal effects often associated with a localist ideology.[102] But the current New York City-centered activism avoids these concerns, because it is based on coalitions and communities of interest that are not tied strictly to a territorial conception of localism.[103]

Even in pre–September 11 New York City, the tradition of locally determined policing policy and priorities had never been a guarantee of harmonious police-community relations (because, as noted, the localist orientation of the NYPD is not the equivalent of a community-based, community-empowering approach). Since September 11 a new layer of federal initiatives and operating imperatives has complicated the NYPD's localized practice. Writing of police abuses in New York City in the 1960s, Paul Chevigny observed that the police serve as the "repository" of society's "illiberal impulses."[104] In a time of public panic about national security, local police working in conjunction with federal initiatives are even more likely to embody, and entrench, social biases and anxieties. In this climate, New York City's grassroots groups and immigrant communities may be best situated to serve as the city's true "first responders," if they continue to take up the front line of protection for liberties endangered by an increasingly coordinated federal-local law enforcement effort to police the antiterrorist state.

Notes

1. Declaration of Deputy Commissioner David Cohen, ¶ 61, September 12, 2002, *Handschu v. Special Services Division*, 71 Civ. 2203 (CSH).
2. See 79 No. 15 Interpreter Releases 519, "DOJ Legal Opinion Would Broaden Use of State, Local Personnel in Immigration Enforcement (April 8, 2002); James R. Edwards, Jr., "Officers Need Backup: The Role of State and Local Police In Immigration Law Enforcement," Center for Immigration Studies (April 2003): at http://www.cis.org/articles/2003/back703.html last accessed on January 13, 2006 Although the Department resisted disclosure of the opinion itself, the Attorney General had discussed its contents in an address to the International Association of Chiefs of Police in October 2002. Ibid.
3. *National Council of La Raza v. Department of Justice*, discussed in ACLU/NYCLU Welcome Immigration Ruling, at http://www.nyclu.org/immigration_ruling_pr_092704.html last accessed on January 13, 2006.
4. P.L. 109–113, May 11, 2005, 119 Stat. 231, Emergency Supplemental Appropriations Act for Defense, the Global War on Terror, and Tsunami Relief, 2005, Title II, Improved Security For Drivers' Licenses and Personal Identification Cards.
5. William K. Rashbaum, "Terror Makes All the World a Beat for New York Police," *New York Times* (July 15, 2002), at http://www.nytimese.com/2002/07/15/nyregion/15TERR.html?todaysheadlines accessed on July 16, 2002; Jennifer S. Lee, State Department Link Will Open Visa Database to Police Officers, *New York Times* (January 31, 2003), at http://www.nytimes.com/2003/01/31/national/31COMP.html?th
6. Tom Perrotta, "Police Papers Stir Islamic Groups Ire," *New York Law Journal*, (December 23, 2002), p. 1.

7. Deputy Commissioner of Counter-Terrorism: Michael Sheehan, at http://www.nyc.gov/html/nypd/html/dcct/dcct-bio-page.html last accessed on January 13, 2006.

8. Declaration of Deputy Commissioner Cohen, ¶¶ 1, 16, 48–69, September 12, 2002, *Handschu v. Special Services Division*, 71 Civ. 2203 (CSH).

9. Ibid., ¶ ¶ 17, 31–47.

10. Executive Order No. 41, City-Wide Privacy Policy and Amendment of Executive Order No. 34 Relating to City Policy Concerning Immigrant Access to City Services, September 17, 2003.

11. See discussion of objections to the ordinance, adopted June 28, 2004, concerning the ambiguity of the criteria for determining whether impermissible profiling has occurred, and the removal from the original version of the bill of requirements that the NYPD collect and report data on police stops, and that it discipline officers for engaging in profiling, "NYCLU Calls City Council Racial Profiling Bill 'Unenforceable,' " at http://www.nyclu.org/racial_profiling_ltr_062804.html last accessed on January 13, 2006.

12. See, e.g., Nina Bernstein, "Immigrants Lost in the Din: Security vs. the Dream," New York Times (September 20, 2004), p. B1.

13. Edwards, Jr. "Officers Need Backup," p. 6.

14. See, e.g., Bernstein, "Immigrants Lost in the Din,"; Press Release, ACLU of Massachusetts Applauds Boston Police Commissioner's Opposition to the CLEAR Act, February 14, 2005, at http://www.aclu.org/ImmigrantsRights/ImmigrantsRights.cfm?ID=17472&c=22 last accessed on January 13, 2006.; Enforcing Immigration Law: the Role of State, Tribal, and Local Law Enforcement, at http://www.theiacp.org/documents/pdfs/Publications/ImmigrationEnforcementconf%2Epdf last accessed on January 13, 2006; Rachel L. Swarns, "Local Officers Join Search for Illegal Immigrants," New York Times (April 12, 2004), p. A14. See also Brief of Amicus Curiae, National Latino Officers Association and National Black Police Association in Support of Plaintiffs, *National Council of La Raza v. Ashcroft*, No. 03-CV-6324 (ILG/ASC), Exhibit A, "Organizations Opposed to Local Enforcement of Immigration Laws."

15. Telephone interview with Kavitha Pawria, Legal and Policy Coordinator of DRUM (Desus Rising Up and Moving), June 27, 2005.

16. Telephone interview with Tushar Sheth, Staff Attorney/Open Society Institute Fellow, Asian-American Legal Defense and Education Fund, June 22, 2005.

17. See Wesley G. Skogan and Susan M. Hartnett, Community Policing, Chicago Style 5–9 (1997), cited in Richard C, Schragger, *The Limits of Localism*, 100 Mich. L. Rev. (2001), pp. 371, 383 n. 38 Sarah E. Waldeck, *Cops, Community Policing, and the Social Norms Approach to Crime Control: Should One Make Us More Comfortable with the Others?* 34 Ga. L. Rev. (2000), pp. 1253, 1267–1268.

18. See discussion of Immigration and Naturalization Act, Sec. 287(g), at Edwards, Jr. Officers Need Backup, p. 10.

19. See discussion of Immigration and Naturalization Act, Sec. 103(a)(8), at Edwards, Jr. Officers Need Backup, p. 10.

20. "DOJ Legal Opinion Would Broaden Use of State, Local Personnel," *supra* note 2; Edwards, Jr. Officers Need Backup, p. 9.

21. Michael J. Wishnie, *State and Local Police Enforcement of Immigration Laws*, 6 U. Pa. J. Const. L. (2004), pp. 1084, 1092–1093.

22. See, e.g., Sam Francis, "Should the Cops Enforce the Law?," *VDare*, at http://www.vdare.com/francis/enforce.htm accessed on January 13, 2006.

23. See note 3.

24. *National Council of La Raza v. Department of Justice*, 339 F. Supp. 2d 572 (S.D.N.Y. 2004). The court based its ruling on the ground that the Department had waived the predeliberative process privilege that otherwise attached to the memo. Ibid., p. 585.

25. The Department also obtained a stay of disclosure pending appeal. Information supplied by Omar Jagwat, staff attorney with the ACLU Immigration Rights Project and counsel for petitioners.

26. *National Council of La Raza v. Department of Justice*, 444 F. 3d 350, 2005 WL 1274270 (2d Cir. (N.Y.) The court opined that the Justice Department had waived the privilege by referring to the reasoning of the OLC memorandum, not just its conclusions, in public discussions and advocacy about state and local enforcement of immigration law. Ibid., pp. 357–358.

27. Wishnie, *State and Local Police*, note 21, pp. 1096–1098.

28. Ibid. See also Complaint, paragraphs 22–45, *National Council of La Raza v. Ashcroft*, No. 03-CV-6324 (ILG/ASC).

29. See Complaint, *National Council of La Raza v. Ashcroft*, No. 03-CV-6324 (ILG/ASC). The plaintiffs seek declaratory and injunctive relief to bar the federal government from placing in the National Crime Information Center database information concerning alleged violations of civil immigration laws and from disseminating the information to state and local law-enforcement agencies that use the NCIC database. The federal defendants moved to dismiss the complaint for lack of subject matter jurisdiction (i.e., plaintiffs lacked standing because they were not individual immigration law violators with respect to whom information was entered in the NCIC database) and for failure to state a statutory or constitutional claim. See Memorandum of Law in Support of Defendants' Motion to Dismiss the Complaint, *National Council of La Raza v. Ashcroft*, No. 03-CV-6324 (ILG/ASC). As of this writing, the court has not ruled on the motion. See also Nina Bernstein, "Crime Database Misused for Civil Issues, Suit Says," *New York Times* (December 17, 2003), p. A34.

30. Michael J. Wishnie, *Introduction: Immigration and Federalism*, 58 N.Y.U. Ann. Survey Am. L. (2002), 283, 285–88; see also Michael J. Wishnie, *Laboratories of Bigotry? Devolution of the Immigration Power, Equal Protection, and Federalism*, 76 N.Y.U. L. Rev. (2001), 493, 527–528.

31. 151 Cong. Rec. H 3455 HR 1817, 109th Congress, 1st Session, U.S. House of Representatives, Department of Homeland Security Authorization Act for Fiscal Year 2006.

32. Bill Summary and Status, H.R. 2671, to provide for enhanced Federal, State, and Local Enforcement of the Immigration Laws of the United States, introduced July 9, 2003, at http://thomas.loc.gov/cgi-bin/bdquery/z?d108:HR02671: @@@D &summ2+m& last accessed on January 13, 2006; CLEAR Act of 2005, H.R. 3137, introduced in House of Representatives June 30, 2005, http://thomas.loc.gov/cgi-bin/query/ZPc109:H.R.3137 last accessed on January 13, 2006. The House recently approved H.R.4437, the Border Protection, Antiterrorism, and Illegal Immigration Control Act of 2005, which declares that state and local law enforcement agencies have "inherent authority" to enforce federal immigration law, at http://thomas.loc.gov/cgi-bin/query/F?c109:1:./temp/~c10964mojt:e108366: last accessed on March 27, 2006.

33. Numbers USA, Update on Recent Immigration Related Votes, at http://www.reformpartyct.org/numbersusa/action_alert062404.html last accessed on January 13, 2006.

34. See 8 U.S.C. Sec. 1373.

35. See, *e.g.*, National Catholic Reporter, "Immigration Reformers Target Sanctuary Laws of U.S. Cities," at http://www.findarticles.com/p/articles/mi_m1141/_41_39/ai_108968725 last accessed on January 13, 2006.

36. *City of New York v. United States*, 179 F.3d 29, 35 (2d Cir. 1999).

37. Ibid., at 36–37.

38. Ibid., at 37. The Court also rejected the City's claim that the federal statutes interfered with the City's Republican form of government guaranteed under article IV of the U.S. Constitution. Ibid.

39. Friends of Immigration Law Enforcement, "Sanctuary Laws: Non-enforcement and Non-cooperation by Local Entities," at http://fileus.com/dept/sanctuary/

40. Office of the Mayor of the City of New York, Press Release 262–03, "Mayor Michael R. Bloomberg Signs Executive Order 41 Regarding City Services for Immigrants," September 17, 2003.

41. Sec. 2, 3, Executive Order No. 41, see note10.

42. Sec. 3, Executive Order No. 41, see note10.

43. Sec. 4, Executive Order No. 41, see note10.

44. Telephone interview with Kavitha Pawria, Legal and Policy Coordinator, DRUM (Desus Rising Up and Moving), June 27, 2005; Nina Bernstein, "Police Report Noncitizens to U.S., Official Says," *New York Times* (April 23, 2005), p. B3, cited at 2005 WLNR 6340721.

45. E.g., Statement of Anthony Miranda, Executive Chairman, Latino Officers Association, Panelist, To Serve and Protect: Should New York City Police Play A Role in Immigration Enforcement?, Association of the Bar of the City of New York, Winter 2004.

46. See Brief of Amicus Curiae, National Latino Officers Association and National Black Police Association in Support of Plaintiffs, *National Council of La Raza v. Ashcroft*, No. 03-CV-6324 (ILG/ASC), Exhibit A, "Organizations Opposed to Local Enforcement of Immigration Laws."

47. See, e.g., Philip Shenon and Kevin Flynn, "Mayor Tells Panel 'Pork Barrel Politics' Is Increasing Risk of Terrorism for City," *New York Times* (May 20, 2004), p. B9; William K. Rashbaum, "F.B.I. Message Exposes Rift With Police Over Terror Case," *New York Times* (June 4, 2004), p. B2.

48. See generally Andrew Hsaio, "Mothers of Invention: The Families of Police Brutality Victims and the Movement They've Built," in Andrea McArdle and Tanya Erzen, eds., *Zero Tolerance: Quality of Life and the New Police Brutality in New York City* (NYU Press 2001), pp. 179–195.

49. See. e.g., Ana Joanes, *Does the New York City Police Department Deserve Credit For the Decline in New York City's Homicide Rates? A Cross-City Comparison of Policing Strategies and Homicide Rates*, 33 Colum. J. L. & Soc. Probs. 265, (2000), pp. 292–300 (concluding that in the two-decade period running from the late 1970s to the late 1990s, cities that did not adopt aggressive policing initiatives such as New York's variously named quality-of-life/zero-tolerance policy saw declines in homicide rates that were equal to or greater than New York's, thus placing in question New York City's assertion that its aggressive enforcement strategies accounted for the drop in the city's homicide rates).

50. Tanya Erzen, "Turnstile Jumpers and Broken Windows: Policing Disorder in New York City," in Andrea McArdle and Tanya Erzen, eds. *Zero Tolerance: Quality of Life and the New Police Brutality in New York City* [hereinafter *Zero Tolerance*], pp. 20–24 (NYU Press 2001), pp. 19–49; Heather Barr, "Policing Madness: People with Mental Illness and the NYPD," in McArdle and Erzen, eds., *Zero Tolerance*, pp. 50–84, 61–68; Jeffrey Fagan and Garth Davies, *Street Stops and Broken Windows: Terry, Race, and Disorder in New York City*, 28 Fordham Urb. L. J. 457, 468–472, 475, 489–496, 501 (2000); Waldeck, *Cops, Community Policing*, pp. 1274–1277.

51. Andrea McArdle, "No Justice, No Peace," pp. 147–176; Fagan and Davies, *Street Stops and Broken Windows*, pp. 489–496.

52. McArdle, "No Justice," in McArdle and Erzen, eds., *Zero Tolerance*, p. 154.

53. Andrea McArdle, "Introduction," pp. 1–16, especially p. 6.

54. See note 17 and accompanying text. See also Erzen, "Turnstile Jumpers," pp. 32–33 nn. 48–51; Judith A. Greene, *Zero Tolerance: A Case Study of Police Policies and Practice in New York City*, 45 Crime & Delinq. 171, 173–175, (1999). In a lecture at Fordham University School of Law in January 1996, William Bratton, then NYPD Police Commissioner, described the shift from reliance on the beat officer (often a new recruit)—a distinguishing feature of the policing policy of New York's previous Mayor David Dinkins and his Police Commissioners (Lee Brown and Ray Kelly)—and the Giuliani administration's more aggressive "take the streets back" approach and empowering of more experienced officers. William J. Bratton, *New Strategies for Combating Crime in New York City*, 23 Fordham Urb. L. J. 781, 787–792 (1996). This shift presumably explains the findings in studies showing that various New York City communities were largely unfamiliar with community policing strategies. *See, e.g.*, Robert C. Davis and Joel Miller, *Immigration and Integration: Perceptions of Community Policing Among Members of Six Ethnic Communities in Central Queens, New York City*, 9 Int'l Rev. Victimology 93, 99, 107–108 (2002) (noting shift in community policing policies in New York City toward greater enforcement orientation in mid-1990s and finding that awareness of community policing was lower in recent immigrant communities in Jackson Heights, Queens (Colombians, Dominicans, Equadorians, Indians) than for

more established ethnic groups (Italians and African Americans); Carmen Leonor Solis, "The Impact of Community Policing on New York City's Puerto Rican Communities," 7–8 dissertation on file at CUNY Graduate Center, 2004 (3115291.pdf) (summarizing research findings that show that NYPD has not adequately maintained communication with Puerto Rican communities, that NYPD seems "resistant" to listening to community members and Puerto Rican officers who wish to solve problems, and that most community participants interviewed for the study showed that they had "no knowledge" of community policing in the NYPD).

55. New York City Police Department Operations Order: Department Policy Regarding Racial Profiling, 13 March 2002.

56. Chisun Lee, "The NYPD Wants to Watch You," *Village Voice* (December 18–24, 2002): at http://www.villagevoice.com/issues/0251/lee.php last accessed on January 13, 2006.

57. *Handschu v. Special Services Division*, 605 F. Supp. 1384, 1396 (S.D.N.Y. 1985), *aff'd*, 787 F.2d 828 (2d Cir. 1986).

58. Ibid., 1398.

59. Ibid., 1388.

60. Chisun Lee, "The NYPD Wants to Watch you," see note 56.

61. *Handschu v. Special Services Division*, 605 F. Supp., 1398.

62. Ibid., 1396.

63. Ibid., 1421.

64. Ibid., 1422–1424.

65. Ibid., 1411.

66. Ibid., 1409.

67. *Handschu v. Special Services Division*, 737 F. Supp. 1289, 308 (S.D.N.Y. 1989).

68. Chisun Lee, "The NYPD Wants to Watch You."

69. Declaration of Deputy Commissioner David Cohen, ¶¶ 17, 31–47, September 12, 2002, *Handschu v. Special Services Division*, 71 Civ. 2203 (CSH).

70. Ibid., ¶¶ 1, 16, 48–69.

71. Ibid., ¶¶ 32, 56; Declaration of Deputy Commissioner David Cohen ¶ 9, November 26, 2002, *Handschu v. Special Services Division*, 71 Civ. 2203 (CSH).

72. Declaration of Deputy Commissioner David Cohen, see note 69, ¶¶ 28–29.

73. Plaintiff Class' Memorandum of Law in Further Opposition to Defendants' Motion to Modify the Consent Decree, pp. 6–7, January 17, 2003, *Handschu v. Special Services Division*, 71 Civ. 2203 (CSH).

74. Declaration of Paul G. Chevigny ¶ 13, November 4, 2002, *Handschu v. Special Services Division*, 71 Civ. 2203 (CSH).

75. Declaration of Deputy Commissioner David Cohen ¶ 3, January 24, 2003, *Handschu v. Special Services Division*, 71 Civ. 2203 (CSH).

76. The Attorney General's Guidelines on General Crimes, Racketeering Enterprise and Terrorism Enterprise Investigations, Introduction, § B (May 30, 2002).

77. *Handschu v. Special Services Division*, 71 Civ. 2003 (CSH), 2003 WL 302258, at *1 (S.D.N.Y. Feb. 13, 2003).

78. Declaration of Gail Donohue, March 10, 2003, Exhibit B, § X, *Handschu v. Special Services Division*, 71 Civ. 2203 (CSH).
79. Declaration of Jethro M. Eisenstein ¶¶ 3–6, April 16, 2003, *Handschu v. Special Services Division*, 71 Civ. 2203 (CSH).
80. Ibid., ¶ 4.
81. Ibid., ¶¶ 2, 11, 16.
82. The judge left to the Handschu Authority whether the debriefing procedures (which had been carried out under both the original and the new *Handschu* dispensations) violated the Constitutional rights of any of those arrested.
83. The USA Patriot Act: Preserving Life and Liberty, at http://www.lifeandliberty.gov
84. Eric Lichtblau, "Bush Administration Plans Defense of Terror Law," *New York Times* (August 19, 2003), at http://www.nytimes.com/ 2003/08/19/politics/19PATR.html?th = &pagewanted = print&position = ; Eric Lichtblau, "Ashcroft Blasts Efforts to Weaken Terrorism Law," *New York Times* (August 20, 2003), at http://www.nytimes.com/2003/08/20/politics/20PATR.html?th.
85. David Cole and James X. Dempsey, *Terrorism and the Constitution*, 2nd ed. (2002) pp. 159–161; American Civil Liberties Union, "ACLU Says Justice Dept.'s PATRIOT Act Website Creates New Myths About Controversial Law," (August 26, 2003), at http://www.aclu..org/SafeandFree/SafeandFree. cfm?ID= 13371&c=206 last accessed January 13, 2006.
86. Mike Davis, *City of Quartz: Excavating the Future in Los Angeles* (Vintage 1992), pp. 270–271, 282–284. [1990].
87. See note 18.
88. See, e.g., Sabrina Tavernise, "Prosecutors Won't Pursue Cases of 227 in Disputed Protest," *New York Times* (7 October 2004), p. B1. Police arrested nearly 1,800 protestors during the three-day convention. The decision to dismiss charges against a group of 227 who were arrested as they began to march northward from the vicinity of Ground Zero to Madison Square Garden was prompted, police and prosecutors said, by anticipated difficulties in proving that each protestor intended to obstruct the sidewalks in violation of a police directive. See also Complaint, *Page v. the City of New York*, 05-CV-2088 (S.D.N.Y. 2005), alleging an "unconstitutional zero-tolerance approach towards protest" during the Republican National Convention and challenging the plaintiff's arrest and detention for obstructing a public sidewalk while she stood alone on a curb dressed as a Hummer vehicle in an act of protest, discussed at http://www.rncprotestrights. org/archives/00000042.html last accessed January 13, 2006.
89. Sewell Chan, "In New York, It's Open Bag or Find Exits," *New York Times* (23 July 2005), at http://www.nytimes.com/2005/07/23/nyregion/23york.html?ei= 5070&n=el6700e464f298e6&ex=1123041600&emc=eta l &pagewanted= print; Sewell Chan & Kareem Fahim, "Legal Issues Being Raised on Searches in Subways," *New York Times* 24 July 2005, http://www. nytimes.com/2005/ 07/24/nyregion/24subways.html?ei=5070&en=f5c65043390a4a30&ex=

1123041600&emc=eta 1 &pagewanted=print last accessed on July 26, 2005; "NYCLU Calls Decision To Conduct Random Searches Of Individuals On New York's Subways Unconstitutional," (July 21, 2005), at http://www. nyclu.org/ mta_searches_pr_072105.html last accessed on January 13, 2006.; NYCLU To Appeal Decision in Subway Bag Search Lawsuit (December 5, 2005) at http://www.nyclu.org/mta_searches_ suit_pr_ 120205.html last accessed on March 28, 2006.

90. Testimony of James R. Edwards, Jr., "Adjunct Fellow at the Hudson Institute, House Subcommittee Debates Local Enforcement of Immigration Laws Under Proposed Clear Act," 80 *Interpreter Releases* (October 13, 2003) pp.1407, 1410.

91. See David Cole, *The New McCarthyism: Repeating History in the War on Terrorism*, 38 Harv. Civ. Rts-Civ. Lib. L. Rev. 1, 16–18, 24–26 (2003).

92. http://www.familiesforfreedom.org last accessed on January 13, 2006.

93. http://www.drumnation.org/about.htm last accessed on January 13, 2006.

94. Sin Yen Ling, *Frontline Lawyering: Defending the Attack on Immigrant Communities After September 11*, Clearinghouse Rev. (September–October 2004), pp. 238–243.

95. New York City Council Adopts Forceful Resolution Affirming Rights and Liberties In the Face of Anti-Terrorism Initiatives (February 4, 2004) at http://www.nyclu.org/nycbordc_vote_020404.html last accessed on March 28, 2006.

96. New York City Council Resolution No. 60 (February 4, 2004), at http://www. nyclu.org/nycbordc_council_resolution_020404.html; New York City Bill of Rights Defense Campaign—Patriot Act Expansion Bill Introduced in the Senate, http://www.nycbordc.org/index.php?option=com_content&task= view&id=74&Itemid=1 last accessed on March 28, 2006.

97. Bill of Rights Defense Committee, Local Efforts, at http://www.bordc.org/ Other Local Efforts.htm last accessed on January 13, 2006.

98. "Grassroots America Defends the Bill of Rights: The First National Conference" (October 18–19, 2003), Silver Spring, Maryland.

99. Ibid.; see, e.g., Andrea L. McArdle, "In Defense of State and Local Government Anti-Apartheid Measures: Infusing Democratic Values Into Foreign Policymaking," 62 *Temple Law Review* 813, 846 (1989).

100. See Gerald Frug, *The City as a Legal Concept*, 93 Harv. L. Rev. 1057, 1068–1070 (1980). For an extended discussion of Frug's thesis, see Richard Briffault, *Our Localism: Part II—Localism and Legal Theory*, 90 Colum. L. Rev. 346, 393–397 (1990).

101. Briffault, *Our Localism* note, pp. 412–415; Schragger, *The Limits of Localism*, p. 421.

102. See, e.g., Schragger, *The Limits of Localism*, pp. 462–464, 467.

103. See, e.g., Briffault, *Our Localism*, pp. 446–454; Schragger, *The Limits of Localism*, pp. 421–424.

104. Paul Chevigny, *Police Power: Police Abuses in New York City* (New York: Pantheon, 1969), p. 280.

9

Transformation: The Emergent Growth of Cooperation amongst Police Agencies

Peter K. Manning

Introduction

If the events of September 11, 2001, could not have been predicted, and the ensuing trauma was entirely to be expected, the invasions of Afghanistan and Iraq, and the continuing rhetorical "war on terrorism," do not appear to be the result of a strategically planned, problem-solving approach to protecting national security.[1] What should be done, or what is being done to increase national security is still being debated.[2] The long-term effects of these events and their *sequelae* on security governance (Johnston and Shearing 2003) are yet unknown. In this chapter, I outline some of the consequences of the events of September 11 with respect to reorganizing policing in the United States at the local level and the emerging cooperative arrangements between local police forces and specialized federal police. I assess some of the most visible changes, largely a result of attempts to refine airport security and monitor immigration. I argue that this focus on antiterrorist policing post–September 11 has obscured important changes in policing that emerged in North American cities during the past fifteen years. I suggest that these changes have resulted from innovations transnationally in policing massive public occasions (MPOs) over the past fifteen years that include the potentiality of damage to places, people, or meetings of national and/or international value.[3] These changes suggest that police have developed refined antiterrorist plans and preventive tactics. A brief case study presented here of preparations made in Boston for the Democratic National Convention (DNC) in August of 2004 suggests that refinements in policing protest that thereby reduce the risks of terrorism have developed not only in response to post–September 11, but to MPOs generally. It is this broader transnational security perspective that is transforming policing in the United States, particularly at the local level.

The Aftermath of September 11

The events of September 11 in New York City and Washington D.C. are repeatedly described in terms that imply that they were the result of some clear series of events leading to a particular named outcome, rather than a contingent process with many unpredictable features. It has been assumed, further, that these events have substantially altered the system of security (including private and public police, state, local, and federal agencies) in North America. Let us first consider some rather visible and superficial changes in the context of U.S. policing, and then consider others less visible.

Changes in the Practices of Federal Agencies

These changes were visible, especially as a result of the powers given officially to the FBI as a result of the passage of the PATRIOT Act into law in late 2001. These are attempts to reshape the traditional practices of federal agencies. Changes have included interviewing large numbers of people from non-Jewish Semitic and South Asian communities in cities around the United States, searches and surveillance without warrant, and other dubious enhancements of federal powers. Because the threat of terrorism is vaguely defined, based on intent, and confounded with conventional crimes committed according to U.S. law, it has an umbrella effect suggesting danger from nebulous groups—Arabs and non-Jewish Semitics, vague new categories of people such as "narco-terrorists," financiers of terrorism, money launderers, and the Al Qaeda (see Brandl 2004; Forst 2003). The threat of terrorism has altered these agencies to the possibility of using more sophisticated technologies to profile the content and frequency of selected communication worldwide (Bamford 2002, 2004). These changed powers also enable "data drilling" and analysis of data bases gathered for other purposes such as newly relevant lists: airline passenger lists, watch lists of suspected persons, and profiles of "dangerous" types (Lyons forthcoming; Ericson and Haggerty 1998).

Homeland Security

Most significantly and visibly, establishing the Homeland Security Agency (a merging of Customs, INS, Border Patrol, and the Coast Guard as well as some smaller agencies), and the creation of a Directorate of Intelligence, hold the potential for integrated intelligence efforts. The establishment of the Homeland Security Agency was an attempt to integrate domestic security agencies. This new consolidated entity has proven a bureaucratic nightmare with its 6,000 employees; it comprises a vast number of agencies connected by mysterious dots, and the lines of authority are totally unclear. The actual scope of its functioning, other than to gather all available evidence and pass it on to the public to educate, remains unclear (see www.dhs.gov/dhspublic/index.jsp). Forty percent of the grants given out by DHS are distributed on a state-by-state basis and the rest on the basis of perceived risk or need. The distribution of these funds in total and on average is inversely related to the actual risks encountered in the states. The monies are distributed further within states on dubious criteria resulting in a curious mixture of items. In Massachusetts these included an armed helicopter for Cape Cod, a communications system for a wealthy Boston suburb, and miscellaneous equipment. Homeland Security funding includes grants for making radio frequencies compatible in jurisdictions that cannot communicate outside their own forces. This communication gap is true across the United States. Furthermore, Homeland Security's list of potential terrorist targets is so sweeping that they are located in virtually any jurisdiction in the United States. These include power plants, interstate highways, water and sewer installations, national parks and symbolic places, military bases, and harbors, thus making funding any police department anywhere in the country conceivable under a Homeland Security grant.

    Institutional structures and culture make change difficult. There is what might be called, following Selznick (1949), "organizational character," a lasting and durable pattern of interfacing and coping with the organizational environment that is a result of how organizations have responded in the past to pressures from the environment. This environment, constituted of other organizations and events, shapes an organizational character that is not easily changed. Federal agencies arise in response to perceived gaps in enforcement in the past (Richman 2000), such as the rash of interstate bank robberies that led to the establishment of the FBI, and do not easily or readily adapt to new environmental contingencies. In fact, the early focus of the FBI, a product of the administrative genius of J. Edgar Hoover and his emphasis on monitoring and evaluating a narrow band of observable crimes and close supervision of agents (Wilson 1978), remained thematic in the agency (Kessler 2003).[4] It was apparent that a lack of coordination within agencies including (primarily) the FBI existed because cases were considered personal property of a sort, information was not shared with other agents, and secrecy valued above collaboration.

There has been a similar lack of coordination across agencies. For example, the CIA has a limited mandate in investigating domestic matters, and has a long history of avoiding cooperation with the FBI (Kessler 1994, 2003). Failure of federal agencies to gather relevant information, to analyze it, to share it, to link it to other cases and investigations, and finally, to make inferences about potential future attacks (*Report of the September 11 Commission*), is a dramatic manifestation of the reactive, case-based, law-enforcement mandate (character) of agencies such as the FBI. Fundamental limits on the effectiveness of federal agencies were and are a lack of cultural knowledge, sensitivity, and experience; absence of language skills and translators; limited computer hardware and software; superficial training in intelligence (rather than criminal investigative techniques); and thin resources for such investigations (Kessler 2003; Powers 2004). The *Report of the September 11 Commission* notes repeatedly an unwillingness of federal agencies to alter their traditional perspective and approaches in spite of their ever abundant and in fact growing resources. A long tradition of obedience to hierarchy rather than innovation and creativity remains.

Other broader trends remain that work counter to the integrated approach that organizational charts of Homeland Security might suggest. The blurring of categories of crime and international terror, the globalization of the financing and mobilizing of criminal schema, as well as the cellular, secretive character, and the social organization of planned, orchestrated terrorism, require rethinking the investigative strategies of federal agencies. These developments mean, for example, greater use of and credibility given to betrayers, double agents, marginal figures, and other kinds of secret agents, "spooks," who can monitor and inform about conspiracies, planned crime, and other matters in progress that are not yet crimes (Brodeur 2004).

Other Visible Moves

On the other hand, the federal government made visible and dramatic moves almost immediately after September 11. These include positioning of troops, police, and U.S. Marshals in and at access points to airports and dispatching air marshals in civilian dress on flights; requiring airlines to install locked cabin doors; enhancing security in the pilots' cabins; as well as permitting pilots to carry arms. Some efforts were made to coordinate information gathering and distribution between local and federal agencies. Federal agencies were given new directions, funding, and personnel.[5]

Most dramatic, perhaps, were augmentation of visual and electronic modes of surveillance at local points of entry and passenger movement. The basis of this surveillance was a new interest in intelligence, or information gathered in advance of an incident relevant to organizational response to such an incident. These include:

- Adding video surveillance of harbors and financial districts in large cities. Boston, for example, has installed 128 cameras in the financial district covering around 80 percent of the area's buildings. One source has estimated that in 2003 there were 396 cameras per square mile in Manhattan, but also reported 25 million video cameras and 30 million cell phones, able to film, record, and send images anywhere in the world (*Wired* magazine (2003: 62). The Massachusetts Bay Transport Authority (MBTA), like London Transport, has cameras monitoring all of its platforms and stations 24/7 (*Boston Globe*, "T-Upgrades security . . ." December 31, 2004).
- Increasing the number and kinds of means for systematically watching and recording the movements of people, especially travelers and their baggage. These include virtual (by a number of electronic means including magnetometer, video surveillance, computerized records checks of passports) as well as actual screening and wand-based searches of passengers prior to boarding airplanes. These means, including the requirement that all baggage be screened, are complemented and accompanied by the usual and past practice of visually "profiling" passengers (see Lehman-Langlois 2002) by Border Patrol and Customs and Immigration (now integrated in the Department of Homeland Security) at international points of entry (Gilboy 1993). This is largely informal and based on intuitive assessments— single men traveling without luggage; Arabic-looking people; or passengers who look worried or in a hurry.
- Developing "watch lists" to monitor passengers. Airlines flying from North American airports have developed since 2001 "watch lists" of frequent travelers to certain countries; identified possible terrorists (Lyons, forthcoming).
- Installing computers to scan and store passport information and data on travelers in and out of the United States, and fingerprinting and photographing all foreign visitors (with or without visas). These moves were combined with installing tighter and more elaborate procedures for issuing visas and granting student permissions to study in

the United States (*Boston Globe*, "Fingerprint Database Delayed . . . ," December 30, 2004).

- Massive incompetence in use and installing computer databases (*Boston Globe*, "FBI set to Dump its New 170m Computer System," January 14, 2005).
- Using random searches to broaden coverage of the least likely passengers, who might in theory be used as "dupes" or covers for terrorists.
- Considering requiring elaborate "smart cards" for individual travelers and installing electronic equipment that would identify people by their unique aspects—voice, pupil refraction, handprints, and fingerprints, and so on.[6]
- Developing integrated databases from INS, FEMA, and local police and putting in place (for use in dispatching and planning) in public agencies detailed floor plans for major targets and schools, lists of buildings with explosives and firearms by location, noting staging areas for assembling police and troops in the event of an attack, and modes of controlling traffic access and egress to potential targets (interview with Boston Police Head of Research and Development, June 2004). These maps and plans were not compatible from one agency to another (because of soft and hardware incompatibilities) nor available until post–September 11, but have been funded by the Office of Homeland Security.

Although these visible moves were clearly a new and awkward impediment to travel, and, along with fear of another version of the September 11 attacks, radically reduced air travel for over two years, there were lurking doubts based on data that they were working as intended. The efforts made have been focused on the last security crisis, preventing the use of hijacked airplanes as weapons, ignoring the other vulnerable targets remaining: ports and the movements of natural gas and other explosives; movement by roadway of hazardous materials; nuclear reactors; air and ship cargos; water and sewer works in large cities. The Inspector General of the Homeland Security agencies, in a report, stated that backup for fundamental databases is not carried out; linkages within and across databases are not possible; and that the twelve agency watch lists were incompatible (*Boston Globe*, "Report Faults Homeland Security," October 2, 2004).

The Present

In respect to the most salient developments outside airport security, pressures to move local police into a more defined role in national defense and national security remain. The results of the efforts to federalize local policing in these respects are impossible to assess. Some of the more obvious tactics and places to monitor have been identified, including watching some strategic sites, such as bridges, dams, and power plants, monitoring water and sewer facilities, developing traffic plans and developing cooperative arrangements for "National Security Events" such as the Salt Lake City Olympics, the Democratic and Republican conventions, and public appearance of the President. However, the infrastructure of security preparedness is still a work in progress.

At present (July, 2005), it is not possible to assess fully the degree to which practices of security governance at the federal, state, and local level have changed since September 11, but it appears that police organizations at the local level have adapted, and have been learning for a longer period of time. This change is demonstrable. It is a combination of several forces that have shaped policing internationally in the past fifteen years, focused on large public events that attract protestors as well as the possibly of terrorists. In an interesting fashion, policing of fan-riots, student celebrations, and very large national events have all been a force for change. First, I will examine the present capacity of U.S. public police agencies, beginning with what are called the specialized (federal) agencies, local agencies, and then proceed to examine ongoing changes in the pattern of policing. It is possible that September 11 and antiterrorist symbolization of threat have masked some of these less visible changes.

Specialized Federal Agencies

Federal agents in the United States act as specialized arms of the government, carrying out functions such as tax regulation, gun control (ATF), customs and immigration, the border patrol, domestic violations of other federal laws, drug control, and external operations in connection with national security (NSA, CIA).[7] Although there has been some consolidation and reconfiguring within and across agencies since the events of September 11, it is estimated that there are some thirty federal enforcement agencies and 58, 689 agents of federal and related special agencies.[8] Their mandates have grown without much constitutional direction (Richman 2000) and in the law-enforcement arena, the result is competition and conflict among the CIA, FBI, and other agencies within the Department of Justice (Kessler 2003).[9]

State and Local Public Policing

Local policing is the tradition in North America. There are (approximately, given sampling error and combining and weighting of sample by

Maguire) 21,143 agencies in the United States: 14,628 local, 49 state, 3,156 Sheriff-headed, and 3,280 special agencies. There are approximately 600,000 officers in these agencies. These agencies are primarily small, highly structured, and reactive to calls for service, and "bottom heavy" with emphasis on response to 911 emergency calls and random patrol. They rely heavily on local funding, local political guidance, accountability, and traditions of law enforcement, and use violence (lethal and nonlethal) and criminal and civil sanctions. Moreover, by tradition, they deploy few detectives; have little or no research or development capacities (except in very large urban departments). The working officer is loyal to the idea of policing as a craft or job, to his or her peers, to a lesser extent the top command, and to the citizens of the local community. Local police have never been tasked to defend the stability of a revolutionary state (compare, for example, Liang 1970; Thomas 2001). They are bound to local loyalty rather than to the national government. This becomes a salient issue if and when local policing is required in response to a war, attack, constitutional crisis, or revolution. This has not been a problematic experience for police in the United States in the past 145–150 years—at least not since the Civil War.

Typically local police in the United States are trained for a brief period (around fourteen weeks) in local academies without the benefit of executive training programs, a national police college, or any required systematic training after the academy. There are widely varying standards of recruitment and acceptance. Promotion, demotion, assignment and reassignment, lateral transfer, and movement from force to force are variously patterned by unions and state laws. It is rare to move from department to department except at the rank of chief. Because of its local grounding, public policing serves the executive indirectly with the law as a mediating and constraining force, separate from courts and the legislature.

Policing powers are quite wide and are shared with individuals, private investigators, citizen self-help groups, private policing agencies, and occasionally the military (National Guard, reserves, and regular forces). Territorial limits or jurisdictional boundaries that once bound the operations of Anglo-American policing now are largely irrelevant at the federal level since American law has been extended and applied within foreign nations with startling impunity.

This broad application is seen in the United States rejecting of the territorial limits at sea and enforcement of drug laws at the pleasure of the U.S. Forces (Langweische 2004); invading Afghanistan and Iraq without declarations of war (Woodward 2002, 2004); the use of torture in Afghanistan, at the U.S. Naval Base in Guantanamo, Cuba, and in Iraq at Abu Ghraib (Strasser 2005; Whitney 2005); and kidnapping citizens residing abroad without the cooperation of the host country and rendering them to third countries for "questioning" (e.g., kidnapping by thirteen CIA agents, charged now in Italian courts with the crime, of an Iranian cleric resident in Italy). In addition, global and task force-based transnational policing, sponsored by the European Union and the United Nations (Kosovo and Bosnia), along with the continuing information-gathering functions of INTERPOL, complemented by private corporate war-making (Singer 2003) is growing (DeFleum 2003; Scheptycki 2000; Walker 2004).

This local autonomy with respect to the policing function in the United States has many strengths as is described below, but it also makes collective, cooperative mobilization in response to large diffuse natural or "man-made" disasters very difficult. Because of a long history of local autonomy and development of small, local police, fire, and rescue squads in the United States, the typical, small local department has no plan for coordinated reaction to disasters, little ability to communicate across jurisdictions (radio frequencies, power, and capacities vary), and no systematic means to evaluate past efforts. The mutual agreements guiding local fire and police actions and responses have tended to be personalized, historic, and not put in writing or in legal form. In some counties, especially outside New England, in the West, Midwest, and South, the County Sheriff is a powerful elected official; in others the Sheriff's office is a nominal position that provides traffic control and patrol, or operates a jail (sometimes this is done at a profit). Much of the coordination amongst agencies in disasters is ad hoc, based on informal hierarchy of state police, officers of larger local jurisdictions, and adjoining agencies. The equipment of cities is highly variable from those with full SWAT teams and "hazmat" (hazardous materials) capacities to those with none, or a few nominal squads (men and women who are assigned as and when needed to carry out dives or rescues). There has been no clear connection made for the local jurisdictions between the warning levels used nationally (green, yellow, and red), and the actions expected from these agencies. Traditionally, police organizations communicate with each other via telephone, and their trust is based on personal knowledge, rather than on the basis of formal, written mutual aid documents. In Massachusetts, for example, local officers have no legal arrest powers in other cities.

New Forms of Policing: Strategies and Tactics

This pattern of local policing has been altered during the past fifteen years by development of a *modified form of policing* of demonstrations, mass gatherings, protests, and even massive public spectacles, such as the World Cup (soccer), Super Bowl (football), and the World Series (baseball).

The problem of policing such *massive public occasions* (MPOs) is exacerbated by the growth of rapid, cheap transportation and communication, globalization of the economy, "massification" of public opinion in industrialized nations, (and) a networked society in which public police organizations are viewed collectively as but one member of a nodal security system (Shearing 2005). What has been less noticeable is the diffusion of new techniques and approaches, shared policing knowledge across police agencies, and even across national borders as well as the growth of a "third culture," a product of the interaction of the culture of the police organization and the culture of students of policing.[10] If "culture" is a way to understand what others understand, a third culture arises when two cultures interact and intersect. This culture, an amalgam of academics and police, is composed of the beliefs, values, experiences, and stories that are shared among police officers, former police officers, academics, and researchers. This is a point of reference that enables people to "point to" matters of mutual regard (see Shearing and Ericson 1991).

While focus has shifted to antiterrorism, policing of MPOs with international dimensions has been vexing for at least the past fifteen years in North America. It is possible to identify at least eight public events meeting the criteria of these MPOs. Although space does not allow an analysis of the unique features of each (see King 2004), they include: the Quebec City Summit of the Americas (April 20–22, 2001); the Salt Lake City Olympics in February, 2002 (see Decker et al., forthcoming); G8 summit in Kananaskis (near Calgary, Alberta, that also involved events in Ottawa and Calgary, June 26–27, 2002); and previously the Asian Pacific Economic Cooperation Conference in Vancouver, B.C. (at the UBC campus) November 16–25, 1997; Organization of American States Senate in Windsor, Ontario (June 4–6, 2000); World Petroleum Congress meetings in Calgary, June 11–15, 2000; and the G20 meetings in Ottawa, November 16–18, 2001).[11] While the organization of policing is slightly more centralized in Canada, the problem remains essentially a local (state or provincial) one in both countries. This is so because while the Royal Canadian Mounted Police (RCMP) is a national police force, they are severely limited in their remit in local policing, and are prohibited from gathering intelligence. The weight of policing an MPO falls on the Provincial police (the RCMP serves as the provincial police in the Western Provinces but not in Newfoundland, Ontario, or Quebec, and serves under contract in cities across Canada). In both countries, the local police are the operational center of control even as they are trumped by federal assets and power.

The Seattle demonstrations (Stamper 2005) and the demonstrations at the 2000 Republican Party convention in Philadelphia have not been as well analyzed in print, but are also relevant to police learning. These gatherings marked a dramatic shift also in the *causes* that were being advanced by the protestors, demonstrators, citizen-activists, or local concerned groups. They reflected a change from concern with local ethnic, class, or economic issues to more international and global questions such as the role of international franchises, oil monopolies, environmental destruction, and miscellaneous symbolic (rather than material) concerns. These were *status politics* events, partially spectacle, partially protest, partially carnival and mockery (King 2004). They became staged and rehearsed events on both sides.[12] Systematic analysis of rioting in New York State suggests that the success comes from two sources—changes in tactics toward a more negotiated presence by police and protestors and a growing sense of cooperation between the partners to the dance (Earle et al. 2003).

As this implies, the targets of concern varied as well, being more about ideas, symbols, and the future than about past wrongs, needed remedies, or demanded corrective actions. Those involved in these demonstrations, like the people protesting U.S. plans to attack and conquer Iraq (Keegan 2005: 107–108), included a heavy proportion of educated, middle-class people, students, and union members protesting free market trade agreements. Their organizers had resources, were not without political capital, and were amenable to negotiation and mediation. They were themselves organized and had leadership; organizers on the ground, marshals, and otherwise were connected rather than ad hoc gatherings of angry people.

As responses developed to these MPOs, both responses anticipating and looking back to best practices that had emerged, police organizations of more than one nation cooperated with shared intelligence. Some MPOs featured incidents that touched off visible and violent police response, confrontations, injury, and arrest, while some did not. In the case of an MPO documenting an incident and response, it is perhaps easier to assign fault or errors in planning, whereas for those events that proceed without incident, such as the Boston case discussed below and the Salt Lake City Olympics, it is more difficult to assess the adequacy of the planning. This focus, however, overlooks the most fundamental conclusion that must be drawn from the policing of such events: police practices have been transformed quite markedly.

The developments in policing such events are reported in several important sources (King 2004; Waddington 1991, 2003). These include (my inference) at least four major clusters of innovation. I have confined my attention to those that are used in more than one event, and used in more than one subsequent policing deployment. Bear in mind also that the success of such strategies and tactics is entirely dependent on the cooperation and compliance of the parties to the conflict and not merely a function of policing ingenuity. Having said that, it is also important to note that the evolution of police tactics has produced a series of police outings that depended heavily for their "success" on a display of force.

I would include the following innovations that have diffused apparently from agency to agency (I have no independent evidence of how they diffused): *simple tactical innovations* (using bike patrols as intelligence sources; establishing a *cordon sanitaire* and zones extending outward from the central place; and visible soft-hat policing near the central sites [to be distinguished from armed, specially suited and equipped riot police units]); *strategic innovations* (using video surveillance, pictures, and tracking on known demonstrators in advance (see *Boston Globe,* "Police Unveil Surveillance Script," December 26, 2004; Police Eye Videotape . . . . December 4, 2004; layering police response based on training, skills, weapons, units involved, and targets of the protest [commercial establishments, people, places, symbolic targets]; and making strong distinctions between visible policing presence and available contingency materiel such as tear gas, pepper spray, dogs, horses, and the military); *coordination of police efforts and practices* (planning in advance with other agencies about responsibilities, resources, command, and control; meeting with potential demonstrators or stakeholders in the events; coordinating ecological factors [the specific circumstances—the who, where, and what—of police protective responses in routine or emergency conditions?], and specifying legal duties in advance by written agreements); *response to, reflection upon, and refining practices* based on after-action products (commissions of inquiry, written responses of Royal Canadian Mounted Police Commissioners, media criticisms, and consultation with academic experts); *an awareness of the crucial need to take into account in advance the contingent role of federal assets.* The term assets is significant, and does not refer simply to equipment, but, as a term of art in the federal government "assets" includes people, weapons, special aircraft, electronic equipment, and so on. The word makes a general gesture toward the almost unlimited power and resources of the federal government. These tactical elements have been communicated widely among police managers, the lessons absorbed, and put into place, as they appear over and over in each next event both in Canada and in the United States.[13]

Case Study: Policing and Preparation for the Democratic National Convention (DNC) meeting in Boston 2004.[14]

Background Facts: Police in the Commonwealth of Massachusetts

The Commonwealth is a fiercely colonial, local, parochial, fragmented state whose politics are vital; party politics still play a very active role in public life. There are some fourteen counties in the Commonwealth with politically weak county sheriffs who primarily transport prisoners to and from court and keep a jail. The state police and the Boston police are quite powerful within the state and the region. Each of the 351 towns and cities has a police and fire agency. There are two formal groups of chiefs, the Western Massachusetts chiefs and the Massachusetts chiefs, both with web sites, and a third informal group of chiefs representing the ten or so largest cities in the Commonwealth. The Chiefs, given their locations, are organized around small town politics and issues. The Boston police, given its size, location in the capital, and its national stature makes its concerns and security obligations fundamentally of a different order and more aligned with those of the larger cities than the formal associations of chiefs.

The police personnel in the cities of Massachusetts are strongly protected by a combination of contracts, union bargaining agreements, and a very elaborate and union-dominated civil service system. It is rare for officers to transfer from one to another department, and all positions up through captain are controlled by civil service exams as well as seniority. This system makes it very difficult to hire talented specialist officers from outside, and resources make specialized training too expensive. Local police departments are both like pyramids and silos, with information collected at the bottom and rarely moving up, and bias for local people in hiring.

The legal powers of police officers in the Commonwealth are in theory rather fragmented. Officers in local city police departments in Massachusetts have no state-wide arrest powers; they cannot easily share personnel for the visitors must shadow a local officer and observe obsequious manners and deference to the local officers and chief. Much of this is done through courtesy calls and reciprocity rather than formal agreements. The state police, called "troopers" and dressed often in wide brimmed Stetson hats and high polished leather cavalry boots, are quite visible at main roads and airports in the Commonwealth, patrol the highways, and investigate serious crimes outside the larger cities.

Police agencies communicate largely by word-of-mouth or phone or fax with other departments. Until recently, as a result of inexpensive encryption, even faxes were little used or police feared that the information could be intercepted. Smaller departments use teletypes. They have few scientific capacities (labs, crime analysis, etc.) and rely on the state or Boston police for forensics, ballistics, and scientific support for evidence analysis. Top command officers (who may be officers who hold the rank of sergeant) variously cultivate relationships with the local schools, school boards, fire chiefs, emergency medical people, and state agencies as well as the media. They do not share databases, information, problems, or personnel except in the rare case of a school-based officer who may organize efforts to coordinate with teachers, principals, and parents as well as other agents and agencies in a community.[15] Police radio frequencies do not permit regional communications and their radios use different frequencies from the federal and state agencies. Often even within a town, or in a large city such as Boston, several radio channels can be used to communicate, but this requires shifting back and forth between channels and often means messages are lost and confusion results. Small cities that adjoin each other cannot communicate quickly and nonproblematically by radio even in emergency situations. Their radio systems cannot easily shift frequencies to send and receive. Massachusetts police have little or no formal organization-to-organization contact with private security organizations, nor do they share radio or other communications facilities with them.

These 351 mainly small Massachusetts cities have local plans that are not state-coordinated for evaluation and handling of hazardous materials, fires, and disasters. Every incident is negotiated in the event, for example, between the officers in the fire department and police present at disasters or at large accidents where arson or other crimes may have taken place. The approach to incidents differs by training, local tradition, and developments in recent years in fire service tactics.[16] In large-scale disasters, negotiation takes place that is largely based on personalities, the hierarchy of status among law-enforcement agencies, and local traditions of deference. Relationships between schools, fire departments, and emergency services are ad hoc, negotiated from incident to incident and not guided by any formal legal hierarchy. Federal agencies have only periodic case-based operations in Massachusetts's cities, and the U.S. Attorney's Office is a presence only in Boston and in the western part of the Commonwealth.

Boston

Boston is the dominant city in New England and in the Commonwealth, and its police department is a center of federal, regional, and state agencies. Boston is one of the oldest cities in North America, and arguably has one of the oldest police departments. The police wear a shoulder patch dating to the beginning of the city in 1630, and the same patch is displayed on the seal above the door to police headquarters. With a population of 589,141 and covering 378.9 square miles, the city sits on a peninsula of land that has been extended into Boston Harbor and is intersected by several rivers. It has three tunnels and two bridges that connect Boston proper to East Boston, Logan Airport, and the North shore. Two major interstate highways run through Boston and a ring road (Route 128) circles the western edge of the city. The city is governed by a historically strong Democratic machine, based on deep roots in the Italian and Irish sections of the city and the highly educated population of the city. The links between city hall and the police department are historic, powerful, and continuing. The mayor now unofficially approves hiring, firing, promotions, and appointments to top command, although this previously was official. The mayor appoints the police commissioner, who serves at his pleasure. Boston is also a strong union city, and this influence shapes decisions involving city personnel matters, including those in the police department.[17]

The Democratic National Convention (DNC)
as a National Security Risk

The police in the New England region planned for about eighteen months to contain the threats to the DNC from demonstrators, terrorists, and imagined dangers.[18] One command center was established under the control of the Boston Commissioner, and staffed by the Boston Police Department (BPD). An electronic bulletin board (WEBEOC) was established to permit input of information by agencies involved in the event (small cities outside Boston were neither included in this network nor in planning and operations). Facilities for jailing and holding prisoners were anticipated by Boston police at the Suffolk County Jail near the Convention center. A free speech zone where talks could be given without police interference was established by negotiation with ACLU, and a huge razor-wired enclosure was built near the center for temporary holding of those detained. All of these were organized and put in place by the BPD. These ecological zonal markings were a development from the experiences in Quebec City, and the involvement of stakeholders in the community, including unions, the ACLU, property owners, and businesses near the convention center reflected tactics used in Ottawa in June 2002 (King 2004: 13).

One acknowledged center of attention, that is, the symbolic center that was not to be breached, was the convention "sacred zone." This center zone around the Convention Center or Fleet Center (named after a local bank now part of the Bank of America) was cordoned off, patrolled on the outside by officers either in "soft" or "normal" uniforms, or in the shorts and t-shirts of bike patrol officers, not SWAT-like ensembles, entry and exit monitored by using magnetometers to check bags, and controlled on the inside by federal agents primarily. This inside/outside pattern of assigning responsibility was used also by police and federal agents at the Salt Lake City Olympics in 2002 (see Decker et al. forthcoming). This arrangement arose in part because Secret Service and Treasury were given responsibilities for the important political figures present. From this center zone radiated out unevenly (Boston ecologically is a colonial city) less controlled zones. Many party and gathering venues at hotels, the harbor, and high status residential areas such as Beacon Hill were patrolled and controlled less visibly. Security was provided at the delegates' hotels. Aside from the candidates, delegates traveling by vans, buses, and cabs were not accompanied by secret service agents.

A network of video surveillance was put in place. There were already some 128 cameras in the financial district adjoining the Fleet Center, and the Globe estimated that about 80 percent of the areas around the Convention Center were being filmed 24 hours a day. Seventeen special cameras were focused on the "sacred zone" immediately around the Convention Center (*Globe*, "Police Unveil Surveillance Script," December 26, 2004).

Major demonstrations were anticipated, but there were no known, named, groups of protestors that had been identified. There was no general name attributed to the "others" who might demonstrate, although "anarchists" was used informally.[19] There were no parades, attempts to breach the bounded zones, and no carnival-like ridicule of politicians. The latter did occur in New York City in 2004 and Philadelphia in 2000 at the Republican convention. Arrests of between 1,500 and 2,000 were anticipated and the County jail made ready, but only six arrests around the Center were made and four of those were not DNC-related.

The precise role of the federal Department of Homeland Security was unclear, although Tom Ridge, then secretary, visited the site and praised the close cooperative arrangements among the many agencies. His picture was taken standing in front of the harbor. The precise role of the State Secretary for Public Security was also unclear throughout, although his office and the DNC supplied a considerable part of the funding needed for the security. According to Ed Flynn, Secretary of Public Safety of the Commonwealth, the budget for the security of the convention was approximately $1 billion. (It was first reported that $25 million was to be supplied by the Federal government, but this later was actually estimated at over 36 million (*Boston Globe*, "Convention Overtime . . . ," October 11, 2004)). Ironically, according to the *Boston Globe* (2004c), although the overtime for police (not all of whom were Boston officers) was estimated as costing at least $6.6 million, the City claimed a profit of over $8 million after this and other costs were recovered (*Boston Globe*, "Convention Overtime . . . ," October 11, 2004).

Personnel involved included the Boston Police and their special units such as harbor, special operations, mounted police, riot police (stationed nearby but not visible to the conventioneers), and undercover officers; officers from nearby cities and states; federal agents; and the state police (1,700 officers of the total strength of 2,300 troopers were assigned to the convention, primarily to traffic duties). The full Boston force, as well as officers from twenty other federal and state agencies, was held ready. Training was to include ". . . suspicious package detection, bomb threats, hazardous materials response and evacuation procedures" (*Boston Globe,* "Police Getting Expert Aid . . .," May 9, 2004). Federal and local agencies did not undertake more elaborate joint training.

The Boston Police and the Massachusetts State Police conceived of and executed a traffic plan to close off the two interstate highways for periods during the convention (four nights), the tramlines across the River Charles, and the tunnels under the river that virtually adjoin and run under the Fleet Center. The center of Boston, the North End, a nearby region very popular with tourists, and the adjoining financial district were virtually deserted during the convention, and businesses, restaurants, and shops complained of lack of business. The huge Boston commuting population and that of the region were essentially staved off and the city was surprisingly quiet. On the other hand, the nearby coastal vacation area was packed with people avoiding and/or having left Boston.

In the eighteen months prior to the convention, the Boston Police Department conceived of and developed a major plan with regional cooperation. This plan involved a strategy of control, according to Commissioner O'Toole (2004), that had four components. The first was advanced planning over eighteen months with a BPD captain fully detailed to this duty. The second was emphasis on intelligence (undercover officers posed as "anarchists") and gathering advance knowledge of potential risks. The third was, in her words, to "change the paradigm" of policing public order. This entailed, according to the Commissioner, positioning uniformed officers on the site and around the center on foot and on mountain bikes in "normal" uniforms, soft hats, and with the usual equipment. They were not dressed in specialized equipment and did not carry weapons associated with control of large-scale disorders. A second level of mobile field forces and federal equipment was held in reserve out of sight. These forces were fully dressed and ready, if and when called. The experiences of reducing social distance between the police and the public in Northern Ireland were used as a model. O'Toole argued that "if you are dressed for battle, you will do battle." Finally, she emphasized the fourth component, cooperation between and among federal and local forces and between local forces. There was no visible test of this aura of cooperation and post-event celebration. However, A written agreement for cooperation between regional State Police Agencies, New England State Police Agreement Compact (NESPAC), had been signed in the 1970s. She also noted that command officers from the various forces (the large local and state forces) learned from the "Super Bowl Model" of gathering top command of the several forces involved in a single command center.

The Boston Police Department was nominally in charge of coordination and federal agents in charge of dignitaries and matters inside the convention center, but any incident would have raised questions of authority, and informal hierarchy giving deference to federal agents would have doubtless ensued. Some examples of tension in the course of the planning are revealing of matters that are difficult to control or alter in a large city with a complex and quite fragile infrastructure of roads and traffic, electrical connections, sewer, and water systems. It must be said that in the absence of a precipitating incident, such as a riot, shooting, or spraying of demonstrators, or a rallying point for further actions, it is not possible to know what was at work in producing an uneventful convention.

Reflections on Risks

Police "think" morally and in terms of control of persons, places, and things. The key areas at the DNC were policed according to the attributed moral importance of control of the area from the police perspective. These areas were a result of traditional policing ideas as well as the newly developed zonal and security warnings (red, orange, yellow, and green) that the office of Homeland Security had institutionalized after September 11. The key areas around the Convention Center were policed according to their degree of moral risk or sacredness. The closer one came to the Convention Center, the tighter the security procedures. The Convention Center itself was under the control of the Secret Service, while the outer perimeter was the responsibility of the Boston Police Department. The newly developed levels of alert of Homeland Security for the country as a whole were irrelevant in this event, since it was a designated National Security Special Event. Thus, the area surrounding the Convention Center was made secure, closed, and traffic rerouted, but the airways, the sea and waterways, in addition to the underground areas adjoining the Center, were not secure. The area under Boston City Hall is honeycombed with tunnels and station routines left over from the razing, closing, and sealing of the former Sculley Square T station.[20] The area under the Convention Center is built over catacombs, adjoins a circle of rotaries, bridge approaches, and an interstate highway. Although patrols were assigned to the harbor, it is not difficult to imagine access via a small boat to the area. The traffic plans, the communication system, and the command center, were not coordinated with the chiefs of the numerous surrounding small, suburban communities. This was particularly awkward for these communities when the closure of the I-93 poured commuters onto Route 128, the ring road around Boston, and other local roads leading in and out of Boston. In the event of a nuclear disaster, traffic on one interstate would be routed north and the other south, a clear recipe for disaster (interview with chief of a large Massachusetts city).

The symbolic and actual dominance of the Boston Police in the area, respect given informally, and past agreements, meant that their overt rank, status, and control were roughly deferred to in everyday activity. If, however, a question required immediate action by an officer, his or her rank and command status would be problematic. The officers who were hired and paid from other regional police departments were in practice under the command of the BPD, regardless of rank. Another informal rule of hierarchy prevailed in that federal agents, namely Secret Service Agents, controlled the symbolic venues and Boston police provided back up. In fact, the federal agents had actual control of the use of resources called "assets" in federal jargon, especially federal agents and the military, not the BPD.

One of the more striking aspects of the fragmented loyalty of police and their obligations was revealed when the Boston police threatened to strike during the national convention. A last-minute strike by Boston police officers, who had been working without a contract for several years, was avoided in late July of 2004. This took concerted efforts by the Governor, the Mayor, negotiators for the unions and the city, and, in the end, arbitrators. The police picketed preconvention events, held street demonstrations in the Back Bay neighborhood, and just before the convention forced John Kerry, the Democratic nominee and a Boston resident, to declare that he would not cross the picket lines to give a planned speech. The potential chaos of a labor action was avoided but always remains a possibility in a strongly Democratic city with solid municipal unions.

No legal problems were encountered with protestors or demonstrators during the event, but U.S. attorneys in the civil division (in the Office of U.S. Attorney—an appointed federal official with considerable power in the region) were denied access to security-related documents as they lacked high enough security clearance (Sullivan speech September 30, 2004). The only visible problem during the convention that brought police action arose when a small group of protestors appeared at the rear entrance to the Fleet Center. It was closed and two people tried to cut through a fence. Uniformed secret service agents closed off the entrance magnetometer and Boston police took over.

Concluding Comment

The changes in the governance of security since September 11, 2001, have been considerable, particularly the visible and public efforts to prevent the use of hijacked planes as weapons against domestic targets outside the context of war. This chapter has reviewed some ongoing visible changes and reorganization at the federal level in the United States. These are works in progress. The changes in local policing, especially those required for policing events that might attract activists and or terrorist attention, appear to be more subtle yet far more transformative of police practices. Although the events of September 11 may be considered a catalyst, these practices have emerged in the policing of massive public occasions (MPOs) over the past fifteen years in North America.

A review of innovations in policing MPOs in Canada and the United States shows that they are consistent with the planning and actions seen in Boston. Almost all of the integral features in policing earlier MPOs were used in Boston. They were present if not deployed visibly. The differences were in the presence of known protest or threat groups in the earlier MPOs. Ironically, while terrorists were a notional opponent, they by definition would be invisible, whereas protestors want to be visible and indeed crave media attention. There was less need to track demonstrators or engage in consultation in Boston as was done in Ottawa and Seattle. There were no recognized, named groups or even vaguely recognized interested parties to oppose the apparent police control. The ACLU was consulted as a kind of surrogate or representative of the civil liberties of the potential protestors.

In summary, the rise of specialized police units, refined tactics, strategies, management approaches, and political negotiations for managing public protest and demonstration has been obscured in the United States because most of the major media-covered developments (except Seattle, Philadelphia, the Salt Lake City Winter Olympics, and the Boston and New York City 2004 political party conventions) have taken place in Canada and Europe, not in this country. Events in these MPOs (except in Seattle) have not escalated into ugly, violent incidents, while those in Canada did so repeatedly with worldwide attention given to the use of pepper spray (in the UBC event); massive arrests (in the Quebec demonstrations); rather awkward coordination and uneven deployment of excessive force (dogs and the equivalent to SWAT teams), and failure to declare the riot act even while acting as if the situation called for martial law (Quebec City demonstrations (see King 2004: 6–9)). The recent experience in the United States has been traumatically marked by the September 11 attacks, and our focus remains there, blocking the fact that major developments have been unfolding outside of the United States. From the perspective of planning for public safety, police forces recognize that the same vulnerabilities of major symbolic places and meetings can be exploited or tested by protestors, as well as terrorists (whether domestic like Nichols and McVeigh or foreign such as the twelve who attacked the Pentagon and World Trade Center on September 11, 2001).

This case study indicates that while antiterrorist activities in policing have been visible and dramatic, especially post–September 11, perhaps a more important transformation in policing of MPOs, as the term has come to be understood, is in process. This is an example of organizational learning. The idea of organizational learning is an inference, as the learning and the tactics displayed were similar across sites, the violence less, the elements of the control approach the same, and the execution parallel. Boston Commissioner O'Toole's role on the Patten Commission (which investigated the Royal Ulster Constabulary) is perhaps the most obvious source of shared learning about nonviolent policing of terrorism and potential terrorism. I would argue that organizational learning is occurring in large urban police organizations, and this learning is being lodged in the symbolic "institutional memory." That is, it can be recalled, used, and applied, refined, and seen as a tool. It stands ready—available for future use. There is a diffusion process in action—spreading policing techniques, strategies, planning, and coordination modes—and in consequence, a more sophisticated pattern of policing is emerging. This is in part responsive to the education, sophistication, and resources of demonstrators, protestors, and other participants in these events. This combination of experience, learning, and maintaining knowledge moves police in the direction of proactive or advance planning based, of necessity, on refined intelligence, as distinguished from a reactive, case-based policing model. The differentiation of units, skills, and training, and the role of tactics and weapons in different points in different kinds of events, are noteworthy in this process, and the implications for federal-local coordination within the United States, as well as transnational circulation and exchange of knowledge, are considerable.

There are several implications from this pattern of organizational learning seen in Boston. North American police departments are small, insular, and unsophisticated; the officers are loyal to local governments, small, generalists with little training and unskilled in many ways; outside large cities, they lack experience in dealing with MPOs. They have little capacity for advanced planning or research, and must face each new occasion afresh. The experience of Boston and New York and to a lesser extent Los Angeles, and Chicago in the first years of the twenty-first century, in handling large-scale protest is now augmented by the protests in Canada,

Seattle, and Philadelphia that were based on reaction against globalization. Are the Boston convention and the Salt Lake Olympics successes more significant than the near disaster in Philadelphia and the riots in Seattle? Is organizational learning ongoing? What are the implications for civil liberties of ratcheting up the use of surveillance cameras in the city of Boston, Logan Airport, and the advanced weapons and other equipment now available to local departments? The recent tragic events in London (July 2005) again remind us that terrorism is in fact not completely preventable, and that modern urban centers are in fact very fragile with respect to their transportation systems, sewers, water supply, and sources of power. No amount of planning, screening, prevention, or intelligence can avert massive damage from time to time if terrorists are willing to risk the personal consequences.

Notes

1. The journalist, Bob Woodward (2002, 2004), who interviewed the principal figures in instigating, rationalizing, and mounting both invasions, suggests there was a drift to these invasions rather than a political and economic plan. The military plan, cobbled together as it was, was at least a plan (Keegan 2005: 6, 97). The rationales he recorded were assembled without coherent analysis or integration, a mixture of personal vendetta against Hussein and bin Laden, a compulsion to act, and concern for national morale and unity.

2. Although there are some text-like treatments of terrorism, there is nothing written on the direct impact of these events on governance of security at the local or national level. Much of what is known about threats to national security is taken from the serious media, i.e., news magazines, journals of opinion, and literary magazines such as the *New Yorker, Atlantic*, and *Harper's*. It should be noted that the Congressional Committee that investigated the failures to anticipate and prevent the Japanese bombing of Pearl Harbor issued a thirty-nine-volume report that led to major changes in U.S intelligence gathering. See Roberta Wohlstetter's magnificent analysis in *Pearl Harbor: Warning and Decision* (1962).

3. In early 2002, the Department of Homeland Security, following President Clinton's Directive 62, allowed certain MPOs to be designated national special security events (NSSEs). This designation qualified them for federal funding and meant federal control over policing such events. Treasury was designated as the lead agency in such events and Secret Service Agents were designated as the lead agents. This designation was used for the Salt Lake City Winter Olympics in February 2002, and the Democratic National Convention (DNC) discussed below.

4. The blurred line between maintaining domestic security, waging war, sustaining anti-terrorism, and international conquest, has led to the crude and ineffectual sweeps, arrests, and detention, including torture of citizens held without legal counsel for some time, that have yielded only limited new intelligence

(Hersh 2004). Internally, the situation is unclear. It was said in congressional testimony by an FBI agent that a crime scene is a crime scene. Perhaps reflecting that view that context is irrelevant, the present executive leader of the terrorist unit in the FBI has had no training in the language, culture, or politics of Islam, nor in antiterrorist work (*Metro*, July 20, 2005).

5. Federal agencies in addition to the Homeland Security Office itself were augmented in budget and personnel. The budget allocations of DEA and FBI included more agents as well as additional money and foreign stations. In a related idea, in these agencies narcotics and terrorism were connected with a neologism, "narco-terrorism" (DEA.gov website, 2002). This is of course counter-factual and counter intuitive since these federal agencies had massively failed to be responsive to the threat of terror.

6. The *Boston Globe* (December 30, 2004a) reports intra-agency conflict on the development of a universal fingerprint database. The conflict resides in practices; Homeland Security and State urge a two-fingerprint approach, and the Department of Justice urge the ten-finger approach. The taking of ten fingerprints adds some one minute to processing time and would add to the workload of processing "7 million VISA applications annually." The FBI retains more than 47 million fingerprint records. It is reported that only an estimated 1% of the 118,000 daily U.S. visitors are actually run through FBI files.

7. Some of this material is modified in Manning, forthcoming (2005).

8. The number of specialized federal agencies involved in some form of law enforcement (this includes regulation as well as use of the criminal sanction) is not known precisely. Morris and Geller (1992) estimated forty-two agencies and Manning (forthcoming in Wood and Dupont) estimates more than fifty. The number depends on how "law enforcement" is defined.

9. These include those in special agencies and 47,129 in federal agencies. Two modes of case-working exist. While the traditional model of case-working is reactive and focused on a violation of federal law, there are also border areas, such as domestic espionage and national security in which a more proactive case-creation model is used. This distinction deserves some elaboration, but it does not figure in the analysis below except indirectly. The first is a sanctioning, case-based model of reacting to known events aiming to eradicate or radically reduce offenses. It thrives on punishment, demonizing of particular targets and criminals known for their past activity, and closing cases as a sign of activity/productivity. Information is property, kept secret, seen as a symbolic good representing the skills and competence of the individual agent, and shared rarely with colleagues. It is reactive, case-based, and responsive to known crimes. It is ill-suited to respond to anticipated crime, conspiracies, domestic, and international terrorism. It begins with a crime and works backwards to find the perpetrator. Fears for security of data and the commodification of information make the introduction of effective electronic infrastructure difficult and resisted (Kessler 2003; *Report of the 9/11 Commission* 2004). The second is a negotiating model which rests on compromise, reducing risk, managing negative consequences of risk and in part preventing or anticipating future deviance. Going to law is the last resort of these agencies (Hawkins 2003). Their

contingency is the irregular aspects of human conduct that lie just outside the criminal and immediate and is projected into the future of present trends and difficulties (see Manning 1992). Information is negotiated between the regulators and the regulated. Compliance is the aim and restorative justice a hoped-for outcome. Spies and informants may be required. Court is avoided in general. Rather than pursing those who have broken a law, this model seeks advance identification of risks and risk management tactics that will reduce future threats rather than pin down past offenders.

10. While clearly this is not an exclusive classification, since some students of police are police or have been police, and many police are not students of policing, the third culture connotes a mutual set of interests that differentiate them from "police" and "students or professors."

11. I draw heavily in this list and the points that follow from the very rich descriptions provided by King (2004) and Decker, et al., forthcoming. As I was revising this draft (July 7, 2005), the demonstrations at Gleneagles, Scotland, at the time of the G8 meetings took place and the horrendous bombings in the London Underground and one bus were reported.

12. For example, during the World Series in baseball in the United States, in October, 2004, the riot police in heavy combat gear, weapons, and supporting personnel and other equipment (pepper pellet guns, dogs, horses) were deployed to a park in Back Bay near the Fenway Baseball Park, and were photographed by the *Boston Globe* (October 4, 2005) rehearsing.

13. These shared ideas include well-known tactics such as undercover work, gathering and coordinating special squads, assembling backup units such as the National Guard, creating a command center, placing magnetometers and screening at the entrance to the Fleet Convention Center (named after a banking corporation), and deploying visible walking officers under close supervision around the perimeter. I have not done a systematic content analysis of the presence of each of these in the MPOs I noted above, although this would be essential to any confirmation of my argument. I do believe that the clustering of these elements in successfully managed events would support the claim that they are necessary if not sufficient to successful (improved) management of MPO occasions.

14. I draw on background material gathered at roundtable meetings with groups of Massachusetts chiefs who met at Northeastern University in August 2003 (I attended as an observer), and the panel discussion on September 30, 2004, at Northeastern University, Boston, by Boston Commissioner of Police Kathleen O'Toole, State Police Colonel Tom Robbins, Secretary of Public Safety in Massachusetts Ed Flynn, and U.S. Attorney Michael Sullivan. Additional materials came from my interviews with Amy Farrell and Jack McDevitt who carried out systematic observations at the DNC on the streets, in the command center, and in the Fleet Convention Center. I also have interviewed ranking officers in some ten local Massachusetts police departments, August 2003–June, 2005.

15. Consistent with local traditions, local school officers have to build a role and a network of colleagues inside and outside the schools and the content of these

roles differs widely (McDevitt, personal communication, June 2001). These observations are based on McDevitt's national study of school safety officers.

16. Space limitations preclude going into detail on this matter, but the national fire standards coordinates approaches to various types of fires, by materials, causation, ecology, height of the building, and weather conditions. Furthermore, the approach deems that the first on the scene coordinates and leads the fire control efforts, marshalling resources and personnel until he or she is satisfied that command can be relinquished. The police, on the other hand, have no national standards for preventing, reducing, investigating, or suppressing crime or disorder, assume that rank takes command (there are often of course officers of the same senior rank at the scene of a hostage situation, disaster, or large fire), and are consistently plagued by questions of authority in ongoing matters including even routine chases.

17. The Boston department is old-fashioned with its strong influences of unions, ethnicity (especially Irish and Italian), the party politics of the Democratic Party, and the state Civil Service Commission, which reviews firings. In many respects the key players inside and outside the department are linked to internal politics of the department and the constant issues of succession, "juice," as a result of being in the inner clique supporting the current commissioner, or in the cabals (those who seek power, resist the current networks of power, or are direct enemies of the top command).

18. I use the term "imagined" carefully because if an organization cannot imagine new forms of threat and correspondingly adjust its strategies and tactics, it will continue to respond in the conventional and traditional fashion to known and well-understood threats. It is not surprising that the primary preparations for policing the DNC were well-known tactics such as undercover work, equipment, and specialized units closeted out of sight, a visible command center (itself of course a vulnerable target), magnetometers and screening at entrances, and visible walking officers.

19. I am grateful to Carsten Andresen, who observed both front and backstage policing at the DNC, for this point.

20. Interview with Jim Jordan, Director of Strategic Planning, Boston Police Department, former, October 26, 2004.

References

Bamford, James. 2002. *The Puzzle Palace*. New York: Simon and Schuster.
Bamford, James. 2005. *Pretext for War*. New York: Simon and Schuster.
Boston Globe
—May 9, 2004. "Police Getting Expert Aid."
—October 10, 2004. "Report faults Homeland Security."
—October 11, 2004. "Convention Overtime at 6.6. Million."
—December 4, 2004. "Police Eye Video Surveillance."
—December 26, 2004. "Police Unveil Surveillance Script."
—December 30, 2004. "Fingerprint Base Faulted."

—December 31, 2004. "T Upgrades Security."

—April 8, 2005. "Government Nearly Doubles use of Patriot Act Search Power."

Brandl, S. 2004. "Back to the Future: The Implications of September 11, 2001 on Law Enforcement Practice and Policy," *Ohio State Journal of Criminal Law*, 1: 133–154.

Brodeur, J.-P. 2004. *Visages de La Police*. Montreal: University of Montreal Press.

Congressional Hearings on Pearl Harbor. U.S. Congress, 1946. 39 volumes.

Decker, Scott, et al., forthcoming. "Safety and Security at Special Events: The Case of the Salt Lake City Olympic Games" *Security Journal*.

Defleum, M. 2003. *Policing World Society*. Oxford: Oxford University Press.

Earl, J. S. Soule, and J.D. McCarthy 2003. "Protest Under Fire?: Explaining the Policing of Protest" *Amercian Sociological Review*, 68: 581–606.

Ericson, R. and K. Haggerty 1998. *Policing the Risk Society*. Toronto: University of Toronto Press.

Forst, B. 2004. "Terrorism" unpublished presentation to ASC, Denver, 2003.

Gilboy, Janet 1993. "Profiling at Airports," *Law and Policy*.

Greenway, H.D.S. "The Kidnapping Case that Irritated Italy" *Boston Globe* (July 15, 2005) editorial page.

Hawkins, Keith 2003. *Law as Last Resort*. Oxford: Oxford University Press.

Hersh, S. 2004. *Chain of Command*. New York: Harper Collins.

Johnston and Shearing. 2003. *Governing Security*. London and New York: Routledge Kegan Paul.

Kessler, Ronald 1994. *Inside the CIA*. New York: Pocket Books.

Kessler, Ronald 2003. *The Bureau*. New York: St. Martin's paperbacks.

Keegan, John 2004. *Intelligence in War*. New York; Random House.

Keegan, John 2005. *The Iraq War*. New York: Vintage.

King, M. 2004. "From Reactive Policing to Crowd Management: Policing Anti-globalization Protest in Canada" unpublished paper, University of Leicester, June.

Langweische, Frank 2004. *American Ground*. New York: North Point Books.

Lehman-Langlois, S. 2002. "The Myopic Panopticon," *Policing and Society*, 13: 43–58.

Liang, Hsi-Huey 1970. *The Berlin Police Force in the Weimar Republic*. Berkeley: University of California Press.

Lyons, D. "Threats of New Data Bases and Screening" forthcoming in *Canadian Journal of Sociology*.

Manning, Peter K. 1992. " 'Big Bang' Decisions" in K. Hawkins ed. *Uses of Discretion*, Oxford: Oxford University Press.

Manning, Peter K. forthcoming. "Two Cases of American Anti-Terrorist Policing" in Jennifer Wood and Benoit DuPont eds. *Democracy and Policing*. Cambridge: Cambridge University Press.

Manning, Peter K. forthcoming. "American Policing," in T. Newburn and T. Jones eds. *Plural Policing*. Collompton, Devon: Willan.

Metro Newspaper (Boston) July 20, 2005. "Selling Security."

Morris, N. and W. Geller 1992. "Relations between Federal and Local Police Agencies" in N. Morris and M. Tonry eds. *Modern Policing*. Chicago: University of Chicago Press.

O'Toole, Kathleen Address, Seminar on Management of the Democratic National Convention, Northeastern University, Boston, MA, September 30, 2004.

Powers, Thomas 2004. *Intelligence Wars*. New York: Simon and Schuster.

Report of the 9/11 Commission. 2004. Washington D.C.: USPGO.

Richman, Daniel 2000. "The Changing Boundaries between Federal and Local Law Enforcement," pp. 81–110 in J. Horney ed. *Changing Boundaries in Criminal Justice Organizations*. Washington, D.C. Department of Justice: USGPO.

Scheptycki, James, ed. 2000. *Issues in Transnational Policing*. London: RKP.

Selznick, Phillip 1949. *TVA and the Grassroots*. Berkeley: University of California Press.

Shearing, Clifford 2005. Nodal Security. *Police Quarterly*, 8 (1) March: 57–63.

Shearing, C. and R. Ericson 1991. "Culture as Configurative Action," *British Journal of Sociology*, 42: 481–506.

Singer, Peter 2003. *Corporate Warriors*. Ithaca, NY: Cornell University Press.

Stamper, N. 2005. *Breaking Rank*. New York: Nation Press.

Strasser, S. 2005. *The Abu Ghraib Investigations*. New York: Public Affairs Press.

Thomas, H. 2001. *The Spanish Civil War*. Revised edition. New York. Harper Torchbooks.

Waddington, P.A. J. 1991. *The Strong Arm of the Law*. Oxford: Clarendon University Press.

Waddington, P.A. J. 2003. "Policing Public Order," in Tim Newburn, ed. *Handbook of Policing*. Cullompton, Devon: Willan.

Walker, Neil 2004. "The Pattern of Transnational Policing," in T. Newburn ed. *Handbook of Policing*. Cullompton: Willan.

Whitney, C. 2005. Abu Ghraib ed. *The Politics of Torture*. Berkeley: North Atlantic Books.

Wilson, James Q. 1978. *The Investigators*. New York: Basic Books.

Wired magazine "You're Being Watched" (December 2003).

Wohlstetter, R. 1962. *Pearl Harbor: Warning and Decision*. Palo Alto: Stanford University Press.

Woodward, B. 2002. *Bush at War*. New York: Simon and Schuster.

Woodward, B. 2004. *Plan of Attack*. New York: Simon and Schuster.

10

The Scales of Justice: Federal–Local Tensions in the War on Terror

Kris Erickson, John Carr, and Steve Herbert

Recently, the city of Portland, Oregon, found itself willing to just say no to the Federal Bureau of Investigation (FBI). After eight years of participation with the FBI in a joint task force to investigate residents suspected of plotting terrorist acts, the city decided to withdraw. The task force was an example of a federal-local law-enforcement partnership that is now quite common in the United States, especially in the age of heightened concern about terrorism. Such partnerships bring together the investigatory expertise of federal agencies with the local knowledge of city or county law enforcement.

The decision to withdraw was the focus of much local controversy, and followed a protracted and impassioned public debate. Portland officials cited two main reasons for ending its cooperation with the FBI. The first involved strong suspicions from the city's Muslim community that they were being illegitimately targeted in investigations of alleged terrorist activity. Second, there was a concern that local officials were not sufficiently able to oversee the work the Portland police were doing in conjunction with the FBI. The FBI, citing the sensitivity of their investigations, did not want elected officials, including the mayor, to have access to their files. City officials thus felt prevented from assuming their responsibility to oversee the practices of law enforcement.

In an age in which the "war on terror" appears both unremitting and unwinnable, such conflicts between federal and local law-enforcement agencies may become commonplace (see Thacher 2005, for an analysis of similar dynamics in Dearborn, Michigan). But these conflicts are hardly new. Instead, they reflect longstanding tensions within American political culture over the proper balance of political power between central and local authorities. There remain persistent conflicts over the geographic scale—national, regional, state, or local—of governance. These struggles are typically most ardent when actors at one scale seek an expansion of power that might reduce the power of actors at other scales.

These political tensions over the geographic scale of authority have a long pedigree; they have appeared in a range of policy arenas throughout American history. Most famously, perhaps, they were a central component of the struggle for the expansion of civil rights for African Americans; federal efforts to enhance equal opportunity were met with resistance couched in the language of local control and states' rights. These tensions over the scale of governance also emerge, understandably, in the area of law enforcement, where the coercive power of governmental authorities is at its most evident. As the Portland story illustrates, strong political passions can emerge in contests over where to situate the power to investigate suspected criminals and to bring them into the criminal justice process.

In this chapter, we hope to show that what may appear, in the Portland case, as a new story about the politics of fighting terror is in fact a much older one about the scales of justice. This timeworn story about the balance of power between different geographical scales often focuses upon law-enforcement practice, but it is hardly limited to that policy arena. In elaborating our argument, we reinforce the work of numerous scholars who recognize the significance of geographic scale. Their central insight is a simple but often neglected one: that the scalar location of social phenomena is critical to understanding how those phenomena operate (see, for starters, Brenner 2001; Cox 1993; Delaney and Leitner 1997; Marston 2000; McMaster and Sheppard 2002). The significance of geographic scale is nowhere more evident than in discussions of political authority. Political actors and institutions with a global reach, for example, exert a different power from that of entities having a more limited scope. In short, to understand the extent and capacity of political power, one must understand the geographic scale at which it operates.

We seek to reinforce this line of work, but to focus attention more particularly on the *ideology* of scale, on the discursive political significance of situating practices at one jurisdictional level versus another. The ideological power of scale is especially obvious in the robust debates about where to locate the surveillance and arrest powers of law-enforcement authorities.[1] As we will show, strong arguments can be made for situating this power at both federal and local levels. Because of the significance of the coercive capacity of law-enforcement agents, political debates that rehash these arguments in the context of policing can be vigorous, as they were in Portland.

It is no great surprise that ideological struggles over the geographic scale of political authority are longstanding and impassioned in the United States. Such debates date to the formation of the republic. Certainly, the authors of the U.S. Constitution wrestled ardently with competing claims for federal and state governmental dominance; they sought to balance the need for centralized authority against the desire for an autonomous sphere for state governments. Such a balance is ever elusive, because the alignment of interests favoring more expansive federal or state power continually shifts depending on the issues and context. A political progressive, for instance, may favor centralized authority to reduce poverty but fear its exercise in acts of surveillance. A conservative, by contrast, may see things completely differently, favoring a hands-off approach on economic issues but a stronger hand on matters cultural and criminal.

In sum, there is an ongoing and contentious politics around the scale of governance. We use the war on terror, and the story of Portland, to illustrate the *potency and indeterminacy* of the political struggles over scale. We move through five sections. In the first, we review the history of federalism in the United States, noting the ongoing struggle over where to situate political authority. We consider, second, the specific case of crime control, and review those forces that grant increased—though never complete—legitimacy to more centralized law-enforcement efforts. In our third section, we focus on the war on terror and the federal response to it, most notably in the form of the U.S.A. PATRIOT Act. We follow this with an analysis of the political contest in Portland. A concluding section summarizes and extends our analysis.

U.S. Federalism and the Constitutionally Embodied Struggle Over Scale of Governance

Questions of federalism have often become imbricated in such contemporary hot-button political debates as abortion, gay marriage, and medical marijuana. Yet the potential of scale of governance to become a focus for political debate is effectively enshrined within the U.S. Constitution. From the beginning, irreconcilable currents of distrust of both local and centralized decision-making have animated the form of the Constitution and subsequent interpretive case law. Thus, current political debates over the scale of governance, as witnessed in Portland, invoke and repeat the framers' original conflicting views about how to strike the right balance of power between central and local political authorities (Blomley 1994: 116–120), the barest outlines of which we sketch here.

In concrete terms, this institutionalized tension finds its most obvious and influential manifestation in the U.S. Constitution. On its face, Article VI, Clause 2—known as the "supremacy clause"—establishes the preeminence of the federal government and federal law, providing that

> This Constitution, and the Laws of the United States which shall be made in Pursuance thereof; and all Treaties made, or which shall be made, under the Authority of the United States, shall be the supreme Law of the Land; and the Judges in every State shall be bound thereby, any Thing in the Constitution or Laws of any State to the Contrary notwithstanding.[2]

This centralized authority was subsequently reinforced by the Fourteenth Amendment, which likewise limits the powers of the states to transgress individual rights under the federal Constitution:

> No State shall make or enforce any law which shall abridge the privileges or immunities of citizens of the United States; nor shall any State deprive any person of life, liberty, or property, without due process of law; nor deny to any person within its jurisdiction the equal protection of the laws.[3]

Such powerful assertions of the authority of a strong central government are offset by language in both the Tenth and Eleventh Amendments, each of which carves out an equally robust state and local governmental sphere. Under the Tenth Amendment, "[t]he powers not delegated to the United States by the Constitution, nor prohibited by it to the States, are reserved to the States respectively, or to the people,"[4] thus promising effectively unrestrained local governmental authority over those matters not explicitly addressed by the Federal Constitution. In a similar vein, the terms of the Eleventh Amendment exempt the states from suit in the federal courts under certain circumstances, providing that, "[t]he Judicial power of the United States shall not be construed to extend to any suit in law or equity, commenced or prosecuted against one of the United States by Citizens of another State, or by Citizens or Subjects of any Foreign State."[5]

While the Constitutional division of power between local and national scales of governance is fairly straightforward in theory—all power to the states except where authority has been explicitly granted to the federal government by the Constitution—in practice it becomes both ambiguous and historically fluid. Indeed, because of the susceptibility of the Constitutional grants of federal authority to widely varying interpretation,[6] the federalist scheme embodied by the Constitution has created a state of permanent struggle between scales of governmental authority.

Indeed, the question of scale of sovereignty was seen as so essential to the survival of the young Republic that it animated the creation of party politics in the United States; Hamilton's Federalist Party advanced the cause of a strong central government, Jefferson's Democrat-Republican Party the need for state and local authority. It was within the courts, however, that much of the struggle between scales of governance has played out. Notwithstanding Jefferson's victory in the 1800 election, the U.S. Supreme Court's 1819 ruling in *McCulloch v. Maryland*[7] solidified the trend toward consolidation of centralized governmental authority by upholding the Federal authority to establish a national bank, in a move that foreshadowed subsequent judicial expansions of federal power, the *McCulloch* court based its decision upon the enumerated Constitutional grant of federal powers of taxation, borrowing, and regulation of interstate commerce along with Article I, Section 8, Clause 18, permitting the national government to, "make all Laws which shall be necessary and proper for carrying into Execution the foregoing Powers, and all other Powers vested by this Constitution in the Government of the United States, or in any Department or Officer thereof."[8]

While the Supreme Court's early decisions set the stage for an expansion of new federal powers, a series of national crises and initiatives—the Civil War and the Depression, Lyndon Johnson's "Great Society" effort to eradicate poverty and promote civil rights, and most recently the "war on terror"—have given impetus to such an expansion. Along with the defeat of the South in the Civil War and the invalidation of slavery by the Thirteenth Amendment, a further shift of governmental power from the local to the national scale developed. Specifically, the post–Civil War period saw both the invalidation of state laws regulating commercial activities such as railroads[9] under notions of federal commerce clause preemption, as well as the creation of the first substantial federal regulatory agencies such as the Interstate Commerce Commission. Shortly after the turn of the twentieth century, the judiciary began interpreting the commerce clause as validating the extension of federal authority to almost all economic activity in the "stream of commerce."[10] Such judicial involvement in the balance of power between governmental scales was essential to the consolidation of federal power, and the birth of the modern centralized regulatory state.

The pull toward the expansion of federal power under the commerce clause grew stronger in years following the Great Depression and World War II. Notwithstanding substantial initial resistance to Roosevelt's "New Deal" efforts to respond to the worldwide economic depression, the Court's decisions in the late 1930s[11] effectively opened the door to unlimited federal economic regulation, enabling the federal government to exert a virtually unchallengeable dominance over an increasingly broad range of economic activities.

Following the pattern set by both post–Civil War federal programs and the New Deal, a strong centralized national government continued to be regarded as the primary tool for enacting sweeping political change in the name of social justice, and overcoming what were perceived to be parochial, and often discriminatory, local practices. This tendency was most strongly manifested by the federal government's championing of the cause of civil rights in the 1950s and 1960s. Thus, *Brown v. Board of Education*,[12]—which extended the Fourteenth Amendment's protections to the racial composition of state classrooms—and Johnson's Great Society project—which led to passage of the Civil Rights Act of 1964 as well as a host of environmental regulations, and an increasingly intertwined system of federal grants to all scales of local government conditioned upon local compliance with an increasingly large number of federal requirements—all typified a judicial move toward larger and larger scales of governmental authority.

While much of the historical jurisprudence interpreting the Constitutional tensions between scales of governance has—as outlined above—favored a centralized federal government, this trend has been resisted by a counter-current favoring state and local authority. For example, before the eruption of federal authority over civil rights in the 1950s and 1960s the Court had previously deferred to southern states' "Jim Crow" laws and practices. Thus as early as the 1890s the Court upheld a state statute requiring railways to provide equal but separate accommodations for white and "colored" passengers,[13] as well as racial segregation in public education as "a matter belonging to the respective states."[14]

Similarly, the modern Supreme Court has begun to reassert the fundamental importance of state governmental authority in a number of landmark cases putting a check on the continued expansion of federal authority. In particular, during the late William $R_h$enquist's tenure as Chief Justice, the Supreme Court began to limit Congress' previously unbounded Commerce Clause powers,[15] while recognizing States' Tenth Amendment immunity from federal mandates for state adoption and/or participation in federal regulatory programs.[16]

It is important to stress that the efforts to increase federal power, often in the name of progressive social change, have been consistently resisted both in the political arena and in the courts through traditional arguments for the virtues and necessity of governance at local and state scales. Southern resistance to federal civil rights programs and court-ordered integration provide the prime example of this trend. In this instance, arguments for racial segregation were rearticulated as more facially neutral assertions of states' rights and inherent local sovereignty. Since the 1950s, similar rhetoric in favor of "state's rights" and "small government federalism" have been mobilized in efforts to oppose a host of federally recognized rights, entitlements, and social programs—as in the case of abortion rights and affirmative action, and to attempt to preempt the creation of such rights, entitlements, and programs—as in the case of gay marriage.

Yet it would be a mistake to make a simple equation between progressive policy and increased federal power, or between reactionary politics and local power. Certainly, local activism is often progressive in its approach (see Andrea McArdle's Chapter 8 in this volume), and skeptical of federal authority. Similarly, as is witnessed in contemporary debates over gay marriage, conservative groups often seek strong assertions of centralized power to limit local autonomy. These concurrent, contradictory developments belie the presumption, often operative in U.S. politics, that centralized federal authority is the tool of progressive, often left-leaning social and economic agenda, and that the assertion of states' rights and the need for localized scales of government largely serve as tropes for conservative opponents of such agenda. These contradictory currents illustrate our central claim: that the ideologies of scale are simultaneously potent and fluid. Advocates of certain policy positions often legitimate those positions by associating them with a particular scale of governance, be it centralized or decentralized. But their allegiance to that scale may be fleeting; in other instances, those same advocates may champion the benefits of situating authority at an alternate scale.

This is what played out in Portland, a politically progressive city that found itself resisting federal interventions in law enforcement. To understand that dynamic, we need first to understand the scale politics of law enforcement.

Federalism and Crime Control

The boundary between federal and local control is often an ill-defined and contentious one; it can be a political fault line riddled with fissures and dislocations. In short, those who favor localized control both fear centralized power and trumpet notions of organic, bottom-up politics. The danger of federal power is that it will go unchecked, and enable central authorities to pry too deeply into, and regulate too completely, the affairs of the citizenry (Fogelson 1971; Marx 1990). The romance of local control is bound up with its association with the citizen-subject, who is close to the dynamics that most directly shape his or her life, and who should possess the capacity to shape those dynamics through localized political action (see Bryan 2003).

On the other hand, centralized power can accomplish worthy social goals. As noted above, the federal government has stepped in to guarantee civil liberties where local authorities refuse to protect them. It also often seeks to provide oversight and direction to large-scale problems of governance. Certainly, efforts to reduce poverty are more likely to succeed if developed on a national scale, given the macroeconomic dynamics that generate income patterns. Isolated efforts by localities will hardly alter those patterns much, if at all (Massey 1979).

These tensions are especially evident in debates over the proper control of law enforcement. The police power is, by tradition, a hallowed *local* power in the United States. As Sandra O'Connor argued in a recent dissent in a key federalism case, *Gonzales v. Raich*,[17] "[t]he States' core police powers have always included authority to define criminal law and to protect the health, safety, and welfare of their citizens."[18] This guarantee of localized control over law enforcement stems, in large part, from suspicions of centralized power that animated the protections in the Bill of Rights against government authority. Because the abuse of such authority is often embodied as the prying federal law-enforcement agent, key provisions of the Bill of Rights, including the Fourth and Fifth Amendments, were written precisely to keep the inquisitive eyes of the central government from any unjustified surveillance.

The favored status of localized policing means that there are an abundance of law-enforcement agencies in the United States. Geller and Morris 1992 document that the United States has nearly 12,000 municipal, seventy-nine county, and more than 18,000 township police agencies; more than 3,000 county sheriff's departments; fifty-one state police and highway patrols; and nearly 1,000 nonfederal special-purpose police agencies. Given this sprawling law-enforcement apparatus, and the resultant potential for duplication, lack of communication, and interjurisdictional disputes, it is not surprising that federal agents tout the efficiency that results from more centralized, and hence coordinated, crime-reduction efforts.

These efforts to centralize law-enforcement practices have historically run in tandem with the wider efforts to assert federal control. The FBI was created coterminously with the New Deal, and was meant to target organized and other forms of trans-state crime (Powers 1987; Theoharis, et al. 1999). In these efforts, the FBI sought to create partnerships with local law enforcement, in no small part through developing centralized databases to collate crime patterns and various key pieces of information, such as fingerprints. In the Great Society era, federal commissions sought to understand crime and law enforcement patterns, especially because these were seen as central dynamics fueling many instances of urban unrest (Kerner Commission 1968; McCone Commission 1965). Out of these commissions emerged centralized efforts to improve the efficiency and effectiveness of policing. The primary example here was the Law Enforcement Assistance Association (LEAA), which subsequently metamorphosed into the National Institute of Justice (NIJ).

These agencies have sought to influence local law enforcement by charting "best practices" and providing resources for departments to adopt these practices (Ross 2000). Reforms such as community policing and problem-solving policing were spurred in large part by these agencies. Local law-enforcement agencies were thus provided incentives to adopt these reforms, because they could lead to an infusion of resources (Crank and Langworthy 1992; Giblin 2004; Herbert 2005). More directly, federal law-enforcement agencies seek to influence local law enforcement through various joint efforts to combat crimes having translocal dynamics, such as drug trafficking. Local police departments often recognize incentives to participate in such task forces; they can gain training, expertise, and status. At the same time, they are sometimes wary of collaboration. Federal agents might usurp local authority or claim excessive credit for any successes that might result. These outside agents might also disrupt relations local police have developed with informants or members of marginal communities, such as undocumented immigrants. Local police may wish not to arrest people who are technically in violation of federal law in order to protect key sources of information that they have cultivated over a long period of time. These delicate relations can possibly be damaged by heavy-handed federal law-enforcement officers who seek quick and well-publicized arrests.

In short, any hope for identifying bright lines that clearly demarcate where federal police power should end and local police power should begin remains elusive. Geller and Morris (1992: 233) summarize the situation well: "The justification usually offered for the hodgepodge of American police forces is that freedom, and a healthy system of checks and balances arising out of interagency competition, precludes the creation of a national police force. This is a deeply, one might say passionately, held belief, and it is for the time being politically unassailable."

Yet this belief *is* politically assailed, in no small part because of the increased prominence of crime as an issue in national politics. This dates most significantly to the 1960s, when Republican presidential candidates Barry Goldwater (1964) and Richard Nixon (1968) employed the so-called Southern strategy to lure conservative whites from their traditional alliance with the Democratic Party. Key to this strategy was the linking of civil rights activism with criminality; the protests of activists were characterized as synonymous with a breakdown in "law and order" (see Beckett 1997). More generally, the law-and-order political discourse that emerged remained a viable vote-getting strategy in the subsequent years, and fueled the massive fourfold increase in incarceration in the United States (Parenti 1999; Wacquant 2001). Given the political prominence of the desire to fight a "war" on crime, federal-level politicians sought to toughen criminal laws and expand federal intervention into criminal investigations.

From this position, it is a short step to a federalized emphasis on fighting a new war, this one on terrorism, despite the continuing importance of local policing institutionally and ideologically. Not surprisingly, the federal-local fault line has once again been disturbed by efforts to combat terrorism, most notably in the form of the U.S.A. PATRIOT Act.

Federalism and Crime Control Under the "War on Terror"

The "war on terror" generally, and such specific measures as the PATRIOT Act ("Uniting and Strengthening America by Providing Appropriate Tools Required to Intercept and Obstruct Terrorism") may represent a substantial break with a number of traditional doctrines of U.S. criminal law. Yet they should also be understood as the most recent chapter in the continuing American struggle over the scale at which crime control is governed, as well as a continuation of the trend toward consolidating and nationalizing authority over crime control.

From its inception, the federal government has framed the "war on terror" as both a multiscalar conflict requiring police efforts ranging from the local to the international, as well as a conflict that must inherently be managed by a strong central authority. Almost two months after the September 11 attacks, President Bush posited the "war on terror" as more than an effort "to defend our homeland," but rather as "a war to save civilization"(Bush 2001). Even given the international scale of such a project, Bush was careful to articulate the war on terror as inherently a local effort, but one that required a strong, supervisory federal government: "To coordinate our efforts we've created the new Office of Homeland Security. Its director . . . reports directly to me—and works with all our federal agencies, state and local governments, and the private sector on a national strategy to strengthen our homeland protections" (Bush 2001). In the context of airport security, Bush explicitly framed safety as directly correlated to federal oversight of local law enforcement: "We have posted the National Guard in America's airports and placed undercover air marshals on many flights. I call on Congress to quickly send me legislation that makes cockpits more secure, baggage screening more thorough, and puts the federal government in charge of all airport screening and security" (Bush 2001).

Moreover, like prior efforts in the "war on crime," the federal government has backed up strong rhetoric regarding the need for centralized leadership with substantial regulatory and economic incentives and initiatives. Specifically, the PATRIOT, which was reauthorized by Congress early in 2006, Act calls for the intensification of federal involvement with, oversight of, and participation from a variety of state and local governmental agencies. For example, Section 215 of the PATRIOT Act permits the federal government to obtain a court order mandating the production of any documents or other information held by any organization—including state agencies and libraries—solely upon the unsupported assertion by an FBI agent that such information is "for an authorized investigation . . . to protect against international terrorism or clandestine intelligence activities."[19] The implications of Section 215 for local government are particularly powerful given that, as of October 2002, a survey conducted by the University of Illinois reported that, "Federal and local law enforcement officials, visited at least 545 (10.7%) libraries to ask for records pursuant to Section 215. Of these, 178 libraries (3.5%) received visits from the FBI" (Estabrook 2002). Because Section 215 as amended makes it generally illegal for an individual or organization approached by the FBI to report that records were requested, the numbers reported by Estabrook almost certainly have underreported FBI efforts to obtain information from such local governmental entities as libraries.[20]

That said, perhaps the greatest potential implication of local authority in the federal prosecution of the "war on terror" is through various programs providing for local/federal crime control partnerships. For example, Section 701 of the PATRIOT Act authorizes the Federal Office of Justice Programs to make grants to and contract with state and local law enforcement agencies and with nonprofit organizations to identify and combat multi-jurisdictional criminal conspiracies.[21] Likewise, Section 816 enables the U.S. Attorney General to establish a variety of "regional computer forensic laboratories," for the purpose of providing training and assistance to "Federal, State, and local law enforcement personnel," in the investigation and prosecution of local and Federal computer crimes, as well as to "facilitate and promote the sharing of Federal law enforcement expertise and information about the investigation, analysis, and prosecution of computer-related crime with State and local law-enforcement personnel."[22] Section 908 provides for the Federal Attorney General and CIA to provide local and state officials training in the identification and use of "foreign intelligence information."[23] The PATRIOT Act even goes so far as to empower the federal government to contract with local law enforcement for the protection of military bases during the duration of Operation Enduring Freedom initiatives, with the Department of Defense footing the bill.[24]

Beyond the specific terms of the PATRIOT Act, the "war on terror" has also brought a redoubled effort to create and maintain Joint Terrorism Task Forces (JTTF). Described by the FBI as "teams of state and local law enforcement officers, FBI Agents, and other federal agents and personnel who work shoulder-to-shoulder to investigate and prevent acts of terrorism," such JTTFs were first created in the 1980s (Federal Bureau of Investigation, 2005). While such partnerships expanded slowly in the 1990s in response to the World Trade Center and Oklahoma City bombings, the "war on terror" has spurred a resurgence in the creation of JTTFs (Dreyfuss 2002).

The incentives for local law enforcement agencies to participate in the "war on terror" are potentially quite substantial. For example, $50 million and $100 million were allocated for local contracts to "identify and combat multi-jurisdictional criminal conspiracies," under Section 701 during fiscal years 2002 and 2003 respectively (Doyle 2001). Likewise, Section 1005 provides $25 million per year from 2003 until 2007 for grants from the Attorney General to "States and units of local government to improve the ability of State and local law enforcement, fire department and first responders to respond to and prevent acts of terrorism," (Doyle 2001).[25] Effectively writing a blank check for local terrorist response readiness projects, Section 1014 provides for appropriations "as necessary for each of fiscal years 2002 through 2007" to "enhance the capability of State and local jurisdictions to prepare for and respond to terrorist acts" (Doyle 2001).[26] Finally, Section 1015 approves appropriations up to $250 million per year for state and local grants supporting "an integrated approach to develop information and identification technologies and systems, through fiscal year 2007 (Doyle 2001).[27]

Not surprisingly, the evidence suggests increased federal-local cooperation. While there were thirty-five formal Joint Terrorism Task Forces before the September 11 attacks, each of the FBI's fifty-six field offices now has a JTTF. In addition, there are another 10 "stand-alone" JTTFs in the FBI's larger resident agencies, plus a large variety of "JTTF annexes" sponsored by other field offices in "small to medium sized resident agencies" (Casey 2004). Indeed, considering the nationwide scope of federal involvement with local law enforcement under the rubric of combating terrorism—even in areas with neither a history nor a substantial threat of terrorist attack (Dreyfuss 2002)—the war on terror represents a previously unprecedented expansion of federal oversight and control over the traditionally local governmental sphere of crime control.

That such joint task forces can enflame longstanding disputes about the scales of justice is best illustrated by one of the places where the debate burned brightest—Portland. Even if expansive federal authority often has been seen as more "progressive" politically, Portland's political culture, for avowedly progressive reasons, rejected a strong federal role in policing.

Local Resistance to the War on Terror:
The Portland Case

The city of Portland devoted local police resources to a JTTF between 1997 and 2005. The tumultuous history of this partnership between local and federal law-enforcement agencies provides a particularly germane example of how scale can be ideologically mobilized by those with both local and federal interests. It also highlights a number of tensions and issues concerning the scale of law enforcement, some of which have traditionally been identified with the expansion of federal jurisdiction in the past, and some of which are new and particular to the political climate since September 11, 2001.

To understand the debate in Portland, we conducted a content analysis of news articles appearing in *The Oregonian*, the lone metropolitan daily newspaper, with a circulation of nearly 350,000 (450,000 on Sunday). This analysis serves as the basis for our discussion of the mobilization of discourses of scale by local and federal law enforcement agencies, politicians, and interest groups. As a mainstream newspaper governed by contemporary journalistic standards of balanced reporting, *The Oregonian* can be presumed to represent the viewpoints of the key actors on either side of this and other prominent public debates. It is thus a good source to use to discern the contours of this debate, and the key tropes mobilized by those on either side.

Our analysis covers a period extending from the inception of the Portland JTTF, to the controversial vote by City Council to withdraw local police officers from the JTTF in April 2005. The JTTF was discussed in 117 articles in the eight-year period. Each news story was assigned a score based on the frequency and nature of discourses present. Articles that devoted more space to perspectives critical of local involvement in the JTTF were classified as being opposed to participation, while articles that devoted a greater amount of attention to issues relating to the benefits of JTTF membership were classified as being in favor of participation (see table 10.1). Overall, a greater number of articles ($n=61$) appearing in *The Oregonian* opposed local participation in the task force. That said, a significant amount of news coverage was favorable to local participation on the task force ($n=46$). A smaller number of articles ($n=10$) devoted an equal amount of attention to both sides of the debate, earning a neutral score.

Editorial space devoted to the JTTF in the years leading up to the September 11 terrorist attacks was limited. Oregon FBI chief Kathleen

Table 10.1 Discourses present in media coverage of JTTF participation, 1997–2005

Position of Article	Discourses	Key Voices
Opposed to participation in JTTF: 61	—Potential abuse of civil rights/racism (49) —Legality; conformity with state constitution (35) —Need for locally elected oversight of police (28) —Potential for police surveillance of legitimate political activity (26) —Not worth expenditure/ should focus in local issues (18) —Participation in federal investigations hinders effective community policing (10)	Mayor Tom Potter; Mayor Vera Katz; City commissioner Randy Leonard; city attorney Jeff Rogers; Stanley Cohen, legal council for Kariye; Dave Fidanque, ACLU spokesperson; Bilal Mosque community; Islamic Center of Portland; Japanese American Citizen's League
In favor of participation in JTTF: 46	—Need to protect local security (33) —Need to protect security at the national scale (24) —Need to combat domestic terrorist groups (22) —Importance of information sharing between local/federal agencies (22) —Portland's exceptionalism; isolation from regional interests (14) —Legality of investigations(13) —Portland's scalar position in wider war on terror (13)	Mayor Vera Katz; Chief of Police Kroeker; Chief of Police Derrick Foxworth; Assistant U.S. Attorney John Kroger; FBI Agent Matthews; FBI Agent Jordan; Beaverton Mayor Ron Drake; local Portland business groups

Neutral: 10
Total: 117

McChesney had pushed for the creation of an antiterror task force in 1997, when local law-enforcement efforts were largely concerned with threats to local infrastructure from domestic activist groups and those accused of "eco-terrorism." This focus was evident in the wording of the initial City Council ordinance, which mandated the use of local law-enforcement resources to "identify and target for prosecution those individuals or groups who are responsible for Right Wing and/or Left Wing movements, as well as acts of the anti-abortion movement and the Animal Liberation Front/Earth Liberation Front" (*Oregonian*, December 1, 2000). The wording of the ordinance troubled local civil rights advocates, who were concerned that the mandate of the JTTF granted too many surveillance powers to both local and federal law enforcement agents. In particular, they cited Portland's troubled history of cases involving misuse of surveillance material by local police forces.

A number of high-profile local cases colored subsequent discussions of law-enforcement powers by local critics. In one case, an officer of the Portland police intelligence unit had leaked a cache of surveillance documents. The embarrassing revelation that the leaked documents contained a photograph of Portland Mayor Vera Katz at an agricultural labor rally in the 1960s helped fuel arguments that local police resources could potentially be used to monitor legitimate political activity. In a separate case, political activist Douglas Squirrel successfully sued the city in 1993, alleging that Portland police officers had conducted illegal surveillance of his political activities by dispatching two undercover agents to a meeting that Squirrel attended in 1992. Multnomah County Circuit Judge Michael Marcus found that the conduct of the Portland Police Bureau violated state law because Squirrel had not committed a crime during the course of the meeting. He ruled that "the mere presence of an individual, group, organization, corporation, business or partnership at an event or activity where criminal behavior is discussed, planned or conducted by others shall not be sufficient basis" for recording the behavior of that individual (*Oregonian*, December 2, 2001).

Thus in the early stages of local participation on the JTTF, critics mobilized arguments about the potential for abuse of police power and the illegitimate surveillance of noncriminal political activity. Prior to September 11, 2001, primarily local actors used these discourses to question the role and motivations of local law enforcement emboldened by federal assistance. These discourses changed following September 11. Local resistance to the JTTF increasingly focused on using state legal precedent to protect local citizens' rights from the potential overreaching of surveillance by federal agencies.

The Marcus ruling formed the basis for criticisms of the legality of police participation on the JTTF in November of 2001, when the FBI planned to conduct interviews with 200 local individuals of Middle Eastern descent. City attorney Jeff Rogers argued that the interviews violated a 1981 Oregon statute that prohibited law-enforcement agents from collecting or maintaining information on individuals who were not suspected of criminal activity. City politicians and attorneys framed their opposition to the planned questioning in legal terms, arguing that partisan politics had no sway over their mobilization of state law.

Yet advocates of federal involvement cited Portland's exceptionalism in challenging the planned participation of local law enforcement agents. Critics of Portland's City Council repeatedly framed the municipal government's actions as unique and uncharacteristic of sentiment in other cities. One U.S. Department of Justice spokeswoman stated that "Portland's actions are not representative of what we're hearing. Fortunately, we're getting a different response from local police around the country" (*Oregonian*, November 22, 2001). The characterization of Portland as alone in its resistance to federal efforts intensified, with critics of the city describing it as "The People's Republic of Portland" and "The Little Beirut." In this way, proponents of the JTTF emphasized the city's scalar position in the national war on terror, and characterized local resistance as a threat to security at the local, regional, and national scales.

Meanwhile, those who opposed the city's participation in the federal investigation increasingly framed the issue in terms of local democratic responsibility. For example, a spokesperson from the Japanese American Citizen's League, Scott Sakamoto, argued that the checks and balances that traditionally kept local law-enforcement agents under the oversight of democratically elected officials did not apply to federal bodies such as the JTTF:

> Because Portland police officers are deputized by the FBI, their activities may not be regulated by state law and administrative rules that prohibit political surveillance. Among those protections are provisions that require files to be audited and purged if no criminal activity is involved. In contrast, FBI records are permanent and may be shared with other agencies. (*Oregonian*, September 26, 2001)

The city's attorneys successfully blocked participation by local members of the JTTF in the federal investigation. This proved something of a pyrrhic victory, however, since the interviews were ultimately allowed to be carried out by federal agents without participation from the local police (cf. Thacher 2005). Furthermore, Portland police continued to participate in other investigations and remained active on the JTTF. One year later, in 2002, *The Oregonian* reported that the relationship between the FBI and local police had in fact grown even stronger, stating that participation in the task force had grown to include forty local law-enforcement agents (*Oregonian*, June 2, 2002).

A series of high-profile arrests in the Portland area helped to galvanize positions on both sides of the issue. When FBI agents detained Sheik Mohamed Kariye at Portland International Airport, local law-enforcement agents complained that the FBI had cordoned off the area and limited their involvement in the case (*Oregonian*, September 9, 2002). Kariye was initially detained because trace amounts of explosive material were detected on his luggage. However, when tests returned negative, the FBI continued to detain him on charges of social security fraud. This angered the local Muslim community, who felt that federal law-enforcement agents were unjustly targeting Kariye. The Islamic Center of Portland mosque emerged as a key voice of opposition to Kariye's detention, and mobilized two main arguments for his release. The first was the charge that federal agencies like the FBI, operating outside of democratically elected oversight, were engaging in a form of racial persecution of Muslims and using archaic legal statutes to detain average citizens without due process. The second discourse appealed to Kariye's role as a prominent member within the local community. That such a key figure could be detained, critics alleged, illustrated a lack of specific cultural knowledge on the part of federal agents unfamiliar with local Muslim knowledge and practices.

Friends and family of Mike Hawash echoed these discourses when he was charged with assisting the Portland Six in March 2003. The Portland Six were a group of Muslims living in the United States who were charged with attempting to enter Afghanistan during the 2001 offensive with the aim of fighting against U.S. forces. Secrecy by federal law enforcement surrounding the arrests of these accused sympathizers served to strengthen opposition to potential abuses by federally mandated investigation teams. Moreover, the potential that the arrests were premised upon racial profiling exacerbated concerns about the abuse of civil liberties. But proponents of local participation in the "war on terror" cited these arrests as evidence of the critical role of Portland in the national fight against terrorism. For example, one report situated Portland on an "Al Qaeda Trail" that linked Osama bin Laden with local Muslim religious leaders (*Oregonian*, September 13, 2002). The ability of the FBI and other federal agencies to track the international movements and relationships of terror suspects was repeatedly cited as a necessary complement to local law enforcement, which lacked sufficient resources to make connections at wider scales. "Portland isn't immune from terrorism," Commissioner Jim Francesconi said on September 19. "We must work with the FBI" (*Oregonian*, September 19, 2002).

Opponents of the JTTF failed to assert sufficient political pressure as Mayor Katz and other city council members voted unanimously to remain involved with the JTTF in 2003 and 2004. The Mayor and Chief of Police Foxworth did yield to public demand for greater official oversight of police activity. Both promised to apply for secret-level FBI security clearance so that they could monitor the activities of Portland police officers participating in the JTTF. However, only Foxworth eventually earned the appropriate clearance.

Local elections in 2004 changed the composition of the City Council and brought Tom Potter into the Mayor's office. These changes caused a shift in focus back to an assessment of the role of city police in the JTTF. In February 2005, the *Oregonian* began reporting that Council Member Randy Leonard and Mayor Potter were opposing continued city involvement and asking the FBI for increased oversight of taskforce activities. On March 23, it was announced that Potter was requesting top-secret-level clearance for himself and Police Chief Foxworth to provide more rigorous supervision of local police resources. Portland FBI Agent Robert Jordan opposed any civilian involvement on the task force, echoing earlier arguments that Portland was alone in its opposition to federal oversight of the JTTF. On March 24, he told the *Oregonian* that the demands by the mayor were "simply not feasible or reasonable . . . No other mayor in the country has been granted the top-secret clearance that Potter wants" (*Oregonian*, March 24, 2005). As debate intensified, local proponents of participation in the JTTF argued that Portland's exceptionalism would harm regional security and the relationship of other neighboring counties with the federal government. In a letter to the mayor, Police Chief Foxworth argued that "Nonsupport of the JTTF would cause long-term damage to our reputation and credibility within the law enforcement community. This will likely weaken our relationships with remaining law-enforcement partners and break down lines of communication" (*Oregonian*, April 23, 2005). An email distributed to local law-enforcement agencies in Oregon by the Department of Homeland Security threatening to withdraw funding for local training partnerships demonstrated that there was some substance to the chief's concerns. Despite this, the City Council voted on April 29 to withdraw support from the JTTF and reassign those police officers to new roles within the Portland Police Bureau.

In their analysis of the relations between federal and local law enforcement agencies, Geller and Morris (1992) outlined some of the primary incentives and disincentives for local participation in task forces, many of which emerged in the Portland case. In terms of incentives, Geller and Morris cite the access to sophisticated investigative and prosecutorial tools as one draw for local community police involvement. Proponents of Portland's participation in federal investigations regularly expressed the need for local police to retain their top-secret clearance in order to have access to FBI computers and crime labs where critical information was exchanged. Similarly, budgetary considerations have been traditionally cited as powerful motivators for local involvement in federal task forces. Proponents of city participation on the JTTF also emphasized the need to share information between jurisdictions, and the possibility that local police forces could benefit from federal preparedness training.

The Portland case is also illustrative of both traditional and new disincentives to local partnership with federal law-enforcement agencies. Certainly the FBI's unwillingness to share sensitive information with elected politicians and local police caused frustration and suspicion among members of the public. There was also a very strong mistrust of centralized federal authority among many Portland citizens, particularly those in the Muslim community. As a result, progressives on the left found themselves in the unusual position of supporting the need for localized government and oversight of police practices, even though the city and the police bureau had a recent history of civil liberties violations and abuse of investigative power. Critics of the task force repeatedly framed Portland's participation as a hindrance to local community policing efforts, because citizens' mistrust of the federal mandate created a rift between community members and law-enforcement agents. Mayor Potter and the City Council mobilized these tropes and committed additional material support to community policing efforts once they withdrew support from the JTTF. "I don't think whether we stay in or out of the JTTF will determine the safety of Portland citizens," Potter said after the City Council vote, "I think what will determine the safety of Portland citizens is when we work together, when we watch out for each and care for each other, that our society is safer" (*Oregonian*, April 29, 2005).

Unsurprisingly, opponents of the mayor's position saw the move by City Council as a knee-jerk reaction that did more symbolic damage to national unity than material good to the citizens of Oregon. While mocking members of the city government, one commentator chillingly evoked a similar period in this country's history when civil liberties were threatened by far-reaching federal surveillance power: "What [this ruling] basically says is that Portland is a very politically correct and very naive city that is also very paranoid. I'm not sure that's going to surprise anyone, but it might surprise the City Council to know that J. Edgar Hoover is dead" (*Oregonian*, April 28, 2005).

Conclusion: Calibrating the Scales of Justice

J. Edgar Hoover may well be dead, but the tensions he fueled by expanding federalized crime control efforts persist. Even if Portland's resistance to the JTTF was unusual in these terror-obsessed times, the city's opposition relied upon well-worn discourses that simultaneously condemned intrusive centralized authority and validated local control of policing. And this resistance to the probing eye of the federal state is hardly unique to Portland; numerous state and local governments have expressed disquiet about, and open resistance to, aspects of the PATRIOT Act (Cambanis 2004).

That such debates rage on shows clearly that the scales of justice can never be brought to a restful balance. No easy resolution is possible because plausible arguments exist for both centralizing *and* devolving political power. This is true in the context of law enforcement, and in numerous other policy arenas. This reality enables political activists to argue for centralization in one context and devolution in another. The ideologies of scale are fluid and ever-changing; yesterday's Great Society liberal arguing in favor of strong national oversight of civil rights and antipoverty initiatives is today's PATRIOT Act opponent arguing against strong national authority to mount national security investigations that threaten basic civil liberties.

Yet even if the ideologies of scale are fluid, they are simultaneously quite potent. Those who support local participation in federal task forces can cite the virtues of a centralized authority that can best protect a vulnerable nation through its efficient practices. Their opponents cite the equally-valued virtues of local control of law enforcement, the better to assure proper oversight of the police's coercive authority and surveillance powers. Each of these broad ideological positions—favoring centralized or decentralized authority—is considered legitimate in American political discourse, in the context of law enforcement and other policy areas. Each can thus be drawn upon in debates about the police power, and other powers, of the state.

In short, geographic scale is a contradictory political object: it is a discursive signifier that is both strong and elusive; both ideologically charged and ideologically promiscuous. This is not inherently problem-atic, because there is no necessary reason why one should advocate solely for one scale to the complete exclusion of others. It is simply that resting one's political argument on the grounds of scale, however robustly, will likely prove an unstable position. Despite the ideological significance often attached to scale, it is a fickle political arrow to fire—it may reverse itself in flight as one moves to a different context.

As the Portland case illustrates, debates about the scale of governance can become especially impassioned when they come to the issues of crime and terror. Political debates about crime and terror are necessarily highly charged, often pursued with moral fervor. As these politics touch upon preexisting concerns about the scale balance of political power, they become even more enflamed. Critics of Portland's decision to withdraw from the JTTF may cite its exceptionalism, but we see this story as anything but exceptional. Rather, it is another chapter in an ongoing saga about the politics of the scale of governance. Other chapters remain to be written, but the story they tell will always be inconclusive, because the scales of justice refuse to be equilibrated.

Notes

1. This is not to suggest, however, that these tensions emerge solely in the area of law enforcement, just that they are often especially impassioned when discussions revolve around the coercive capacity of the police.
2. U.S. Const. art. VI, Cl. 2.
3. U.S. Const. amend. XIV, section 1.
4. U.S. Const. amend. X.
5. U.S. Const. amend. XI.
6. Richard Fallon, The "Conservative" Paths of the Rehnquist Court's Federalism Decisions, 69 U.Chi.L. Rev. 429 (2002) provides a concise overview of the complex field of federalist jurisprudence that has arisen from over two centuries of judicial constitutional interpretation.
7. 17 U.S. (4 Wheat) 316, 4 L. Ed. 579 (1819).
8. Ibid.
9. *Wabash, St. Louis & Pacific Railroad v. Illinois*, 118 U.S. 557 (1886) (invalidating state regulation of railroad rate discrimination).
10. *Swift & Co. v. United States*, 196 U.S. 375 (1905).
11. *NLRB v. Jones & Laughlin Steel*, 301 U.S. 1 (1937).
12. 347 U.S. 483 (1954).
13. *Plessy v. Ferguson*, 163 U.S. 537 (1896).
14. *Cumming v. Richmond County Board of Education*, 175 U.S. 528 (1899).
15. *United States v. Lopez*, 514 U.S.549 (1995), *United States v. Morrison*, 529 U.S. 598, 618 (2000). But see *Gonzales v. Raich*, 125 S. Ct. 2195, 2211–2215 (2005).
16. *New York v. United States*, 505 U.S.144 (1992), *Printz v. United States*, 521 U.S. 898 (1997).
17. 125 S. Ct. 2195 (2005) (upholding the application of the federal Controlled Substances Act criminalizing the manufacture, distribution, or possession of marijuana, to intrastate cultivators and users of marijuana for medical purposes).
18. Ibid., 2221 (O'Connor, J., dissenting).
19. Pub. L. 107–56, § 215.
20. Ibid.
21. Ibid., § 701.
22. Ibid., § 816.
23. Ibid., § 908.
24. Ibid., § 1010.
25. Ibid., § 1005.
26. Ibid., § 1014.
27. Ibid., § 1015.

References

Works Cited

Beckett, K. (1997) *Making Crime Pay: Law and Order in Contemporary American Politics*. New York: Oxford University Press.

Blomley, N. (1994) *Law, Space and the Geographies of Power*. New York: Guilford.

Brenner, N. (2001) "The Limits to Scale? Methodological Reflections on Scalar Structuration." *Progress in Human Geography 25*(4): 591–614.

Bryan, F. (2003) *Real Democracy: The New England Town Meeting and How it Works*. Chicago: University of Chicago Press.

Bush, G. (2001) *Address to the Nation* (Speech). Atlanta.

Cambanis, T. (2004) "Resistance to Patriot Act Gaining Ground: Foes Organizing in Communities." *Boston Globe* January 20, p. A4.

Casey, J. (2004) "Managing Joint Terrorism Task Force Resources." *The FBI Law Enforcement Bulletin 73*(11): 1(6).

Cox, K. (1993) "The Local and the Global in the New Urban Politics: A Critical View." *Environment and Planning D: Society and Space 11*(4): 433–448.

Crank, J. and Langworthy, R. (1992) "An Institutional Perspective on Policing," *Journal of Criminal Law and Criminology 83*(3): 338–363.

Delaney, D. and Leitner, H. (1997) "The Political Construction of Scale," *Political Geography 16*(2): 93–97.

Doyle, C. (2001). *Terrorism: Section by Section Analysis of the USA PATRIOT Act* (RL31200). Washington, D.C.: Congressional Research Service.

Dreyfuss, R. (2002, June 3, 2002) "The Cops are Watching You." *The Nation, 274* 12(14).

Estabrook, L.S. (2002) *Public Libraries and Civil Liberties: A Profession Divided*. Urbana-Champaign: Library Research Center.

Federal Bureau of Investigation (2005) *War on Terrorism, Counterterrorism; Partnerships* [Web Page]. "Federal Bureau of Investigation." Retrieved 12 June 2005, from the World Wide Web:

Fogelson, R. (1971) "White on Black: A Critique of the McCone Commission Report," in A. Platt (ed.), *The Politics of Riot Commissions, 1917–1970*. New York: Macmillan, 307–341.

Geller, W. and Morris, N. (1992) "Relations Between Federal and Local Police," in M. Tonry and N. Morris (eds.) *Modern Policing*. Chicago: University of Chicago Press, 231–348.

Giblin, M. (2004) "Institutional Theory and the Recent Adoption and Activities of Crime Analysis Units in U.S. Law Enforcement Agencies." Ph.D. Dissertation. Department of Criminal Justice, Indiana University.

Herbert, S. (2005) "POP in San Diego: A Not-So-Local Story," *Criminology and Public Policy 4*(2): 181–186.

Johnson, L.B. (1964) "Remarks at the University of Michigan," *Public Papers of the Presidents of the United States: Lyndon B. Johnson, 1963–64. Volume I, entry 357, pp.* (pp. 704–707). Washington, D. C.

Kerner Commission (1968) *Report of the National Advisory Commission on Civil Disorders*. Washington, D.C.: Government Printing Office.

Marston, S. (2000) "The Social Construction of Scale," *Progress in Human Geography 24*(2): 219–242.

Marx, G. (1990) *Undercover: Police Surveillance in America*. Berkeley: University of California Press.

Massey, D. (1979) "In What Sense a Regional Problem?" *Regional Studies 13*(2): 233–243.

McCone Commission (1965) *Violence in the City: A Report of the Governor's Commission on the Los Angeles Riot*. Sacremento: State of California Printing Office.

McMaster, R. and Sheppard, E. (2002) *Scale and Geographic Inquiry: Nature, Society and Method*. Cambridge, MA: Blackwell.

Ross, J. (2000) "Grants-R-Us: Inside a Federal Grant Making Research Agency." *American Behavioral Scientis 43*(7): 1704–1723.

Parenti, C. (1999) *Lockdown America: Police and Prisons in an Age of Crisis*. New York: Verso.

Powers, R. (1987) *Secrecy and Power: The Life of J. Edgar Hoover*. New York: Free Press.

Thacher, D. (2005) "The Local Role in Homeland Security." *Law and Society Review 39*(3): 635–676.

Theoharis, A., Poveda, T., Rosenfeld, S., and Powers, R. (1999) *The FBI: A Comprehensive Reference Guide*. Phoenix: Oryx Press.

Wacquant, L. (2001) "The Penalization of Poverty and the Rise of Neoliberalism." *European Journal on Criminal Policy and Research 9*(4): 401–412.

Newspaper Articles

The *Oregonian*, December 1, 2000. "Activists Urge Council Not to Back Task Force."
The *Oregonian*, November 22, 2001. "State Studies Fed's Request."
The *Oregonian*, September 26, 2001. "In My Opinion Pro & Con."
The *Oregonian*, December 2, 2001. "Controversy Swirls Around Two Laws."
The *Oregonian*, September 9, 2002. "FBI Task Force Stops Man at Airport."
The *Oregonian*, September 13, 2002. "Al-Qaida Trail Tracked to NW."
The *Oregonian*, September 19, 2002. "Police Surveillance Powers Need Watching."
The *Oregonian*, March 24, 2005. "FBI Rules Out Potter Demand on Terror Force."
The *Oregonian*, April 28, 2005. "Portland's Vote on FBI Force Could Have Fallout."
The *Oregonian*, April 29, 2005. "Joy in Galley as Portland Quits FBI Task Force."

Notes on Contributors

William Thomas Allison has been associate professor of history at Weber State University since 1999, where he teaches American diplomatic and military history. He earned his Ph.D. in history from Bowling Green State University in 1995. He is author of *In the Vanguard: American Military Justice and Judge Advocates in Vietnam* (Lawrence: University Press of Kansas, 2007) and coauthor of *To Protect and To Serve: A History of Police in America* (Prentice Hall, 2004).

John Carr is an attorney as well as a Ph.D. candidate in the University of Washington's Department of Geography. His research interests center on public space and how different conceptions of such spaces are mobilized to pursue various social, political, and economic projects.

Kris Erickson is a doctoral candidate in geography at the University of Washington. His research focuses on social control and resistance in both material and virtual public spaces. Before moving to the United States, he lived and studied in Canada and France.

Steve Herbert is an associate professor in the Department of Geography/Law, Societies, and Justice Program at the University of Washington. He is the author of *Policing Space: Territoriality and the Los Angeles Police Department* (Minneapolis: University of Minnesota Press, 1997) and *Citizens, Cops and Power: Recognizing the Limits of Community* (Chicago: University of Chicago, 2006). He has published extensively in the areas of police territoriality, police subculture, and the ethnographic issues presented in research on human geography.

Marilynn Johnson is professor of history at Boston College where she teaches U.S. urban and social history. She is the author of *Street Justice: A History of Police Violence in New York City* (Boston, MA: Beacon Press, 2003) and *The Second Gold Rush: Oakland and the East Bay in World War II* (Berkeley, CA: University of California Press, 1993). She is currently at work on an edited collection on the history of violence in the American West.

Val Marie Johnson is assistant professor in the Sociology and Criminology Department and the Women's Studies Program of Saint Mary's University in Halifax, Nova Scotia. Her scholarly interests center on the theory and history of how we construct and regulate space, identities, communities, and citizenship, particularly in cities. The *Journal of Urban History* nominated her article "Protection, Virtue, and the 'power to detain': The Moral Citizenship of Jewish Women in New York

City, 1890–1920" (JUH 31 [2005]: 655–684) for the 2005 Berkshire Conference Article Prize. She has an article on "New York City Electoral Campaigns Against Vice and the Incorporation of Immigrants" forthcoming in the *Journal of American Ethnic History* (Winter Spring 2006). She is coediting with Michele Byers an interdisciplinary anthology entitled *The "C.S.I. Effect": Television, Crime, and Critical Theory*, which is under contract with Lexington Books (for their Critical Studies in Television Series) and forthcoming in 2006. She is also currently revising her dissertation, "Defining 'Social Evil': Moral Citizenship & Governance in New York City, 1890—1920" for publication as a book. She is working on a second coedited manuscript, *Poverty, Regulation, and Social Exclusion: Readings on the Criminalization of Poverty*.

Joanne Klein is associate professor of Modern Comparative European History at Boise State University. She is active in the criminal justice/legal history network of the Social Science History Association, has served as network chair for four years, and manages the network's web page. She also serves on the Advisory Board of the journal, *Crime, Histoire & Sociétés/Crime, History & Societies*. She writes on policing in Britain, and is at work on her book, *Invisible Men: the Daily Lives of Police Constables in Manchester, Birmingham and Liverpool, 1900–1939*.

Peter K. Manning (Ph.D. Sociology, Duke 1966) is Brooks Professor of Criminal Justice at Northeastern University. Author of some thirteen books, several collections and many articles, he has been a fellow of Wolfson and Balliol College, Oxford, the American Bar Foundation, National Institute of Justice, and The Bellagio Rockefeller Center. He is currently working on a book on theorizing democratic policing and exploring its role in promoting equality and justice.

Andrea McArdle is associate professor of law at City University of New York School of Law, and a Ph.D. candidate in American Studies at NYU Graduate School of Arts and Science. Before joining the CUNY faculty, she taught in the lawyering and clinical programs at NYU School of Law, and practiced law in the public sector, including criminal defense work. She writes on urban police-community relations, and law and humanities. She coedited, and is a contributor to, the anthology *Zero Tolerance: Quality of Life and the New Police Brutality in New York City* (New York: NYU Press, 2001).

Stacy K. McGoldrick is assistant professor of sociology in the Department of Psychology and Sociology, California State Polytechnic University, Pomona. She holds a Ph.D. and MA in Sociology from the Graduate Faculty at the New School for Social Research. She writes on the history and politics of policing in the United States.

Anthony W. Pereira is associate professor in the Department of Political Science at Tulane University, where he teaches courses in State and Society in Developing Countries, Justice and Democracy in Latin America, and The Military, Politics, and Society in Latin America. He is the author of *The End of the Peasantry: The Emergence of the Rural Labor Movement in Northeast Brazil, 1961–1988* (Pittsburgh: University of Pittsburgh Press, 1997) and coedited with Diane Davis, *Irregular*

Armed Forces and Their Role in Politics and State Formation (Cambridge: Cambridge University Press, 2003). He has written and presented extensively on authoritarian regimes and militarized violence in Latin America.

Joseph J. Varga is a doctoral candidate in sociology and historical studies at the New School for Social Research in New York City. His dissertation, "The Spatial Containment of Democracy: Reform, Restructuring, and Citizenship in Progressive Era New York, 1884–1920," examines the relationship between urban space and citizenship. He has also been teaching in the History Department at Brooklyn College CUNY since 2002, offering courses on urban history and the history of European and U.S. social and political movements.

Index